United States
Department
of Agriculture

Forest Service

Rocky Mountain
Research Station

Resource Bulletin
RMRS-RB-15

July 2012

Montana's Forest Resources, 2003–2009

Jim Menlove, John D. Shaw, Michael T. Thompson, Chris Witt, Michael C. Amacher, Todd A. Morgan, Colin Sorenson, Chelsea P. McIver, Chuck Werstak

Abstract

This report presents a summary of the most recent inventory information for Montana's forest lands. The report includes descriptive highlights and tables of area, number of trees, biomass, volume, growth, mortality, and removals. Most of the tables are organized by forest type group, species group, diameter class, or owner group. The report also describes inventory design, inventory terminology, and data reliability. Results show that Montana's forest land totals 25.6 million acres. Sixty percent (15.4 million acres) of this forest land is administered by the USDA Forest Service. Douglas-fir forests cover 7.5 million acres or roughly 29 percent of Montana's forested lands, making it the most abundant forest type in the State. The lodgepole pine type is the second-most common individual forest type comprising 17 percent of Montana's forest land. Lodgepole pine is the most abundant tree species in Montana by number of trees, and Douglas-fir is the most abundant species by volume or biomass. Net annual growth of all live trees 5.0 inches diameter and greater on Montana forest land totaled 289.8 million cubic feet. Average annual mortality totaled nearly 746.3 million cubic feet.

Keywords: Montana, forest resources, inventory methods, forest inventory, forest type

Authors

Jim Menlove is an Ecologist and a member of the Analysis Team with the Interior West Inventory and Analysis Program at the USFS Rocky Mountain Research Station in Ogden, Utah. He holds a B.S. degree in Biology from the University of Utah and an M.S. degree in Zoology and Physiology from the University of Wyoming, both with an emphasis in ecology (contact: jmenlove@fs.fed.us, 801-625-5426).

John D. Shaw is a Biological Scientist and Analysis Team Leader with the Interior West Inventory and Analysis Program at the USFS Rocky Mountain Research Station in Ogden, Utah. He holds B.S. and M.S. degrees in Natural Resources Management from the University of Alaska Fairbanks and a Ph.D. in Forest Ecology from Utah State University.

Michael T. Thompson is a Forester and a member of the Analysis Team with the Interior West Inventory and Analysis Program at the USFS Rocky Mountain Research Station in Ogden, Utah. He holds a B.S. degree in Forestry from North Carolina State University.

Chris Witt is an Ecologist and a member of the Analysis Team with the Interior West Inventory and Analysis Program at the USFS Rocky Mountain Research Station in Ogden, UT. He holds B.S. and M.S. degrees in Ecology from Idaho State University.

Michael C. Amacher is a Research Soil Scientist in the Forest and Woodland Ecosystems Research Program at the USFS Rocky Mountain Research Station in Logan, Utah. He also serves as the western soils Indicator Advisor in the Indicators of Forest Health program. He has B.S. and M.S. degrees in Chemistry and a PhD in Soil Chemistry, all from The Pennsylvania State University.

Todd A. Morgan is the director of the Forest Industry Research Program at The University of Montana's Bureau of Business and Economic Research in Missoula, Montana. He received a B.A. degree in Philosophy and a B.S. degree in Forest Science from Pennsylvania State and an M.S. degree in Forestry from The University of Montana.

Colin Sorenson is a Research Economist with the Forest Industry Research Program at The University of Montana Bureau of Business and Economic Research in Missoula, Montana. He holds a B.S. degree in Social Science with a secondary degree in Natural Resources and Environmental Sciences from Kansas State University and an M.A. degree in Economics from The University of Montana.

Chelsea P. McIver is a Research Assistant with the Forest Industry Research Program at The University of Montana's Bureau of Business and Economic Research in Missoula, Montana. She received her B.A. degree in Rural & Environmental Sociology and is currently working towards her M.S. degree in Forestry, both at The University of Montana.

Chuck Werstak is a Biological Scientist and a member of the Analysis Team with the Interior West Inventory and Analysis Program at the USFS Rocky Mountain Research Station in Ogden, Utah. He holds a B.S. degree in Geography from Western Illinois University and an M.S. degree in Geography from Utah State University.

Cover photo: Looking toward Glacier NP from the west side (photo by Renate Bush, Regional Inventory Specialist, USDA Forest Service, Northern Region).

Acknowledgments

The Rocky Mountain Research Station gratefully acknowledges the cooperation and assistance of the Northern Region, Forest Service, U.S. Department of Agriculture; the Montana State Forester and other Montana Department of Natural Resources and Conservation personnel; the Bureaus of Land Management and Indian Affairs; and the National Park Service, U.S. Department of the Interior. The authors extend a special note of thanks to the field staff who collected the inventory data and to private landowners who provided information and access to field sample plots.

Table of Contents

I. Introduction

This report contains highlights of the status of Montana's forest resources, with discussions of pertinent issues based on the first 7 years of inventory under the new Forest Inventory and Analysis (FIA) annual system (Gillespie 1999). In 1998, the Agricultural Research Extension and Education Reform Act (also known as the Farm Bill) mandated that inventories would be conducted throughout United States' forests on an annual basis. This annual system integrates FIA and Forest Health Monitoring (FHM) sampling designs resulting in the mapped-plot design, which includes a nationally consistent plot configuration with 4-fixed-radius sub-plots; a systematic national sampling design consisting of one plot in each approximately 6,000-acre hexagon; annual measurement of a proportion of permanent plots; data or data summaries within 6 months after yearly sampling is completed; and a State summary report after 5 years.

Interior West Forest Inventory and Analysis (IWFIA) implemented the new annual inventory strategy starting in Montana in 2003. The strategy for the Western United States involves measurement of 10 systematic samples (or subpanels) each of which represents approximately 10 percent of all plots in the State. Because the initial 5-year Montana report was delayed, the decision was made to use the most current available data.

The most recent periodic report for Montana (Conner and O'Brien 1993) was based on inventory data from 1989, and from other data sources for National Forest lands. Reserved areas were not inventoried. Because of differences in plot design, sampling intensity, and measurement and data compilation strategies, comparisons with past inventories are somewhat tenuous. Appendix A discusses in more detail the differences between the current inventory, the 1993 report, and the 1989 data available in the national FIA database.

Although nearly two-thirds of Montana is on the Great Plains, the western portion of the State contains the backbone of the Rocky Mountains, including a portion of the Continental Divide. West of the Continental Divide, Montana has a maritime-influenced climate, with higher precipitation and relatively warmer winters than the rest of the State. As a result, 80 percent or more of the land area is forested, with the highest tree diversity in the State. Species requiring moister site conditions—such as western larch, grand fir, western hemlock, western white pine, and western redcedar—are found here. The climate east of the Continental Divide is increasingly influenced by continental weather patterns, with a slightly lower proportion of forest land and less tree diversity in the mountains. Moving east, out of the mountains onto the Great Plains, forests and tree diversity decrease. On the eastern plains of the State, in areas with varied topography—such as the hills of the Powder River basin and the Missouri Breaks region—forests dominated by ponderosa pine and Rocky Mountain juniper occur. The distribution and composition of forests are determined by many factors such as elevation, aspect, soils, climate, and past fire history, and their influences are discussed in this report.

Annual inventory summaries are updated each spring to include the most recent subpanels of data available to the public. Data may be downloaded in table form or queried using a variety of online tools (http://fia.fs.fed.us/tools-data/default.asp). After 2013, a full assessment of 10 subpanels of data will be included in the upcoming 10-year (full cycle) report. In 2013, the re-measurement phase of the inventory will begin by re-measuring the first subpanel of plot data collected in 2003.

II. Inventory Methods

Plot Configuration

The national FIA plot design consists of four 24-foot radius subplots configured as a central subplot and three peripheral subplots. Centers of the peripheral subplots are located at distances of 120 feet and at azimuths of 360 degrees, 120 degrees, and 240 degrees from the center of the central subplot (USDA Forest Service 2003-2009a). Each standing tree with a diameter at breast height (d.b.h.) for timber trees, or a diameter at root collar (d.r.c.) for woodland trees, 5 inches or larger is measured on these subplots. Each subplot contains a 6.8-foot radius microplot with its center located 12 feet east of the subplot center on which each tree with a d.b.h./d.r.c. from 1.0 -inch to 4.9 inches is measured.

In addition to the trees measured on FIA plots, data are also gathered about the stand or area in which the trees are located. Area classifications are useful for partitioning the forest into meaningful categories for analysis. Some of these area attributes are measured (e.g., percent slope), some are assigned by definition (e.g., ownership group), and some are computed from tree data (e.g., percent stocking).

To enable division of the forest into various domains of interest for analysis, it is important that the tree data recorded on these plots are properly associated with the area classifications. To accomplish this, plots are mapped by condition class. Field crews assign a number to the first condition class encountered on a plot. This condition is then defined by a series of discrete variables attached to it (i.e., land use, stand size, regeneration status, tree density, stand origin, ownership group, and disturbance history). Additional conditions are identified if there is a distinct change in any of the condition-class variables on the plot.

Sample Design

Based on historic national standards, a sampling intensity of approximately one plot per 6,000 acres is necessary to satisfy national FIA precision guidelines for area and volume. Therefore, FIA divided the area of the United States into non-overlapping, 5,937-acre hexagons and established a plot in each hexagon using procedures designed to preserve existing plot locations from previous inventories. This base sample, designated as the Federal base sample, was systematically divided into a number of non-overlapping panels, each of which provides systematic coverage of the State. Each year the plots in a single subpanel are measured, and subpanels are selected on either a 5-year (eastern regions) or 10-year (western regions) rotating basis (Gillespie 1999). For estimation purposes, the measurement of each subpanel of plots can be considered an independent, equal probability sample of all lands in a State, or all plots can be combined to represent the State.

Three-Phase Inventory

FIA conducts inventories in three phases. Phase 1 uses remotely sensed data to obtain initial plot land cover observations (prefield) and to stratify land area in the population of interest to increase the precision of estimates. In Phase 2, field crews visit the physical locations of permanent field plots to measure traditional inventory variables such as tree species, diameter, and height. In Phase 3, field crews visit a subset of Phase 2 plots to obtain measurements for an additional suite of variables associated with forest and ecosystem health. The three phases of the enhanced FIA program are discussed in the following sections.

Phase 1: Remotely sensed data in the form of aerial photographs, digital orthoquads, and satellite imagery are used for initial plot establishment. Each plot is assigned a digitized geographic location, and a human interpreter determines whether a plot has the potential to sample forest or other wooded land. Plot locations that are accessible to field crews and have the potential to sample forest or other wooded land are selected for further measurement via field crew visits in Phase 2.

The only remote sensing medium used for stratification in Montana was 2004 MODIS satellite imagery. The spatial resolution of the MODIS imagery used was 250 meters. Three strata were recognized: forest/other wooded land, nonforest land, and census water. Depending on geography and sampling intensity, geographic divisions are identified within a State for area computation and are referred to as estimation units. In Montana, individual counties served as the estimation units. The area of each estimation unit is divided into strata of known size using the satellite imagery and computer-aided classification. The classified imagery divides the total area of the estimation unit into pixels of equal size and assigns each pixel to one of H strata. Each stratum, h, then contains n_h ground plots where the Phase 2 attributes of interest are observed.

To illustrate, the area estimator for forest land for an estimation unit in Montana is defined as:

$$\hat{A}_g = A_{Tg} \sum_{h=1}^{H} \frac{n'_{hg}}{n'_g} \frac{\sum_{i=1}^{n_{hg}} y_{ihg}}{n_{hg}}$$

where:

$\hat{A}_g$ = total forest area (acres) for estimation unit g

A_{Tg} = total land area (acres) in estimation unit g

H = number of strata (3)

n'_{hg} = number of Phase 1 points in stratum h in estimation unit g

n'_g = total number of Phase 1 points in estimation unit g

y_{thg} = forest land condition proportion on Phase 2 plot i in stratum h in estimation unit g

n_{hg} = number of Phase 2 plots in stratum h in estimation unit g

Phase 2: In Phase 2, field crews record a variety of data for plot locations sent to the field by Phase 1 (USDA Forest Service 2003-2009a). Before visiting privately owned plot locations, field crews consult county land records to determine the ownership of plots and then seek permission from private landowners to measure plots on their lands. The field crews determine the location of the geographic center of the center subplot using geographic positioning system (GPS) receivers. They record condition-level variables that include land use, forest type, stand origin, stand-size class, site productivity class, forest disturbance history, slope, aspect, and physiographic class. For each tree, field crews record a variety of variables including species, live/dead status, diameter, height, crown ratio, crown class, damage, and decay status. Office staff personnel apply statistical models using field crew measurements to calculate values for additional variables such as individual tree volume and per unit area estimates of number of trees, volume, biomass, growth, and mortality. The standard set of Phase 2 variables is collected by all FIA regions in a consistent manner. In addition to these national "core" variables, IWFIA collects data on additional forest attributes that regional stakeholders find informative and useful. These include understory vegetation cover and species dominance, noxious weeds, and down woody material. These data are collected through documented protocols on all accessible Phase 2 forested plots in the Interior West. These regional attributes are used in the "Noxious Weeds" and "Down Woody Material" sections of this report.

Phase 3: The third phase of the enhanced FIA program focuses on forest health. Phase 3 is administered cooperatively by the FIA program, other Forest Service programs, other Federal agencies, State natural resource agencies, universities, and the Forest Health Monitoring (FHM) program. Phase 3 is the ground survey portion of the Forest Health Monitoring (FHM) program and was integrated into the FIA program in 1999. The Phase 3 sample consists of a 1/16 subset of the Phase 2 plots, which equates to one Phase 3 plot for approximately every 95,000 acres. Phase 3 measurements are obtained by field crews during the growing season and include an extended suite of ecological data (USDA Forest Service 2003-2009b). Because each Phase 3 plot is also a Phase 2 plot, the entire suite of Phase 2 measurements is collected on each Phase 3 plot at the same time as the Phase 3 measurements. Phase 3 measurements include detailed assessments of tree crown condition, more detailed down woody material measurements, lichen diversity, and soil structure and chemistry. Phase 3 soil data are used in the "Forest Soil Resources" section of this report.

Sources of Error

Sampling error: The process of sampling (selecting a random subset of a population and calculating estimates from this subset) causes estimates to contain error they would not have if every member of the population had been observed and included in the estimate. The 2003-2009 FIA inventory of Montana is based on a sample of 10,711 plots systematically located across the State (a total area of 94.1 million acres); a sampling rate of approximately one plot for every 8,785 acres.

The statistical estimation procedures used to provide the estimates of the population totals presented in this report are described in detail in Bechtold and Patterson (2005). Included with every estimate is an associated sampling error that is typically expressed as a percentage of the estimated value but that can also be expressed in the same units as the estimate or as a confidence interval (the estimated value plus or minus the sampling error). This sampling error is the primary measure of the reliability of an estimate. An approximate 67 percent confidence interval constructed from the sampling error can be interpreted to mean that under hypothetical repeated sampling, approximately 67 percent of the confidence intervals calculated from the individual repeat samples would include the true population parameter if it were computed from a 100-percent inventory. The sampling errors for State- and county-level estimates are presented in Appendix E table 37.

Users may compute statistical confidence for subdivisions of the reported data using the formula below. Because sampling error increases as the area or volume considered decreases, users should aggregate data categories as much as possible.

Sampling errors obtained from this method are only approximations of reliability because homogeneity of variances is assumed. The formula is:

$$SE_s = SE_t \frac{\sqrt{X_t}}{\sqrt{X_s}}$$

SE_s = sampling error for subdivision of State total.

SE_t = sampling error for State total.

X_s = sum of values for the variable of interest (area, volume, biomass, etc.) for subdivision of State total.

X_t = sum of values (area, volume, biomass, etc.) for State total.

Measurement error: Errors associated with the methods and instruments used to observe and record the sample attributes are called measurement errors. On FIA plots, attributes such as the diameter and height of a tree are measured with different instruments, and other attributes such as species and crown class are observed without the aid of an instrument. On a typical FIA plot, 30 to 70 trees are observed with 15 to 20 attributes recorded on each tree. In addition, many attributes that describe the plot and conditions on the plot are observed. Errors in any of these observations affect the quality of the estimates. If a measurement is biased—such as tree diameter consistently taken at an incorrect place on the tree—then the estimates that use this observation (e.g. calculated volume) will reflect this bias. Even if measurements are unbiased, high levels of random error in the measurements will add to the total random error of the estimation process. A Quality Assurance Program is an integral part of all FIA data collection efforts to ensure that all FIA observations are made to the highest standards possible (see "Quality Assurance Analysis" in Section IV for more details).

Prediction error: Errors associated with using mathematical models (such as volume models) to provide information about attributes of interest based on sample attributes are referred to as prediction errors. Area, number of trees, volume, biomass, growth, removals, and mortality are the primary attributes of interest presented in this report. Area and number of trees estimates are based on direct observation and do not involve the use of prediction models; however, FIA estimates of volume, biomass, growth, and mortality use model-based predictions in the estimation process.

III. Overview of Tables

FIA is currently working on a revised National Core Table set that will expand the suite of tabled information to incorporate more of the core FIA Program, using both Phase 2 and 3 data ("core" refers to elements of data collection, compilation, and reporting that are consistent and required in all State's FIA programs). Appendix E contains an interim set of tables supporting this report, using Montana annual data for the years 2003 through 2009. There are a total of 37 tables with statistics for land area, number of trees, wood volume, biomass (weight), growth, mortality, and sampling errors. Table 1 is the only table that includes all land types or land status; the rest are for accessible forest land or timberland. Table 37 shows sampling errors for area, volume, net growth, and mortality at the 67 percent confidence level. A complete listing of mean soil properties in Montana, organized by forest type, is in the Soil Indicator core tables in Appendix F. Additional tables in the text of this report that supplement specific sections are numbered consecutively as they appear, starting with table 1.

To avoid confusion with tables found in the body of this report and tables found in the appendices, appendix tables will be referred to beginning with the appendix letter (for example, Appendix E) followed by the table number. A list of all report tables and appendix tables with headings appears in the "Table of Contents."

IV. Overview of Montana's Forest Resources

Ecoregion Provinces of Montana

Issues and events that influence forest conditions often occur across forest types, ownerships, and political boundaries. As a result, scientists, researchers, and land managers must also find a way to assess and treat these issues in a boundary-less way. Ecoregions are often used as a non-political land division to help researchers study forest conditions. An ecoregion is a large landscape area that has relatively consistent patterns of physical and biological components that interact to form environments of similar productive capabilities, response to disturbances, and potentials for resource management (McNab and others 2007). Ecoregions are classed in a descending hierarchy of provinces, sections, and subsections.

Montana encompasses parts of five ecoregion provinces (Bailey 1995): (1) the Northern Rocky Mountain Forest-Steppe Province, (2) the Middle Rocky Mountain Steppe Province, (3) the Southern Rocky Mountain Steppe Province, (4) the Great Plains-Palouse Dry Steppe Province, and (5) a very small portion of the Intermountain Semi-Desert Province. All of these provinces contain forest land in Montana, differing in composition and extent. FIA uses the modifications to Bailey (1995) of McNab and others (2007) to assign plots to ecological provinces, sections, and subsections (fig. 1).

The Northern Rocky Mountain Forest-Steppe Province has a maritime-influenced climate, and has the lowest elevations of the three Rocky Mountain provinces. As a result of these and other influences, it has the highest proportion of forest area (83 percent forested) of Montana's provinces. It is also the most diverse in respect to forest trees: moist site species like grand fir, western larch, mountain hemlock, western hemlock, and western redcedar are concentrated here, and nearly all of the conifer species found elsewhere in Montana are found here as well.

From the Northern Rockies through the Middle Rocky Mountain Steppe and to the Southern Rocky Mountain Steppe Provinces, climatic influences shift from maritime to continental, and elevation increases. Some of the tree species found predominantly in the Northern Rockies are present with a limited distribution in the Middle Rockies, and are absent in the Southern Rockies. Douglas-fir, lodgepole pine, Engelmann spruce, subalpine fir, and whitebark pine are common in these provinces.

Although the Great Plains-Palouse Dry Steppe Province is the most sparsely forested (6 percent forested) of Montana's provinces, due to its large area it contains 13 percent of the State's forest land. The forests are dominated by ponderosa pine and Rocky Mountain juniper.

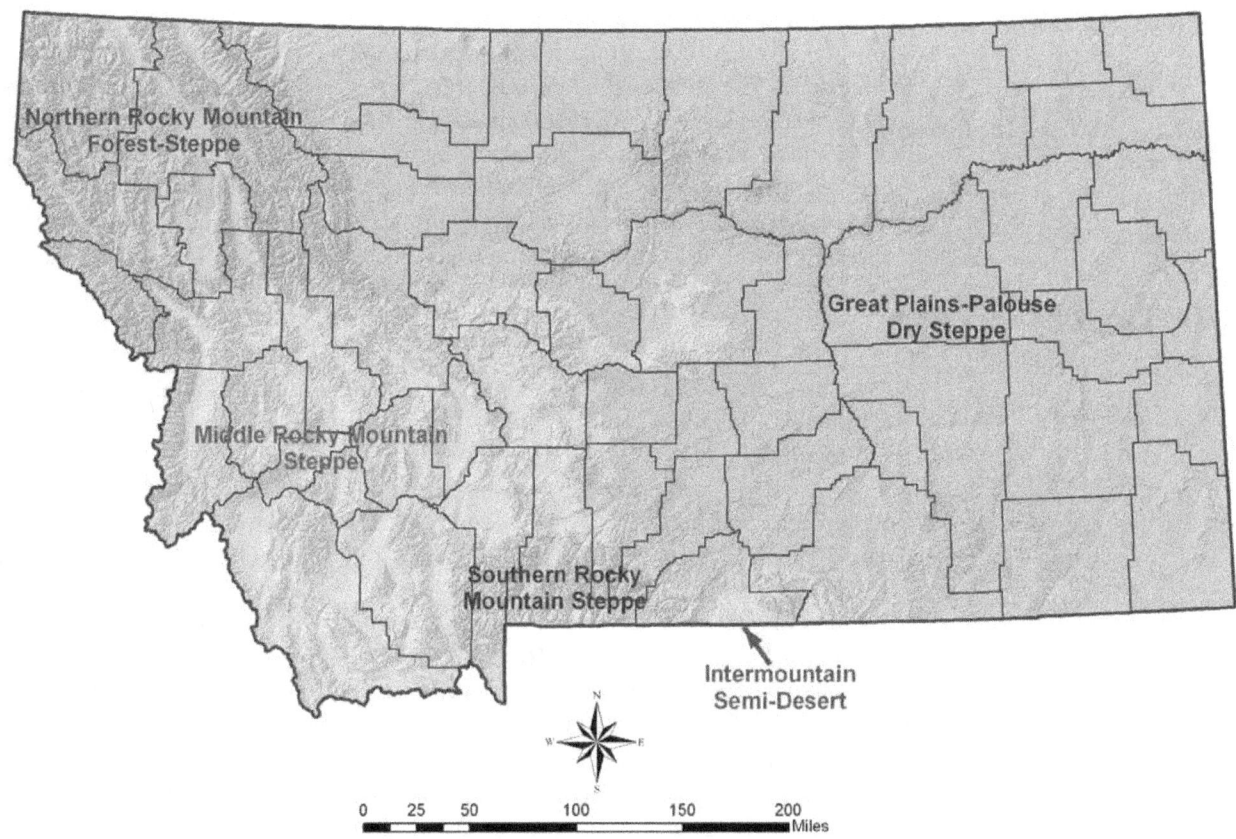

Figure 1—Ecoregion provinces of Montana.

Forest Land Classification

Historically, FIA has used a nationally consistent standard for defining different categories of forest land. These categories were originally developed for the purpose of separating forest land deemed suitable for timber production from forest land that was either not suitable or unavailable for timber harvesting activity. The first division of forest land is unreserved forest land and reserved forest land. Unreserved forest land is considered available for harvesting activity where wood volume can be removed for timber products. Reserved forest land is considered unavailable for any type of wood utilization management practice through administrative legislation.

Unreserved forest land is further divided into timberland and unproductive forests. Timberland is forest land capable of producing 20 cubic feet of wood per acre per year of trees designated as a timber species and not withdrawn from timber production. Unproductive forests, because of species characteristics and site conditions, are not capable of producing 20 cubic feet of wood per acre per year of trees designated as a timber species and not withdrawn from timber production (see Section IX, "Standard Forest Inventory and Analysis Terminology").

Reserved forest land can also be divided by productivity. Some characteristics that contribute to productivity can be visibly obvious, such as the presence or absence of non-commercial species, rocky substrates, and high elevation. While these distinctions may be important to reserved area management concerns, for example, their effect on visitor experience, wood production capability on reserved forest land is probably not the best way to discuss these issues.

USDA Forest Service Resour. Bull. RMRS-RB-15. 2012

7

The State of Montana covers over 94 million acres (Appendix E table 1). Twenty-seven percent, or 25.6 million acres, of the area meets the definition of forest land. The remaining 64 percent or 68.5 million acres are classified as nonforest or water. Unreserved forest land accounts for 84 percent (21.5 million acres) of Montana's forest land, with 92 percent of unreserved forest land classified as timberland, and only 8 percent classified as unproductive. Sixteen percent (4.1 million acres) of the forest land is reserved, with similar proportions of productive and unproductive forest land as in the unreserved portion.

Forest Land Ownership

Table 1 shows that although only 36 percent of Montana's total land area is in the public domain (34.2 million acres: all Forest Service, other Federal, and State and local), this area includes 73 percent of the total forest land area (18.7 million acres). The National Forest Systems (NFS) contains the majority of forest land, at 60 percent, or 15.4 million acres. Over 82 percent of NFS forest land is unreserved, with 79 percent (12.2 million acres) classified as timberland. Seventeen percent, or 2.7 million acres, of NFS forest land is reserved.

Other public agencies managing large portions of Montana's forest land are the Bureau of Land Management (BLM), with 1.2 million acres (69 percent timberland, 10 percent reserved), the State of Montana with 0.9 million acres (89 percent timberland, none reserved), and the National Park Service (NPS) with 0.9 million acres (no timberland, 100 percent reserved). The U.S. Fish and Wildlife Service (USFWS), local (county and municipal) governments, and other Federal agencies combined manage just less than 1 percent of Montana's forest land. The proportion of total managed area that is forested is highest on NFS lands (87 percent) and NPS lands (82 percent).

Privately owned forest land totals 6.9 million acres, or 27 percent of the forest land. Montana's private forest land owners consist of private individuals/families, corporations, and tribes, along with a few unincorporated groups or associations, and non-governmental conservation organizations. All private forest land is considered unreserved, with the exception of some tribal timber reserves. Half of the unreserved, unproductive forest land in Montana is privately owned. Figure 2 shows the spatial distribution of FIA plots by ownership.

Forest Type

Forest type is a classification of forest land based on the species forming a plurality of living trees growing in a particular forest (Arner and others 2001). Forest types are aggregated into forest type groups, which may contain one or several forest types in a particular state. The distribution of forest types across the landscape is determined by factors such as climate, soil, elevation, aspect, and disturbance history. Many of these factors are captured in Montana's ecoregion provinces. Forest type names may be based on a single species or groups of species. Forest types are an important measure of diversity, structure, and successional stage. Loss or gain of a particular forest type over time can be used to assess the impact of major disturbances such as fire, weather, insects, disease, and man-caused disturbances such as timber harvesting activity.

The most abundant forest type group in Montana is the Douglas-fir group, consisting of only one forest type in Montana. The Douglas-fir forest type covers 7.5 million acres and accounts for 29 percent of the forest land in the State,

Table 1—Total area (acres) by ownership class, land status, and forest land classification, Montana, cycle 2, 2003-2009.

Owner class	Forest land					Nonforest	Water	Total area
	Not reserved		Total not reserved	Reserved	Total forest land			
	Timberland	Unproductive						
Forest Service								
National Forest	12,239,635	471,423	12,711,058	2,688,863	15,399,921	2,211,138	101,080	17,712,139
Total Forest Service	**12,239,635**	**471,423**	**12,711,058**	**2,688,863**	**15,399,921**	**2,211,138**	**101,080**	**17,712,139**
Other Federal								
National Park Service	--	--	--	908,085	908,085	194,034	11,135	1,113,254
Bureau of Land Management	851,623	256,111	1,107,734	123,882	1,231,616	6,483,645	--	7,715,261
Fish & Wildlife Service	--	--	--	186,915	186,915	764,273	239,722	1,190,909
Other Federal	--	--	--	8,241	8,241	175,041	58,776	242,058
Total other Federal	**851,623**	**256,111**	**1,107,734**	**1,227,122**	**2,334,856**	**7,616,992**	**309,633**	**10,261,481**
State and local government								
State	825,472	103,140	928,612	--	928,612	5,067,304	174,408	6,170,324
Local	10,227	--	10,227	--	10,227	33,751	--	43,979
Total State and local	**835,700**	**103,140**	**938,839**	**--**	**938,839**	**5,101,056**	**174,408**	**6,214,303**
Private								
Undifferentiated private	5,947,519	803,984	6,751,503	165,672	6,917,176	52,648,592	353,113	59,918,881
Total private	**5,947,519**	**803,984**	**6,751,503**	**165,672**	**6,917,176**	**52,648,592**	**353,113**	**59,918,881**
All owners	**19,874,476**	**1,634,659**	**21,509,135**	**4,081,657**	**25,590,792**	**67,577,778**	**938,234**	**94,106,804**

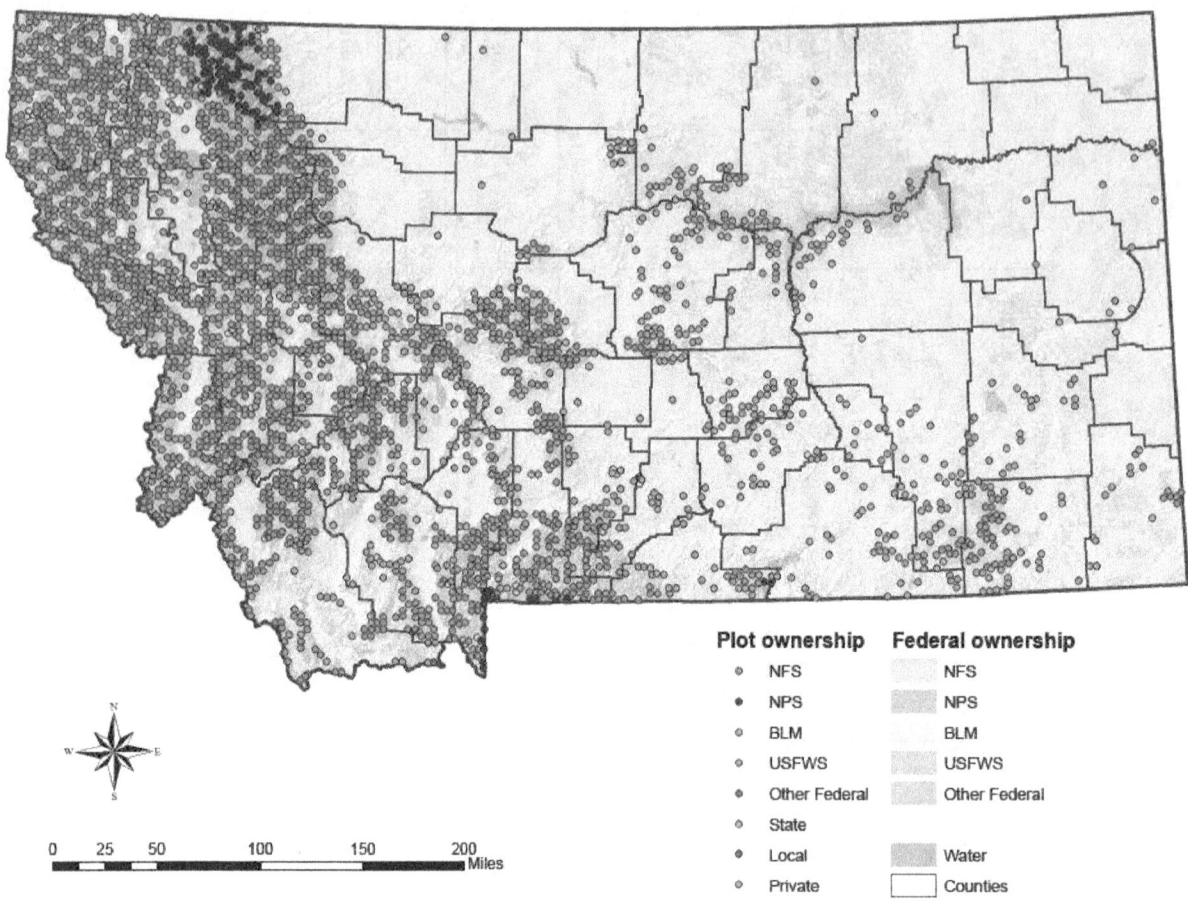

Plot ownership
- ◦ NFS
- • NPS
- ◦ BLM
- ◦ USFWS
- • Other Federal
- ◦ State
- • Local
- ◦ Private

Federal ownership
- NFS
- NPS
- BLM
- USFWS
- Other Federal
- Water
- Counties

Figure 2—Distribution of inventory plots by ownership, showing Federal land management, Montana, cycle 2, 2003-2009. Note: plot locations are approximate and some on private land are randomly swapped.

mostly in the Rocky Mountain ecoregion provinces. Second in abundance is the fir-spruce-mountain hemlock forest type group with 20 percent (5.0 million acres) of the forest land area. This group includes the Engelmann spruce, Engelmann spruce-subalpine fir, subalpine fir, grand fir, and mountain hemlock forest types. The subalpine fir forest type is the most abundant of these, with 45 percent of the area in the forest type group. The fir-spruce-mountain hemlock group occurs only in the Rocky Mountain ecoregion provinces, with the grand fir and mountain hemlock forest types concentrated in the Northern Rocky Mountain province. The lodgepole pine forest type/forest type group includes 17 percent (4.4 million acres) of forest land, primarily in the Rocky Mountain provinces. Ponderosa pine forest type/forest type group makes up 12 percent (3.0 million acres) of Montana's forest land, but 53 percent of ponderosa pine forest is in the Great Plains province, although it occurs in the Rocky Mountain provinces as well. Figure 3A-D shows the spatial distributions of these four most abundant forest type groups.

The other western softwoods group, consisting of the whitebark pine, limber pine, and miscellaneous western softwoods (subalpine larch in Montana) forest types; and the western larch forest type/forest type group each cover 0.9 million acres.

Other forest type groups occurring in the inventory are the pinyon-juniper group (primarily Rocky Mountain juniper), the aspen-birch group, the hemlock-Sitka spruce group, the elm-ash-cottonwood group, the oak-hickory group, the woodland hardwoods group, and the alder-maple group.

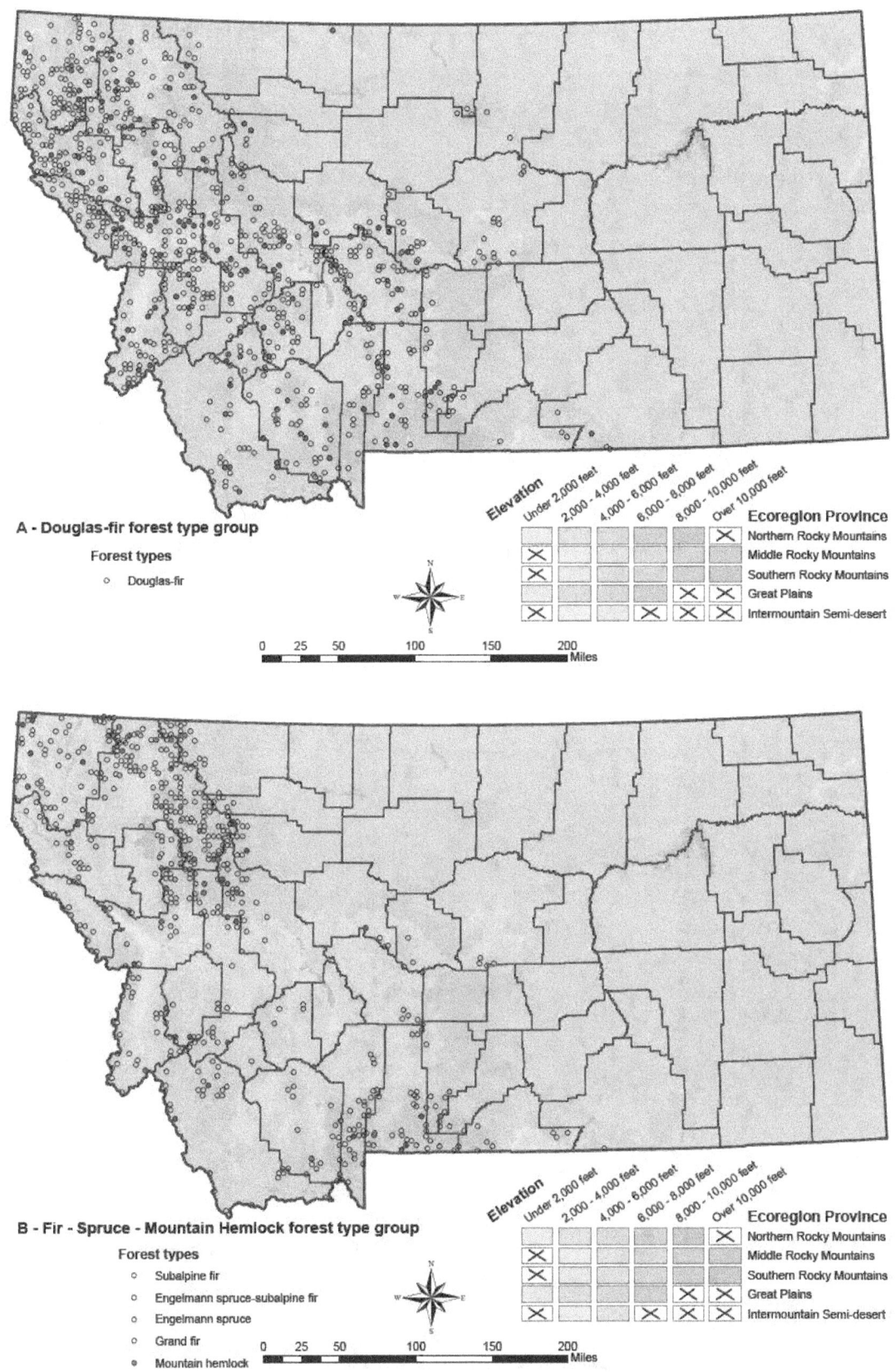

Figure 3—Distribution of inventory plots for four major forest type groups by forest type, ecoregion province, and elevation, Montana, cycle 2, 2003-2009. Note: plot locations are approximate and some on private land are randomly swapped.

USDA Forest Service Resour. Bull. RMRS-RB-15. 2012

11

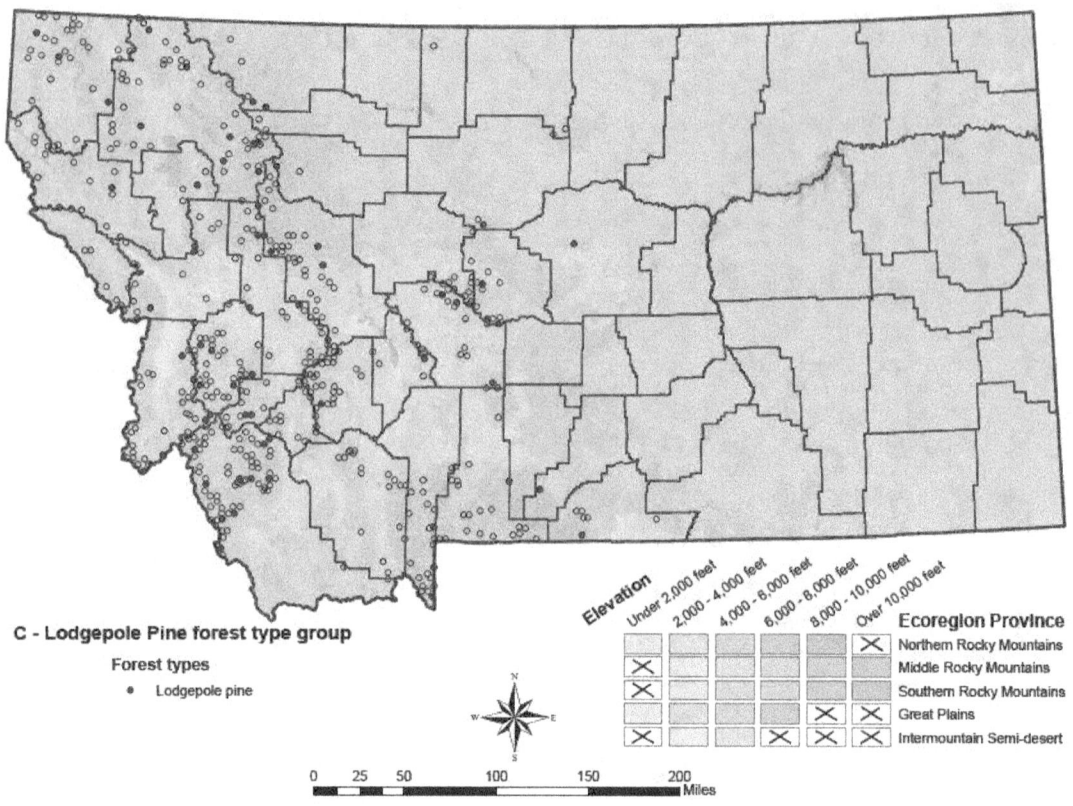

C - Lodgepole Pine forest type group

Forest types

- Lodgepole pine

Elevation

	Under 2,000 feet	2,000 - 4,000 feet	4,000 - 6,000 feet	6,000 - 8,000 feet	8,000 - 10,000 feet	Over 10,000 feet	Ecoregion Province
						☒	Northern Rocky Mountains
☒							Middle Rocky Mountains
☒							Southern Rocky Mountains
					☒	☒	Great Plains
☒			☒	☒	☒		Intermountain Semi-desert

0 25 50 100 150 200 Miles

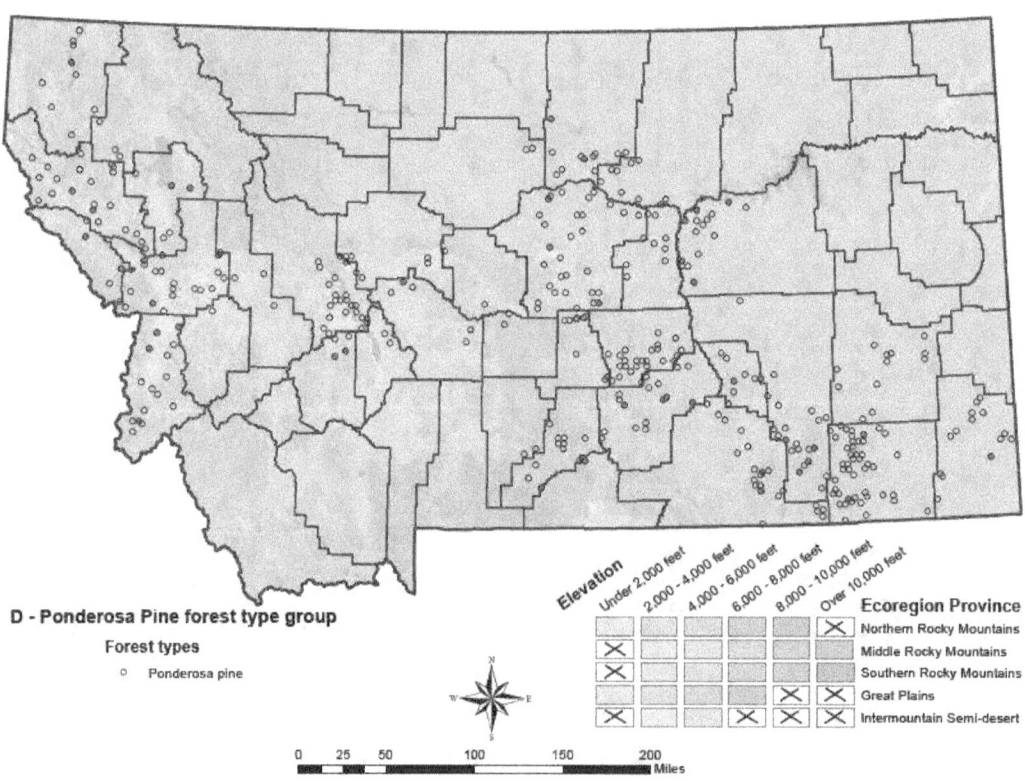

D - Ponderosa Pine forest type group

Forest types

- Ponderosa pine

Elevation

	Under 2,000 feet	2,000 - 4,000 feet	4,000 - 6,000 feet	6,000 - 8,000 feet	8,000 - 10,000 feet	Over 10,000 feet	Ecoregion Province
						☒	Northern Rocky Mountains
☒							Middle Rocky Mountains
☒							Southern Rocky Mountains
					☒		Great Plains
☒			☒	☒	☒		Intermountain Semi-desert

0 25 50 100 150 200 Miles

Figure 3—Continued.

Numbers of Trees

A measure of the numbers of live trees is needed in a variety of silvicultural, forest health, and habitat management applications. To be meaningful, numbers of trees are usually combined with information about the size of the trees. Younger forest stands are usually comprised of large numbers of small-diameter trees whereas older forest stands contain small numbers of large-diameter trees.

There are an estimated 12.0 billion live trees in Montana (Appendix E table 10). Softwood species total 11.7 billion trees or 97 percent of the total (fig. 4). Nearly 66 percent of softwood trees are under 5.0-inches in diameter and over 2 percent are 15.0-inches and larger in diameter. The true fir species group, consisting of subalpine fir and grand fir, is the most abundant species group accounting for 23 percent, or 2.8 billion trees, of the live trees. Next in abundance is lodgepole pine, comprising its own species group, at 2.7 billion trees. Third in abundance is another single- species group, Douglas-fir, with 2.6 billion trees. At 0.9 billion trees, Engelmann spruce (which entirely comprises the Engelmann and other spruces group) is the fourth most abundant species, followed by ponderosa pine (comprising the ponderosa and Jeffrey pine group) with 0.8 billion trees.

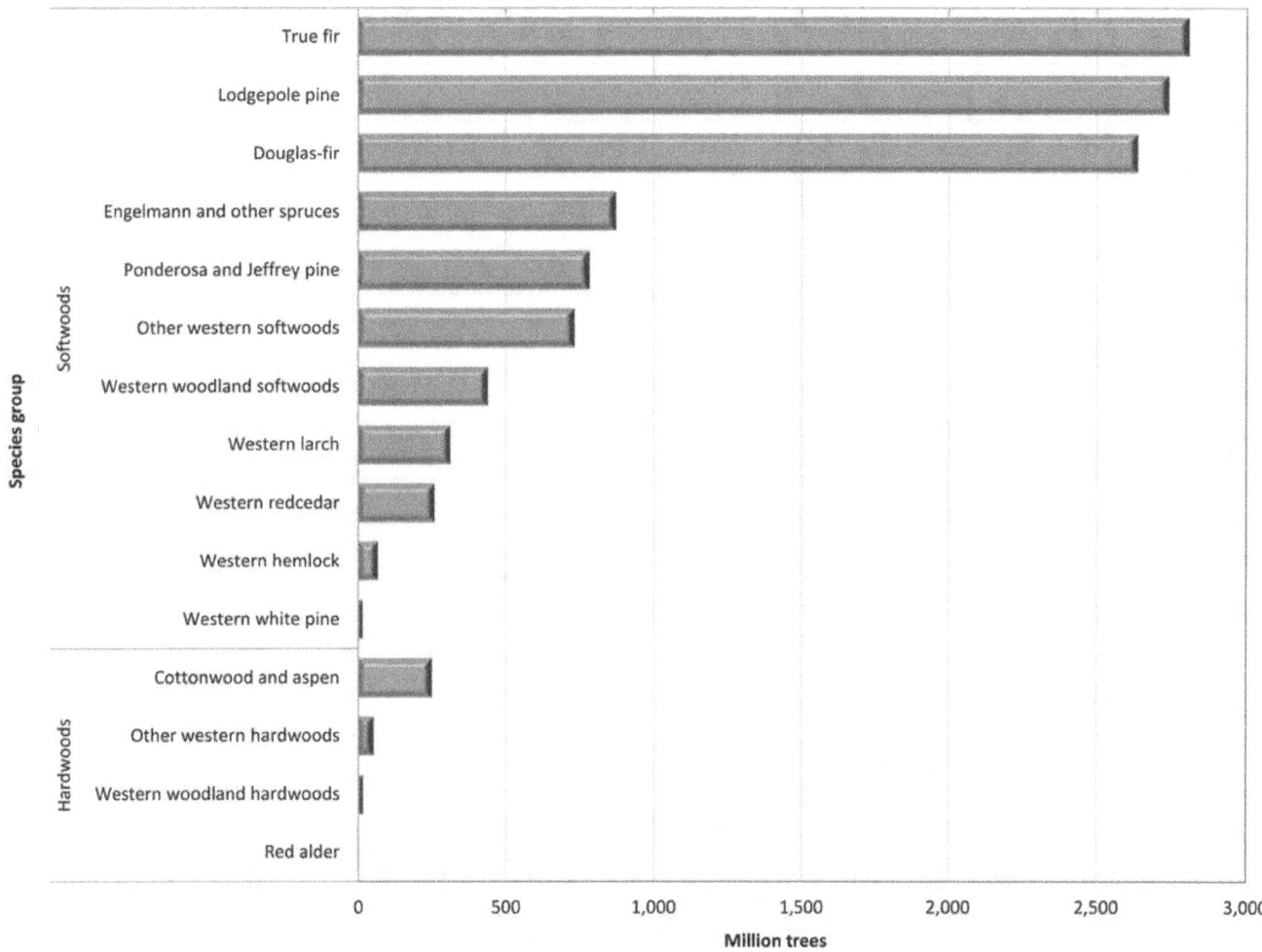

Figure 4—Number of live trees 1.0 inch diameter and greater by species group on forest land, Montana, cycle 2, 2003-2009.

Next in abundance is the other western softwood species group at 0.7 billion trees. The other western softwoods group is a combination of whitebark pine, limber pine, mountain hemlock, pacific yew, and subalpine larch.

Following three other softwood species groups (western woodland softwoods, western larch, and western redcedar), the cottonwood and aspen group is the most abundant hardwood group with 0.25 billion trees. The group consists primarily of quaking aspen, but also includes black cottonwood, plains cottonwood, and narrowleaf cottonwood; and accounts for 2 percent of all trees, but 78 percent of hardwood trees. Seventy-six percent of hardwood trees are under 5.0-inches in diameter and 1.5 percent are 15.0-inches and larger in diameter.

Figure 5 shows numbers of live trees by diameter class for the three most abundant species groups in Montana. It shows the expected distribution of many smaller trees compared to larger trees, and also illustrates the differences in this distribution between species groups that are due to differing ecologies and life histories. For trees less than 5 inches diameter, the true firs are most dominant, with 80 percent of the trees in those size classes compared to 61 percent of Douglas-firs and 56 percent of lodgepole pines. Lodgepole pines are dominant in the 5- to 10.9-inch diameter classes, with 39 percent of the trees, compared to 27 percent of

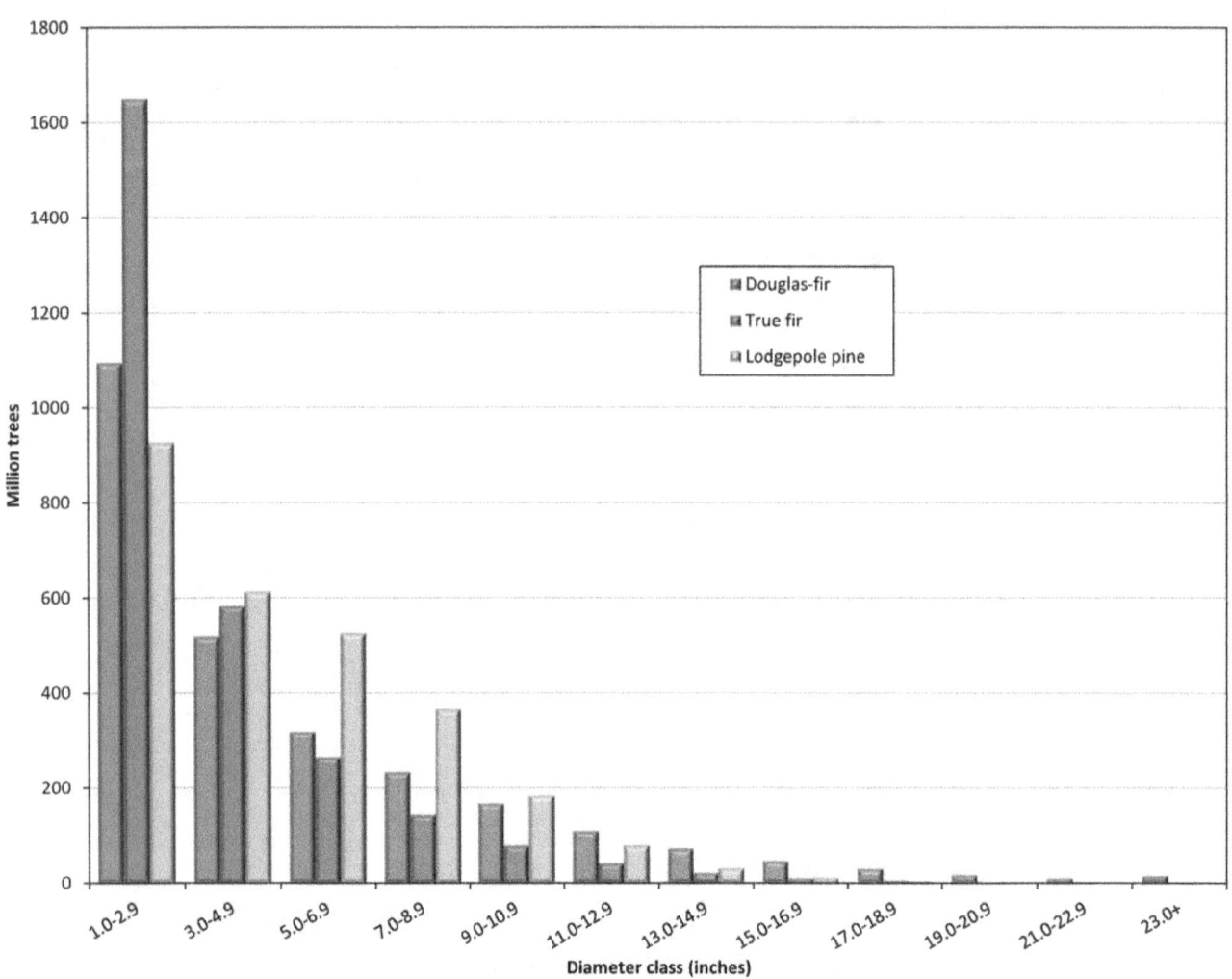

Figure 5—Number of live trees on forest land by three major species groups and diameter class, Montana, cycle 2, 2003-2009.

USDA Forest Service Resour. Bull. RMRS-RB-15. 2012

Douglas-firs and 17 percent of true firs. Twelve percent of all live Douglas-firs are 11 inches diameter and larger, while only 5 percent of lodgepole pines and 3 percent of true firs are that large.

On timberland (nonreserved and productive) in Montana, there are 3.2 billion live growing-stock trees 5.0-inches diameter and greater, of which lodgepole pine is the most common with 31 percent (Appendix E table 11). The next most abundant growing-stock species on timberland are Douglas-fir with over 28 percent, subalpine fir (in the true fir species group) with 11 percent, ponderosa pine with 8 percent, Engelmann spruce with 7 percent, western larch with 4 percent, and whitebark pine (in the other western softwoods group) with over 3 percent.

There are an estimated one billion standing dead trees, or snags, at least 5.0-inches diameter on forest land in Montana, or an average of 39.7 snags per acre (this compares to 159.3 live trees per acre of these diameters). As with live trees, larger snags are less common than smaller snags, and often contribute more significantly to important forest landscape components such as wildlife habitat, nutrient cycles (including carbon), fire fuel loading, and soil formation. Considering snags 11.0-inches diameter and larger, the average density is 8.3 per acre (compared to 33.3 live trees per acre of this size). Very large snags, 19.0-inches diameter and larger, occur on Montana forests at about 1.1 per acre (3.8 live trees per acre of this size). Overall, the most common species for snags is lodgepole pine, which is also the most common in the 11.0-inches and over snag class. In the 19.0-inches and over class, the most abundant species for snags is Douglas-fir. Snag densities are calculated over all forest land in the State, and do not take into account irregular distributions of dead trees caused by localized mortality events like fires, insect outbreaks, and diseases. Densities may vary considerably when looked at by sublevels of forest land like ownerships, counties, or forest types.

Volume and Biomass

The amount of cubic-foot volume of wood in a forest is important for determining the sustainability of current and future wood utilization. The forest products industry is interested in knowing where available timber volume is located, who owns it, the species composition, and the size distribution. Estimates of gross and net volume include only the merchantable portion or saw-log portion (e.g., cubic-foot or board-foot) of trees, while biomass describes aboveground tree weight (oven-dry) by various components (merchantable bole and bark, tops and limbs, saplings). Net volumes are computed by deducting rotten, missing, or form defect from gross volume. Biomass estimates for this report are those obtained using IWFIA regional equations (Appendix E tables 29a and 30a), which are based on gross volumes and exclude foliage. These volume and biomass equation sources are documented in Appendix D. For comparison, biomass estimates using the FIA national component ratio method are presented in tables 29b and 30b. For explanation of the component ratio method, see Appendix J in Woudenberg and others (2010).

Appendix E tables 12 through 16 show net volume of live trees 5.0-inches diameter and greater on Montana forest land by various categories. The total net volume of wood in live and standing dead trees 5.0-inches diameter and greater on Montana forest land is 44.6 and 9.2 billion cubic-feet, respectively. Over 75 percent, or 33.7 billion cubic feet, is located on lands administered by National Forest System. Fifteen percent, or 6.5 billion cubic feet, is under private ownership. Seven percent, or 3.1 billion cubic feet is on lands administered by various Federal

USDA Forest Service Resour. Bull. RMRS-RB-15. 2012

15

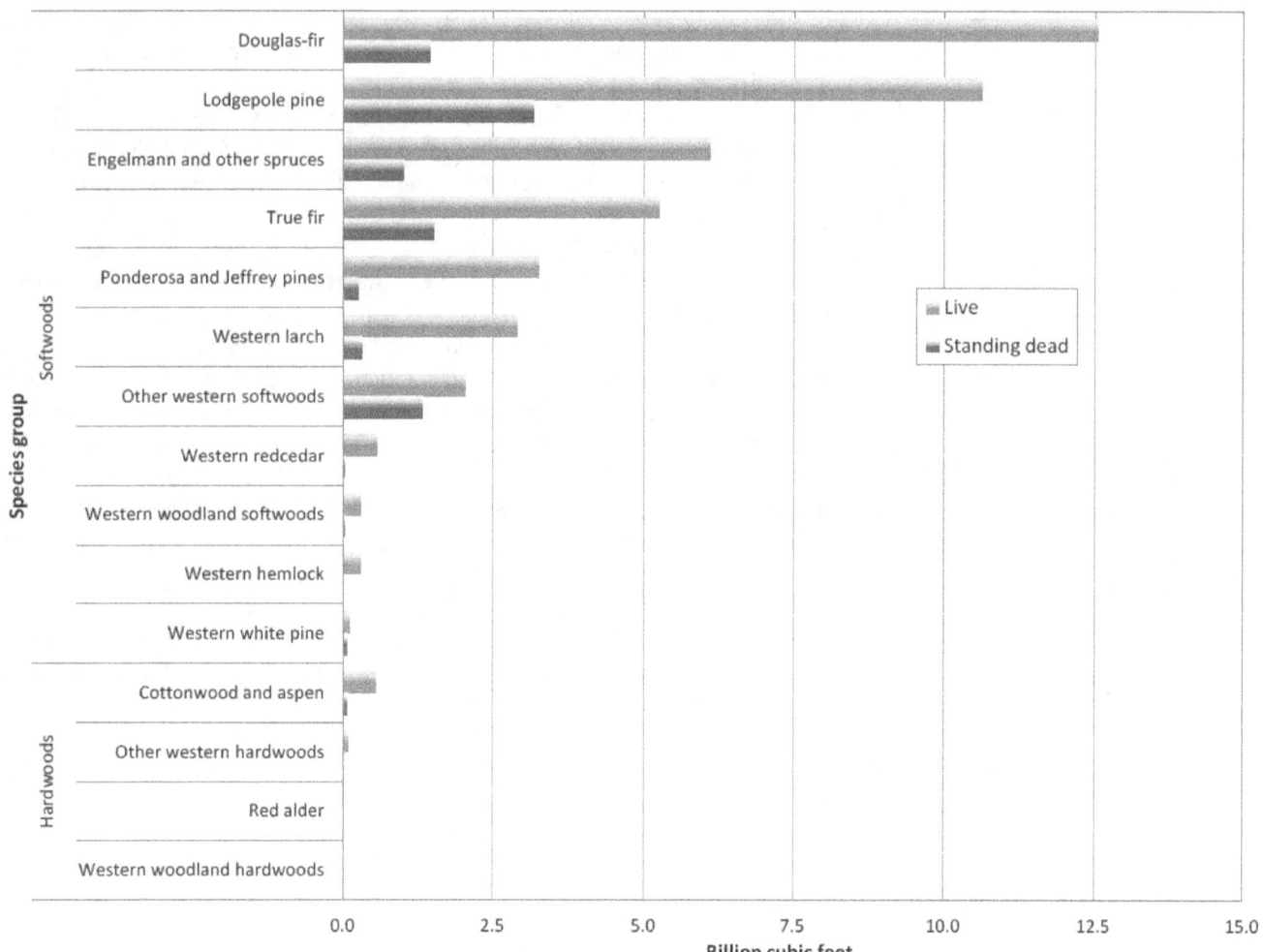

Figure 6—Net cubic-foot volume of all live and standing dead trees 5.0 inches diameter and greater by species group on forest land, Montana, cycle 2, 2003-2009.

agencies other than the National Forest System. The remainder, about 1.3 billion cubic feet, is on lands administered by State and local governments.

The predominant species are Douglas-fir, which comprises 28 percent of the total live net cubic-foot volume, followed by lodgepole pine at 24 percent, Engelmann spruce at 14 percent, subalpine fir at 10 percent, and ponderosa pine at 7 percent. Lodgepole pine comprises 35 percent of the total standing dead volume, followed by 16 percent for Dougas-fir, 15 percent for subalpine fir, 12 percent for whitebark pine, and 11 percent for Engelmann spruce (fig. 6). The total weight of oven-dry biomass in live (1.0 inches diameter and greater) and standing dead trees (5.0 inches diameter and greater) on Montana forest land is 870 and 200 million tons, respectively (fig. 7).

Another way to look at volume and biomass is by forest type, for which net volume and biomass per acre can be computed (table 2). These estimates include the different species that occur within each forest type. Because estimates for forest types with small samples may not be representative, only forest types sampled on at least 20 plots are included in this discussion. Western redcedar has the highest per-acre net volume of live trees 5.0 inches diameter and greater at 4,226 cubic-feet per acre, and the highest biomass of live trees 1.0 inches diameter and greater

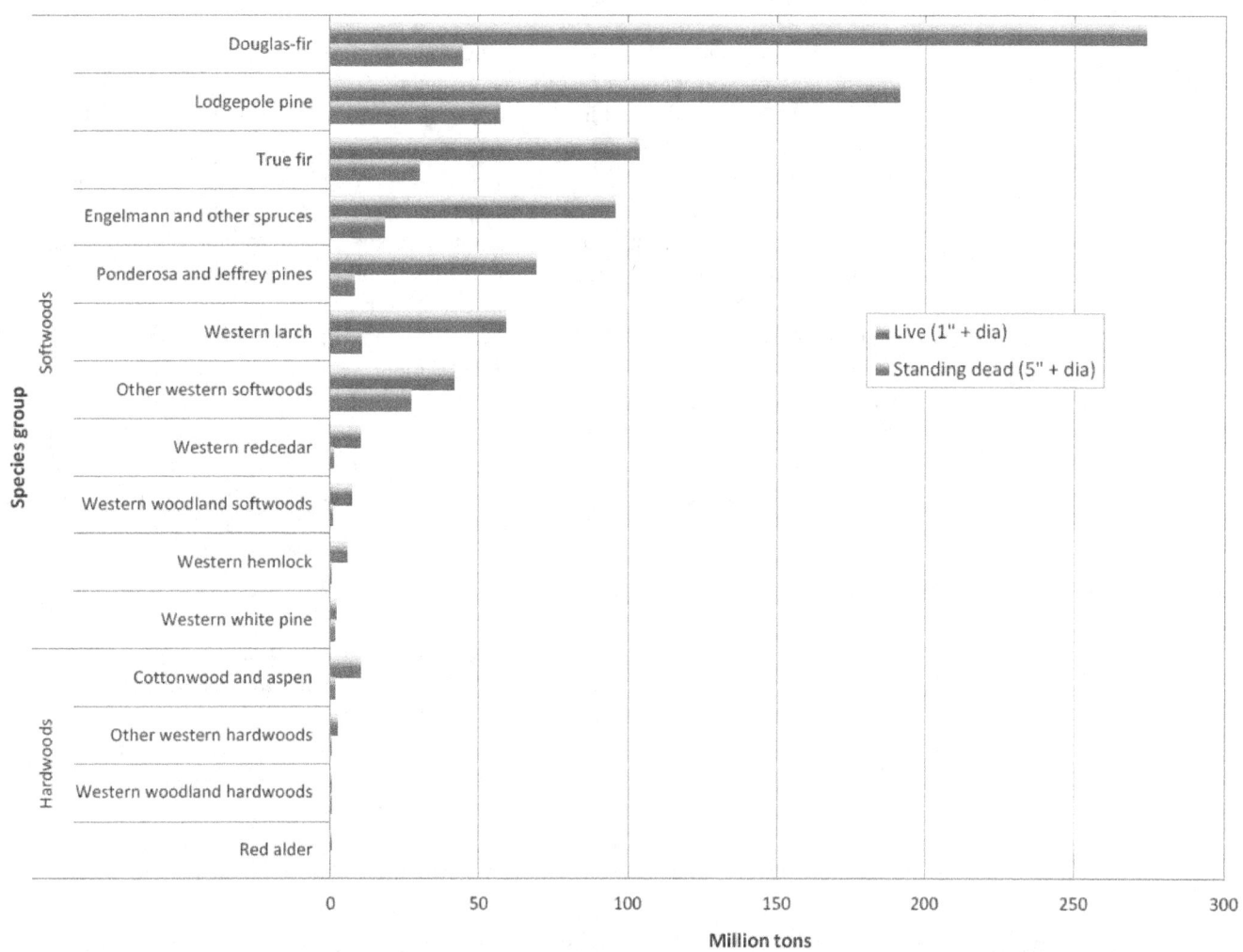

Figure 7—Oven-dry weight biomass of live and standing dead trees by species group on forest land, Montana, cycle 2, 2003-2009.

Table 2—Net volume (cubic-feet) and biomass (tons) per acre of live trees by common forest types on forest land, Montana, cycle 2, 2003-2009.

Forest type	Net volume	Biomass
Western redcedar	4,226	74.6
Engelmann spruce	3,038	48.2
Engelmann spruce-subalpine fir	2,998	52.6
Western larch	2,723	53.8
Grand fir	2,486	44.1
Lodgepole pine	2,211	41.9
Whitebark pine	1,906	36.9
Douglas-fir	1,836	38.9
Subalpine fir	1,669	32.2
Cottonwood	1,325	22.1
Ponderosa pine	964	20.9
Aspen	571	12.2
Limber pine	517	13.0
Rocky Mountain juniper	329	7.5
Nonstocked	59	1.3
All types	**1,742**	**34.0**

USDA Forest Service Resour. Bull. RMRS-RB-15. 2012

17

at 74.6 tons per acre. Douglas-fir, the most common forest type in Montana, has about 1,836 cubic-feet per acre of volume and 38.9 tons per acre of biomass.

The net volume of growing stock trees on nonreserved productive timberland in Montana is 36 billion cubic feet (Appendix E table 17). Douglas-fir makes up 31 percent of the total growing stock volume, followed by lodgepole pine at 24 percent, Engelmann spruce at 12 percent, and subalpine fir and lodgepole pine, each with 9 percent. Appendix E table 19 shows the volume of sawtimber trees (International ¼-inch rule) on nonreserved productive timberland at about 149.5 billion board feet. Douglas-fir accounts for the majority of sawtimber at 30 percent, followed by lodgepole pine at 18 percent, Engelmann spruce at 15 percent, and ponderosa pine at 10 percent. The total weight of oven-dry biomass in live trees 1.0 inches diameter and greater on nonreserved productive timberland land is 715 million tons (Appendix E table 29a). Although biomass is usually sold by green weight, the water content of wood is highly variable geographically, seasonally, and even across portions of a single tree. This makes live-tree inventory estimates of green biomass unreliable and potentially misleading.

Forest Growth and Mortality

Two common measures of forest vigor and sustainability are tree growth and mortality. Growth, as reported here, is the average annual growth volume calculated from a sample of tree increment core measurements based on the previous 10 years of radial growth. Mortality, as reported here, is the average annual net volume of trees that have died in the 5 years prior to the year of measurement. The reason behind this growth and mortality estimation procedure in Montana is that the inventory data are limited to initial plot measurements. Complete remeasurement data for the State—where the status of the plot and all trees on the plot are known at two points in time—will not be available until all ten panels of data are completed and remeasurement begins in the eleventh year.

The relationship between growth and mortality quantifies the change in inventory volume over time. Net growth is gross, or total, growth minus mortality, which approximates the average annual change in inventory volume, but does not include the average annual volume removed through timber harvesting.

Net annual growth of all live trees 5.0 inches diameter and greater on Montana forest land totaled 289.8 million cubic feet while mortality totaled nearly 746.3 million cubic feet (Appendix E tables 22 and 25). Figure 8 illustrates the relationship between net growth and mortality by ownership group in Montana. Mortality of all trees on forest land administered by the National Forest System totaled 578 million cubic feet and exceeded net growth on this owner group by more than threefold. In contrast, net growth exceeded mortality on privately owned forests. Net growth totaled 126.9 million cubic feet on private forest land compared to 58.8 million cubic feet of mortality.

Figure 9 illustrates the relationship between net growth and mortality for the major species and species groups in Montana. Of the nine species and one species group listed, mortality exceeded net growth for five. A striking relationship between net growth and mortality occurred in lodgepole pine. The 252.6 million cubic feet of lodgepole pine mortality was over 25 times higher than the 10 million cubic feet of net growth. Whitebark pine—an important producer of food for wildlife in Montana and other States—actually recorded a negative net growth of −30.4 million cubic feet compared to 53.8 million cubic feet of mortality. Mortality of the true fir species group, consisting of grand fir and subalpine fir, totaled

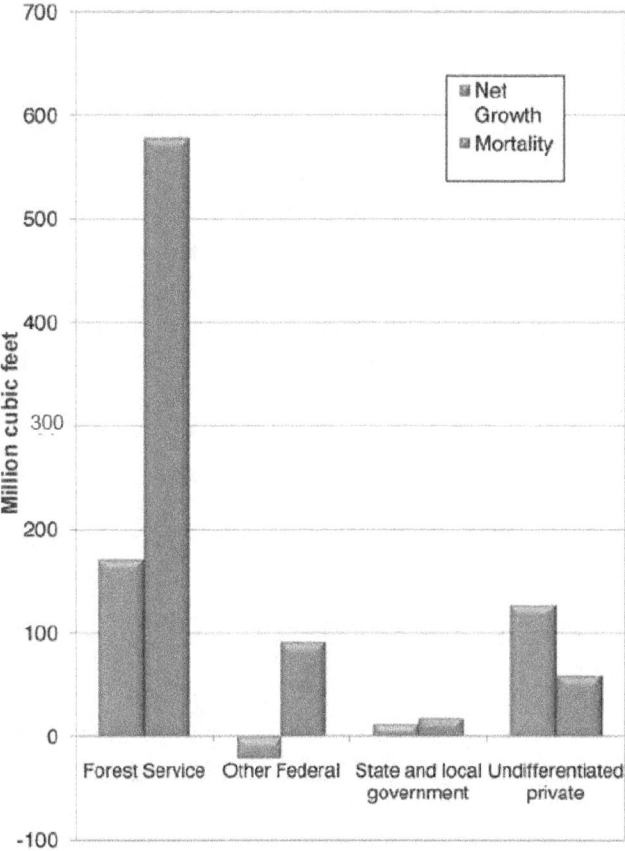

Figure 8—Net annual growth and mortality of live trees on forest land by ownership group, Montana, cycle 2, 2003-2009.

138.5 million cubic feet compared to only 34.4 million cubic feet of net growth. Ponderosa pine, western larch, western redcedar, western hemlock, and aspen indicated positive relationships between net growth and mortality.

As mentioned in the "Introduction" and further explained in Appendix A, comparisons of current inventory estimates with previous inventories are tenuous. In previous inventories, reserved lands were not inventoried, sampling intensities varied, and data compilation strategies were different. However, general comparisons between current estimates of net growth and mortality and previous estimates do provide some historical perspective. For the current inventory, net annual growth of growing-stock trees averaged 361.5 million cubic feet and growing stock mortality averaged 492.1 million cubic feet on forest land defined as timberland. In the 1989 inventory, net annual growth averaged 658.0 million cubic feet and mortality averaged 199.4 million cubic feet on forest land classified as timberland at that time (Conner and O'Brien 1993). Net growth also exceeded mortality in the 1979 inventory (Green and others 1985) as well as in the inventory that occurred during the period between 1943 and 1949 on land defined as timberland (Hutchison and Kemp 1952). Despite the differences in inventory procedures over time, the 2003-2009 inventory of Montana undoubtedly marks the first period since the State began inventories where mortality exceeded net growth.

Since high mortality is the driving force behind the large reductions in gross growth, further examination of this change component by other resource attributes can help explain the factors behind the high level of tree volume estimated to have died in the previous 5 years. Significant differences were observed in per-acre estimates of mortality between major ownership groups and reserved status. Converting the State-level estimates of mortality into per-acre estimates removes

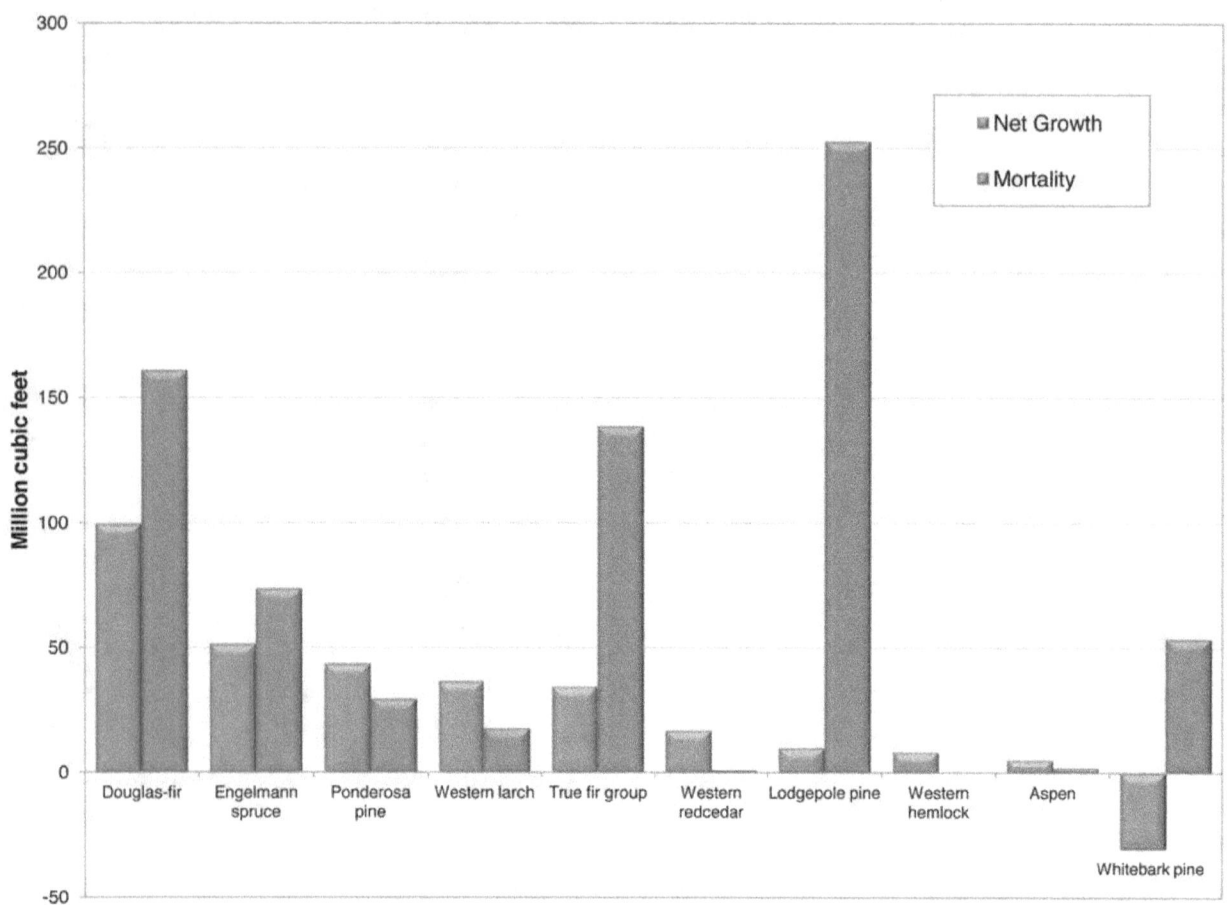

Figure 9—Net annual growth and mortality of live trees on forest land by species or species group, Montana, cycle 2, 2003-2009.

the effect of differences in the amount of forest land administered by different ownership groups. Across all ownerships, the per-acre estimate of annual mortality volume averages 29.2 cubic feet per year on forest land. Mortality on reserved forest land was significantly higher than unreserved land. Average annual mortality on reserved land averaged 58.4 cubic feet per acre compared to 23.6 cubic feet per acre on unreserved forest land. Figure 10 illustrates per-acre estimates of mortality by two major owner categories and reserved status. Reserved forest land administered by private landowners, other Federal agencies, and State agencies recorded the highest average level of per-acre mortality at 59.3 cubic feet per acre followed by National Forest System's lands classified as reserved at 58 cubic feet per acre.

Figure 11 illustrates per-acre estimates of mortality by reserved status and cause of death. All trees classified as mortality are assigned a cause of death in the field. Drawing conclusions from mortality estimates by cause of death should be done with caution. The actual agent that caused a tree's death may be difficult, if not impossible, to determine. The cause of death category of other includes trees that have died due to reasons the field crews are unable to determine. Interactions between insects and diseases are complex and make identification of damaging agents difficult. Mortality due to fire accounted for the majority (46.9 percent) of total mortality. Insects were the second leading contributor to mortality, accounting for 34.5 percent of the total. Disease accounted for 13 percent. There was a very significant difference in the level of fire-caused per-acre mortality recorded on reserved forest land (fig. 11).

USDA Forest Service Resour. Bull. RMRS-RB-15. 2012

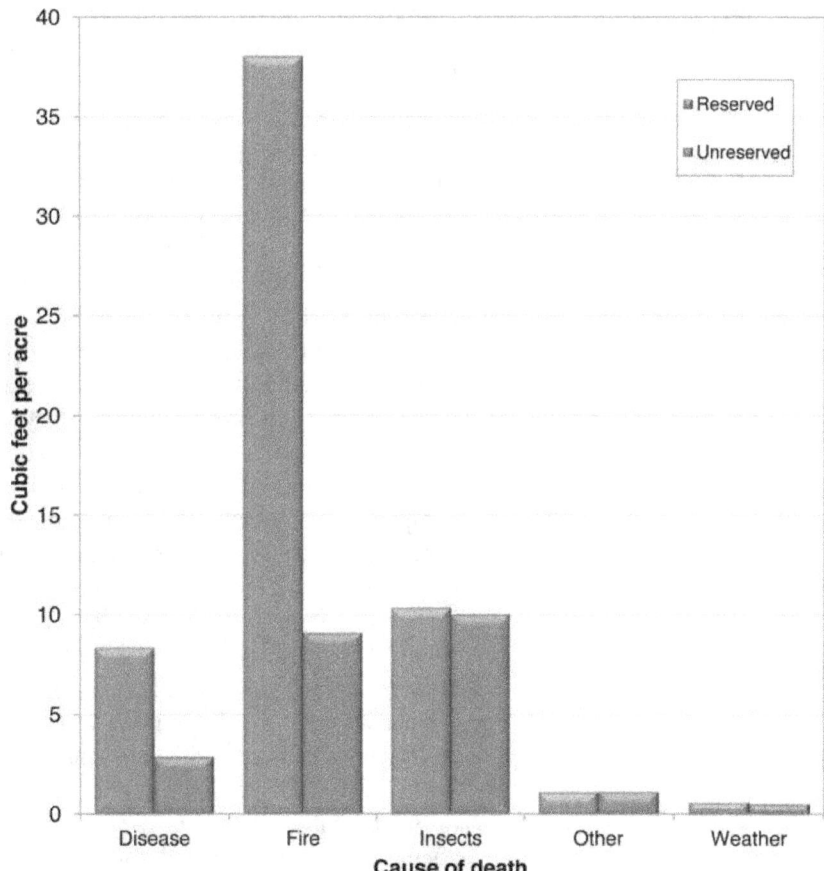

Figure 10—Average annual per-acre mortality on forest land by two major owner categories and reserved status, Montana, 2003-2009.

Figure 11—Average annual per-acre mortality on forest land by reserved status and cause of death, Montana, 2003-2009.

USDA Forest Service Resour. Bull. RMRS-RB-15. 2012

21

The high mortality resulted in a very significant reduction in gross growth for several species and species groups. Mortality is highest on forest land classified as reserved. Mountain pine beetle infestations are likely contributing to much of the lodgepole pine mortality. Lodgepole pine accounted for 57 percent of the mortality volume determined to be caused by insects. Trends in lodgepole pine mortality believed to have been caused by mountain pine beetle are examined in "Mountain Pine Beetle" in Section V.

Stand Density Index (SDI)

Stand density index (SDI; Reineke 1933) is a relative measure of stand density, based on quadratic mean diameter of the stand and the number of live trees per acre. In the western States, silviculturists often use SDI as one measure of stand structure to meet diverse objectives such as ecological restoration and wildlife habitat (e.g., Smith and Long 1987; Lilieholm and others 1994; Long and Shaw 2005).

SDI is usually presented as a percentage of a maximum SDI for each forest type. Maximum SDI is rarely, if ever, observed in nature at the stand scale because the onset of competition-induced (self-thinning) mortality begins to occur at about 60 percent of the maximum SDI. Average maximum density, which is used in normal yield tables and is equivalent to the A-line in Gingrich-type stocking diagrams (Gingrich 1967), is equal to approximately 80 percent of maximum SDI. There are several reasons why stands may have low SDI. Stands typically have low SDI following major disturbances, such as fire, insect attack, or harvesting. These stands remain in a low-density condition until regeneration fills available growing space. Stands that are over-mature can also have low SDI, because growing space may not be re-occupied as fast as it is released by the mortality of large, old trees. Finally, stands that occur on very thin soils or rocky sites may remain at low density indefinitely, because limitations on physical growing space do not permit full site occupancy. A site is considered to be fully occupied at 35 percent of maximum SDI. At lower densities, individual tree growth is maximized but stand growth is below potential, while at higher densities, individual tree growth is below potential but stand growth is maximized (Long 1985).

Originally developed for even-aged stands, SDI can also be applied to uneven-aged stands (Long and Daniel 1990; Shaw 2000). Stand structure can influence the computation of SDI, so the definition of maximum SDI must be compatible with the computation method. Because FIA data include stands covering the full range of structure, the maximum SDIs are currently being revised for FIA forest types (Shaw and Long, in prep.). The provisional revised maximum SDIs, which are compatible with FIA computation methods, are shown in table 3. SDI was computed for each condition that sampled forest land using the summation method (Shaw 2000), and the SDI percentage was calculated using the maximum SDI for the forest type found on the condition.

The distribution of SDI values in Montana is relatively balanced. Figure 12 shows that stands appear to be well-stocked, with over 52 percent of forest acres at least fully occupied (SDI equal to 35 percent or greater). The other 48 percent is relatively evenly distributed over the lower range of stocking. Over 19 percent of Montana's forests are in the range where competition-induced mortality is expected (SDI equal to 60 percent or greater).

Stands with SDI between 35 and 60 percent of maximum SDI (full stocking zone) are desirable from a forest management perspective because that density

Table 3—Maximum SDI by forest type, Montana, cycle 2, 2003-2009.

Forest type	Maximum SDI
182 Rocky Mountain juniper	425
184 Juniper woodland	385
201 Douglas-fir	485
221 Ponderosa pine	375
265 Engelmann spruce	500
266 Engelmann spruce / subalpine fir	485
267 Grand fir	475
268 Subalpine fir	470
270 Mountain hemlock	560
281 Lodgepole pine	530
301 Western hemlock	600
304 Western redcedar	630
321 Western larch	430
366 Limber pine	410
367 Whitebark pine	500
368 Misc. western softwoods	450
517 Elm / ash / black locust	458
703 Cottonwood	360
706 Sugarberry / hackberry / elm / green ash	504
709 Cottonwood / willow	420
901 Aspen	490
902 Paper birch	440
911 Red alder	445
974 *Cercocarpus* woodland	415
999 Unknown / nonstocked	475

range maximizes stand growth and minimizes competition-induced mortality; other objectives, such as fuel reduction or maintenance of wildlife habitat characteristics, may warrant lower relative densities. The proportion of Montana's forests in the full stocking zone (32.5 percent) is comparable to the proportions found in other interior Western States (Arizona, 25.2 percent; Colorado, 34.9 percent; Idaho, 32.7 percent; Utah, 32.0 percent). At 19.6 percent, the proportion of area in the competition mortality zone is about in the middle of the range found in other interior Western States (Arizona, 15.8 percent; Colorado, 25.3 percent; Idaho, 14.4 percent; Utah, 20.0 percent). The proportion of acreage in this density range is likely to decrease over time because excessive density is considered a risk factor for many damaging agents. Several damaging agents, such as mountain pine beetle and spruce budworm, are currently active in Montana and are expected to disproportionately affect high-density stands. Management activities designed to reduce risks, such as thinnings and fuel reduction treatments, will also reduce the proportion of stands in high-density condition. At the same time, many lower-density stands should increase in relative density. Depending on the severity of insect infestations, the combined effects of growth, mortality, and management activities may lead to an eventual increase in the area of well-stocked forest land, or possibly an increase in the area of lower-stocked stands.

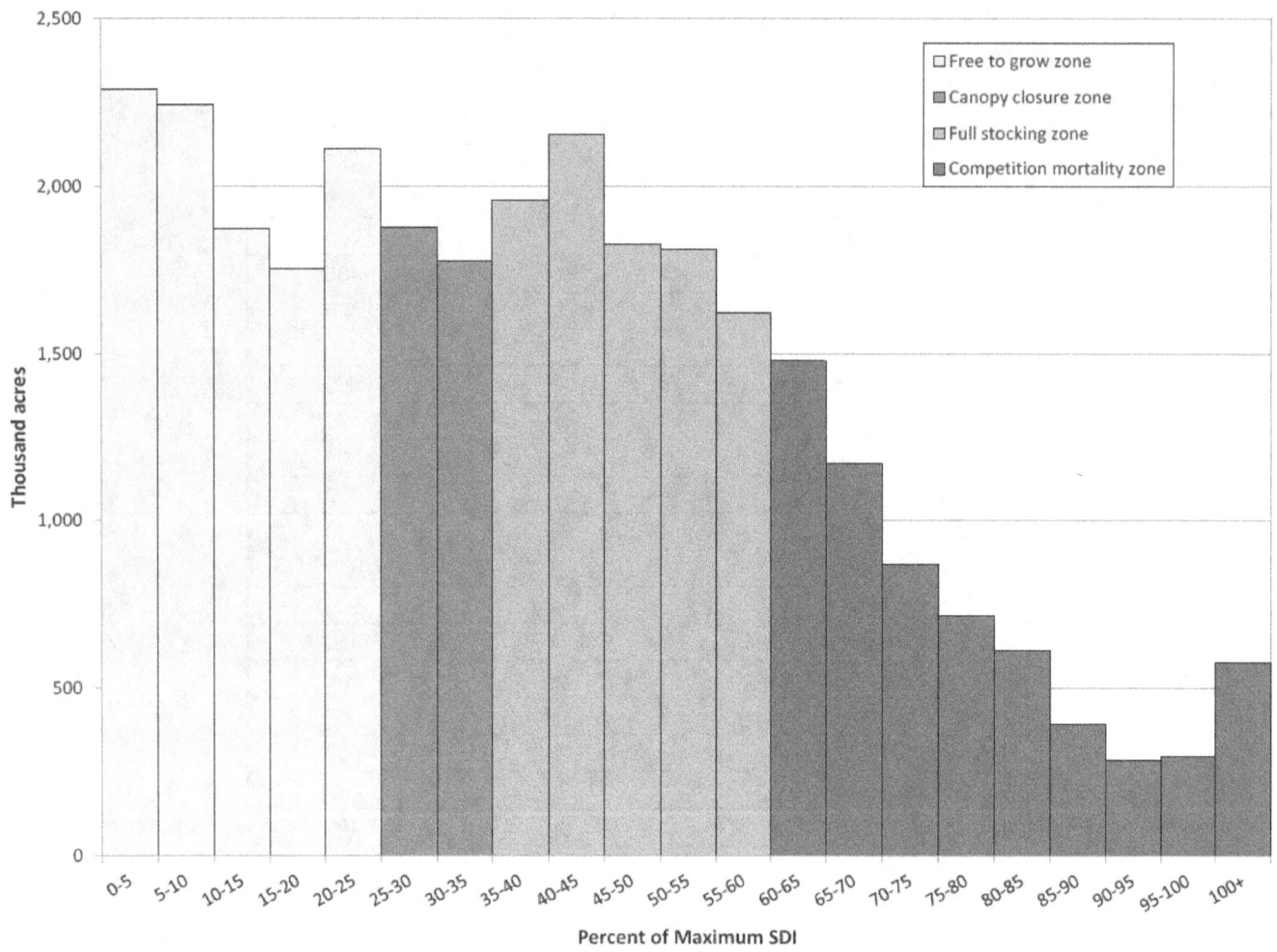

Figure 12—Distribution of stand density on Montana forest land, cycle 2, 2003-2009.

Quality Assurance Analysis

FIA employs a Quality Assurance (QA) Program to ensure the quality of all collected data. The goal of the QA program is to provide a framework to assure the production of complete, accurate, and unbiased forest information of known quality. Specific Measurement Quality Objectives (MQO) for precision are designed to provide a performance objective that FIA strives to achieve for every field measurement. These data quality objectives were developed from knowledge of measurement processes in forestry and forest ecology, as well as the program needs of FIA.

The practicality of these MQO, as well as the measurement uncertainty associated with a given field measurement can be tested by comparing data from blind check plots. Blind check data are paired observations where, in addition to the field measurements of the standard FIA crew, a second QA measurement of the plot is taken by a crew without knowledge of the first crew's results (Pollard and others 2006). The QA data for this analysis were collected between 2003 and 2009, in the same year as the standard field measurements, and then compared for measurement precision between two independent FIA crews' observations. Therefore, for many FIA variables the data quality is measured by the repeatability of two independent measurements.

The results of the QA analysis for this reporting period are presented in tables 4 and 5. Table 4 describes tolerances for condition-level variables, and table 5 describes tree-level variables. Tolerances are the "accepted" range of variability between two independent observations, for checking or comparison purposes. Each variable and its associated tolerance are followed by the percentage of total paired records that fell within one, two, three, and four times the tolerance. The last four columns show the number of times out of the total records the data fell outside the tolerance.

For example, table 5 shows that there were 3,358 paired records for the variable "d.b.h." (diameter at breast height). At the 1X tolerance level, over 91 percent of those records fell within plus or minus one-tenth inch of each other, for each 20.0 inches of d.b.h. observed. This percentage is referred to as the observed compliance rate. MQO for each variable consists of two parts: a compliance standard and a measurement tolerance, and can be compared to the observed compliance rate to determine that variable's performance.

The information in tables 4 and 5 shows variables with varying degrees of repeatability. For example, one condition-level regional variable that appears fairly repeatable is "percent bare ground." At the 1X tolerance level, its observed compliance rate was 94 percent for 146 paired observations that were within plus or minus 10 percent of each other. In contrast, the compliance rate for "habitat type 1," which has no tolerance variability, was only 62 percent for the same observations. Habitat types, often grouped in various ways, are an important variable for forest management. Accurate determination could provide an insight to successional status when combined with existing vegetation, such as tree numbers, size class, and species by habitat types or series, thus warranting further investigations into the potential repeatability issues associated with evaluating habitat types and/or groups.

The tree-level variable "d.b.h.," as mentioned above, is more repeatable when compared to the regional variable "tree age," which has a 1X tolerance compliance rate of 18 percent. This is probably due to the difficulty of obtaining accurate tree ages. Several factors might affect inconsistent tree ages: (1) tree too large to reach the center, (2) rings too close or faded to read accurately, or (3) variation in age estimation when not hitting tree center (pith). Although not much can be done about the first two situations, QA data can be used to develop better field procedures for the last, especially for critical variables such as tree age.

As more blind check information becomes available, it might become apparent that a variable's MQO needs to be adjusted accordingly to better reflect the realistic expectation of quality for that variable. As a result, MQO should be used not only to assess the reliability of FIA measurements and whether current standards are being met, but also to provide data collection experts with the information necessary to improve the current data collection system. This process can improve repeatability, or lead to elimination of variables that prove to be unrepeatable.

USDA Forest Service Resour. Bull. RMRS-RB-15. 2012

25

Table 4—QA results for condition-level variables from 169 conditions in Montana, cycle 2, 2003-2009.

Variable	Tolerance	Percentage of data within tolerance				Number of times data exceeded tolerance				Records
		@1x	@2x	@3x	@4x	@1x	@2x	@3x	@4x	
Condition status	No tolerance	99.4				1				169
Reserve status	No tolerance	98.8				2				169
Owner group	No tolerance	98.8				2				169
Forest type (Type)	No tolerance	91.1				13				146
Stand size	No tolerance	87.0				19				146
Regeneration status	No tolerance	99.3				1				146
Tree density	No tolerance	100.0				0				146
Owner class	No tolerance	95.9				7				169
Owner status	No tolerance	92.5				3				40
Stand age	±10 %	99.3	99.3	99.3	99.3	1	1	1	1	145
Disturbance 1	No tolerance	79.5				30				146
Disturbance year 1	±1 yr	63.6	72.7	72.7	72.7	4	3	3	3	11
Disturbance 2	No tolerance	98.6				2				146
Disturbance year 2	±1 yr									
Disturbance 3	No tolerance	100.0				0				146
Disturbance year 3	±1 yr									
Treatment 1	No tolerance	95.9				6				146
Treatment year 1	±1 yr	50.0	100.0			1	0			2
Treatment 2	No tolerance	99.3				1				146
Treatment year 2	±1 yr									
Treatment 3	No tolerance	100.0				0				146
Treatment year 3	±1 yr									
Physiographic class	No tolerance	61.0				57				146
Present nonforest use	No tolerance	95.0				1				20
Regional variables										
Percent crown cover	±10 %	83.6	99.3	99.3	99.3	24	1	1	1	146
Percent bare ground	±10 %	94.5	97.3	98.6	99.3	8	4	2	1	146
Habitat type 1	No tolerance	61.6				56				146
Habitat type 2	No tolerance	54.8				66				146

Table 5—QA results for tree variables from 3471 trees in Montana, cycle 2, 2003-2009.

Variable	Tolerance	Percentage of data within tolerance				Number of times data exceeded tolerance				Records
		@1x	@2x	@3x	@4x	@1x	@2x	@3x	@4x	
DBH	±0.1 /20 in.	91.5	96.8	98.2	98.7	285	107	61	44	3358
DRC	±0.1 /20 in.	52.2	59.3	64.6	70.8	54	46	40	33	113
Azimuth	±10 °	97.5	99.2	99.5	99.5	86	29	19	17	3471
Horizontal distance	±0.2 /1.0 ft	93.7	97.4	98.3	98.8	218	89	58	43	3471
Species	No tolerance	98.8				41				3471
Tree status	No tolerance	99.6				15				3471
Rotten/Missing cull	±10 %	95.3	98.2	99.1	99.6	146	56	28	11	3118
Total length	±10 %	80.9	94.2	97.7	99.0	662	200	80	33	3471
Actual length	±10 %	81.8	94.9	98.3	99.5	633	176	59	19	3471
Compacted crown ratio	±10 %	72.7	93.9	98.4	99.5	800	180	47	14	2932
Uncompacted crown ratio (P3)	±10 %	87.2	96.1	98.4	99.5	334	102	41	12	2611
Crown class	No tolerance	81.9				530				2932
Decay class		100.0				0				524
Cause of death	No tolerance	83.7				23				141
Mortality year	No tolerance					61				141
Condition class	No tolerance					30				3471
New tree	No tolerance	99.1								
Regional variables										
Mistletoe	±1 class	98.4	98.9	99.4	99.8	48	33	19	5	2932
Number of stems	No tolerance	54.9				51				113
Percent missing top	±10 %	97.4	98.1	98.7	99.0	81	59	41	32	3118
Sound dead	±10 %	90.1	94.4	96.4	97.3	310	176	112	84	3118
Form defect	±10 %	93.6	97.1	98.0	98.3	159	73	50	43	2499
Current tree class	No tolerance					151				3471
Tree Age	±5 %	18.0	23.4	35.1	48.6	91	85	72	57	111
DRC using IW MQO	±0.2 in/stem	90.3	92.0	96.5	97.3	11	9	4	3	113
Horiz Dist-timberland	±0.2 /1.0 ft	95.4	98.3	99.0	99.2	154	58	35	27	3358
Horiz Dist-woodland	±0.2 /1.0 ft	43.4	72.6	79.6	85.8	64	31	23	16	113

V. Current Issues

Mountain Pine Beetle

High tree mortality rates associated with mountain pine beetle infestations have become a serious issue in many western forests. Since the primary host of mountain pine beetle is lodgepole pine, and lodgepole pine comprises a significant component of many western North American forests, recent epidemics of this insect have raised significant concerns about the health, stand structure, and composition of lodgepole pine stands.

The mountain pine beetle is a native insect to western pine forests in North America and innocuous populations are almost always present in forests. Transition to epidemic populations is a function of the beetle's capacity to locate, colonize, and reproduce within suitable host trees in a weather pattern conducive to over-wintering survival, emergence, and dispersal (Caroll and others 2004). The reasons behind the recent outbreaks have received considerable discussion. Most bark beetles prefer to invade trees that are in poor physiological condition (Rudinsky 1962). Temperature is known to influence insect outbreaks, especially species such as the mountain pine beetle (Amman 1973). Because of the recent interest in climate change, the effect of global warming is believed by some researchers to be a contributing factor in the severity of mountain pine beetle infestations (Logan and others 2003). Another significant factor is the presence of large areas of lodgepole pine stands comprised of ideal host trees homogeneous in age, composition, and structure.

Figure 13 illustrates the average annual volume of lodgepole trees killed by insects by measurement year in Montana. The estimates in figure 13 illustrate a moving average trend that accumulates information from successive annual inventory measurements. The assumption is that most of the lodgepole classified as mortality and assigned a cause of death of insects is due to the mountain pine beetle. It is clearly evident that a pronounced upward trend has occurred during the 7 years of annual inventories in Montana. As of 2009, the average annual volume of insect-killed lodgepole pines is 121 million cubic feet, which is nearly five times higher than the average of 25 million cubic feet recorded in 2003.

Aspen Mortality

Aspen is the widest-ranging species in North America. It is present in all States in the Interior West and occupies a wide elevational range from 2,000 ft in northern Idaho to 11,700 ft in Colorado. It is also found on a wide range of sites, and occurs in 26 of the forest types that occur in the Interior West. The species is intolerant of shade and relatively short-lived, which makes it prone to replacement by conifers through successional change. In the Interior West, it also reproduces infrequently by seeding, relying mostly on root sprouting for reproduction. However, aspen responds well to fire and cutting, and it is able to dominate heavily disturbed sites for many years following severe disturbance. In addition, there is some evidence that aspen is able to persist in conifer-dominated forests by exploiting gaps in the conifer canopy that are caused by insects, disease, windthrow, and other smaller-scale disturbances.

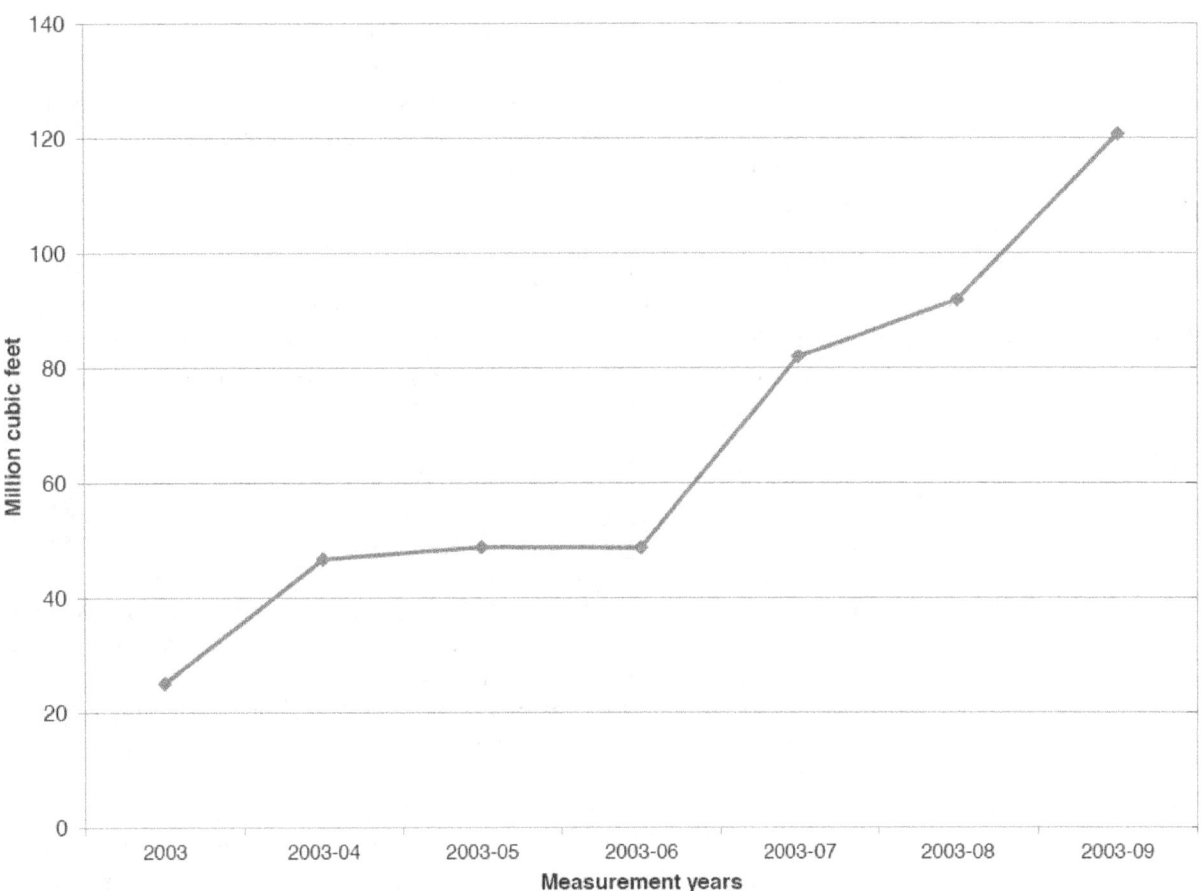

Figure 13—Moving average estimate of average annual volume of lodgepole pine killed by insects by measurement years, Montana, cycle 2, 2003-2009.

In recent years there has been concern about the future of aspen on the landscape, primarily due to the characteristics of aspen and how they relate to changes in disturbance regimes. The earliest concerns were related to successional change in the Interior West, where fire suppression has decreased disturbance rates and, as a result, aspen regeneration rates. In addition, it has been shown that large populations of herbivores can inhibit aspen regeneration where it occurs spontaneously or after disturbance (e.g., Hessl and Graumlich 2002). The lack of disturbance allows conifers to gain dominance where they are present, and in pure aspen stands, consumption of regeneration by ungulates could lead to loss of senescing overstory trees without replacement. More recent concerns are related to a period of drought that has an impact on aspen and other forest types (e.g., Shaw and others 2005; Thompson 2009). Drought appears to have contributed to mortality in many low-elevation stands (Worrall and others 2008); in some of these stands, regeneration is either lacking or suppressed by herbivores.

Johnson (1994) suggested that the acreage of aspen-dominated stands had declined as much as 46 percent in Arizona since the 1960s, with most of these acres becoming dominated by mixed conifer forest types. Bartos (2001) suggested that similar changes—aspen acres decreasing by 64 percent—had occurred in Montana. These assessments of "lost" aspen acres were based on the assumption that forested acres with a minority aspen component were, at one time in the recent past, dominated by aspen in pure, or nearly pure, stands. This assumption may not be reasonable because there are many situations where aspen may persist normally as a minor stand component.

USDA Forest Service Resour. Bull. RMRS-RB-15. 2012

29

It is not possible to estimate trends in the aspen forests of Montana with great certainty because of differences between the coverage of periodic and annual inventories (see Appendix A: Inventory History). However, it is possible to make a limited set of comparisons when looking at certain characteristics that are indicative of aspen status, such as the proportion of aspen acreage to total forest acreage, number of acres with only dead aspen present, and number of acres with aspen reproduction present.

Current inventory data show that there are just nearly 450,000 acres of the aspen forest type in Montana, as compared to over 263,000 acres found during the previous inventory. When considering all acres where aspen is present, the current inventory data show that at least one live aspen stem is present on over 791,000 acres, while the previous inventory showed live aspen present on just over 671,000 acres.

Statistics on live trees may overlook "relict" aspen stands, and both inventories show that some stands had only dead aspen present at the time of inventory. The 1990s periodic inventory showed that only dead aspen 1.0 inch diameter and greater were found on approximately 34,000 acres, or about 4.6 percent of all acres with aspen present. The current inventory shows an apparent increase to over 65,000 acres, or about 7.6 percent of all acres with aspen present. However, when seedling-sized trees are taken into account the area with only dead aspen decreases substantially, and there are many more acres where only aspen seedlings (or suckers) are recorded. Of the plots where aspen is only found as seedlings or suckers, disturbances such as fire are frequently recorded (see "Fire in Montana's Forests" in Section V).

Another way to compare the previous and current inventories is to normalize data on a common basis, for example, basal area per acre. During the 1990s periodic inventory in aspen-dominated stands (aspen forest type), the average basal area per acre of all aspen (live and standing dead) was just over 68 square feet per acre, with nearly 62 square feet per acre in live aspen. In the current annual inventory, aspen-dominated stands averaged just over 42 square feet of live and dead aspen basal area, with just under 37 square feet per acre of live aspen. The results are similar for all stands with an aspen component of trees at least 1 inch diameter. Total aspen basal area in these stands averaged just over 34 square feet of basal area in the periodic inventory, with about 31 square feet of basal area in live aspen. As with the aspen-dominated acres, the numbers were lower in the annual inventory: nearly 29 square feet per acre of live and dead aspen, and slightly more than 24 square feet of live aspen. These figures suggest that live aspen basal area has fallen approximately 40 percent on a per-acre basis since the periodic inventory. However, it is not yet possible to tell if this is a real decrease possibly caused by successional changes and disturbances or an apparent increase that may have been caused by capturing a high proportion of regenerating aspen acres in the annual inventory that were not captured in the periodic inventory.

In contrast with apparent trends in live aspen stocking, mortality rates do not appear to be increasing in recent years, at least in comparison to the mortality rates observed during the periodic inventory. Mortality is expressed here as the proportion of basal area estimated to have died in the 5 years prior to the plot visit. During the 1990s periodic inventory, mortality was estimated at almost 7 percent in aspen-dominated stands and over 6 percent in stands with an aspen component. This equates to an average annual mortality of about 1.3 percent. During the annual inventory, mortality was estimated at 4 percent in aspen-dominated stands and less than 4 percent in stands with an aspen component. This equates to an average annual mortality of about 0.8 percent. Because the annual inventory is spatially unbiased over time, it is possible to look at year-by-year mortality estimates for possible trends. Figure 14 shows the mortality estimates for annual inventory years 2003-2009. Although the annual trend data might be somewhat noisy due to small sample size within any given year, it does not appear that there has been any substantial change in mortality rates since 2003. Individual annual estimates vary about the 7-year average.

Comparisons between the mid-1990s periodic inventory results and the current annual inventory data in Montana give somewhat conflicting results, so aspen trends are difficult to interpret at this point in the inventory. Total acreage with aspen present appears to be somewhat higher than in the 1990s, but the aspen component appears to have decreased when considered on a basal area per acre basis. Several disturbance agents, including fire and drought, have apparently reduced aspen basal area. However, there are a substantial number of plots with aspen reproduction present. On many of these plots there are no large, standing live or dead aspen, so it is difficult to ascertain whether these plots are capturing re-occupation of the sites by aspen or expansion of aspen into other forest types. However, continued monitoring of these plots in the future will tell whether or not the young aspen reproduction is able to persist.

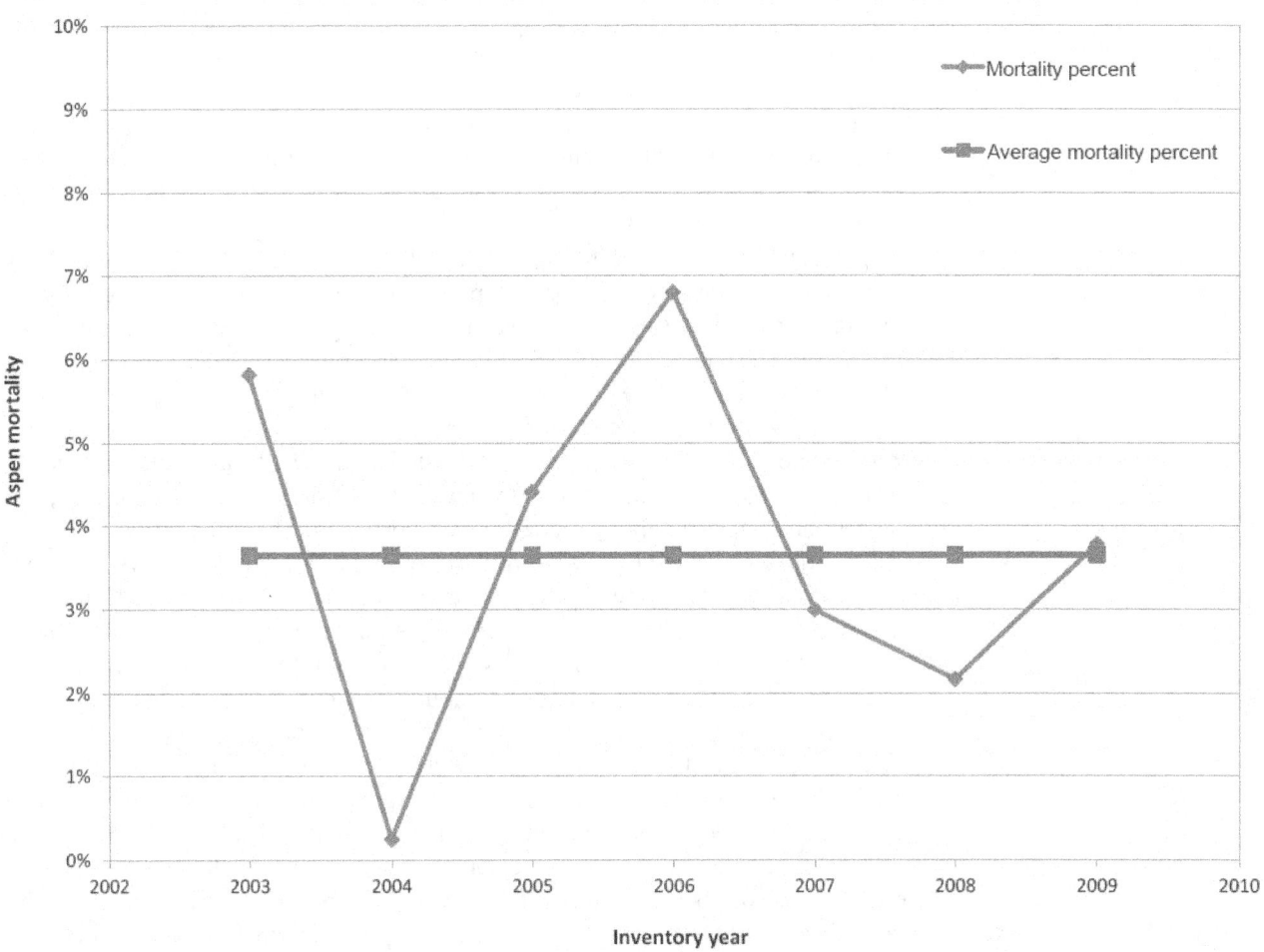

Figure 14—Estimated 5-year mortality rates for individual measurement years and average 5-year mortality for all annual inventory years (2003-2009) of aspen in Montana, cycle 2, 2003-2009.

USDA Forest Service Resour. Bull. RMRS-RB-15. 2012

31

There have been many studies that have shown aspen to be in decline at local scales (e.g., Bartos and Campbell 1998; Di Orio and others 2005; Worrall and others 2008), while other analyses have shown increased dominance of aspen in some landscapes (Kulakowski and others 2004). It is not surprising that studies documenting loss are more numerous, because unexplained or unexpectedly high mortality events tend to attract the attention of managers, researchers, and the public. Because these changes are evident to a wide range of observers, there is a tendency to extrapolate local conditions to larger areas. Aspen is found in many forest types with a wide variety of associate tree species, so the characteristics of aspen-dominated stands and stands with aspen as a minor component vary considerably over the range of the species. This makes generalization difficult. In addition, local or regional trends may differ from those of the population as a whole, because agents like drought and fire are not regularly distributed over the landscape. However, with continued monitoring under the annual inventory system, FIA will be able to assess regional- and population-scale trends in aspen.

Whitebark Pine Status

Whitebark pine has become recognized as an important component of high-elevation ecosystems in western North America. Its periodic crops of large wingless seeds provide a major food source for several species of birds and mammals including the black bear and grizzly bear (Schmidt and McDonald 1990). Wildlife biologists have noted that for several months after production of a large whitebark pine cone crop, bears concentrate their feeding on cone caches made by squirrels and tend to stay away from lower elevation encounters with humans and their habituations (Kendall 1980). Whitebark pine aids in the protection of watersheds by stabilizing soil and rock on the harshest sites and by catching and retaining snowpack (Arno and Hoff 1989).

Compared to other conifer species in Montana, whitebark pine is relatively uncommon. Whitebark pine forest types comprise about 679 thousand acres in Montana or about 2.7 percent of total forest area in the State. The number of all live whitebark pine trees 1.0-inches d.b.h. and larger totals 491 million trees in Montana or about 4 percent of all live trees in the State.

In many areas in the West, whitebark pine stands have experienced heavy mortality (Arno 1986). The principal agents named in the decline are white pine blister rust (*Cronartium ribicola*), mountain pine beetle (*Dendroctonus ponderosae*), and successional replacement by shade-tolerant trees in the absence of fire.

To address the decline issue in whitebark pine in Montana, an analysis of long-term trends was performed using remeasurement data from permanently established FIA plots. In the previous 1988 to 1998 periodic inventories of Montana, field plots used a variable-radius tree sampling design. When the annual inventory began in 2003, IWFIA changed the sampling design to the fixed-radius national mapped-plot design. In addition to the initial establishment of the mapped plot, field crews were instructed to relocate and remeasure trees tallied on the previously established variable-radius plot. All trees measured in the previous inventory (time 1) were accounted for and current status recorded (live, dead, cut) in the current inventory (time 2). This remeasurement and accounting for trees on previously established plots provides an accurate measure of growth, removal, and mortality rates since the status of trees are known at both points in time. The procedures used to remeasure the previous variable-radius plot and a description of the plot layout is described in USDA Forest Service 2011.

Remeasurement of permanent FIA plots can produce estimates of change that quantify the net change in inventory between two points in time. For this analysis, mean basal area per acre of whitebark pines 5.0-inches d.b.h. and larger was the attribute of interest. The following components were generated for the analysis:

- Initial Inventory—Basal area/acre of live whitebark pines 5.0 inches d.b.h. and larger measured at the previous visit.
- Survivor growth—Change in basal area/acre of live whitebark pine trees 5.0 inches d.b.h. and larger measured at the previous visit and the basal area/acre of live whitebark pine trees 5.0 inches d.b.h. and larger measured at the second visit.
- Ingrowth—Basal area/acre of live whitebark pine trees 5.0 inches d.b.h. and larger at time of second visit but were less than 5.0 inches d.b.h. at time of previous visit (trees that grew on to the inventory during the remeasurement period).
- Mortality—Basal area/acre of live whitebark pine trees 5.0 inches d.b.h. and larger measured at the previous visit that was dead due to natural causes at time of second visit.
- Removals—Basal area/acre of live whitebark pine trees 5.0 inches d.b.h. and larger measured at the previous visit that was cut at time of second visit.
- Terminal Inventory—Basal area/acre of live whitebark pines 5.0 inches d.b.h. and larger measured at the second or current visit.

For this analysis, only remeasured plots where at least one live whitebark pine 5.0 inches d.b.h. and larger was measured in the initial inventory were selected. A total of 199 remeasured plots in Montana met the criteria. The initial inventory measurement years ranged from 1988 to 1998. The terminal inventory measurement years ranged from 2003 to 2009. Plots measured prior to 1991 were on non-National Forest Systems (NFS) land and those measured after 1990 were on NFS land. The average interval between plot measurements was 10.4 years. The procedure used to estimate the basal area per acre for the six components is described in Beers and Miller 1964.

Mean basal area per acre of whitebark pine for the six change components are illustrated in figure 15. Mean basal area per acre of whitebark pine in Montana decreased 22 percent or by about 2.2 percent per year. Mortality reduced the estimate of initial inventory by 27 percent. Mortality rate of whitebark pine averaged 2.6 percent per year. The leading cause of death of the whitebark pines classified as mortality was disease, which accounted for 38 percent of the trees that died during the remeasurement interval. The second leading cause of death was attributed to insects at 29 percent. Fire accounted for 23 percent of the whitebark pine mortality.

These results indicate a very significant decline in live basal area of whitebark pine. The annual level of mortality is currently outpacing the combined annual basal area growth of survivor trees and ingrowth trees. Similar studies conducted in the early 1970s in western Montana also indicated significant basal area reductions in whitebark pine due to heavy mortality (Keane and Arno 1993). Figure 16 illustrates the numbers of live whitebark pine trees by diameter class. Numbers of 2- and 4-inch whitebark pines comprise 62 percent of all live whitebark pines in Montana. The high proportion of sapling-size trees might suggest enough regeneration is occurring to offset losses due to mortality in the larger diameter classes. However, blister rust can cause mortality and top kill in whitebark pine seedlings and saplings resulting in fewer saplings reaching maturity. Blister rust incidence is particularly high in southwestern Montana (Kegley and others 2011). Whitebark

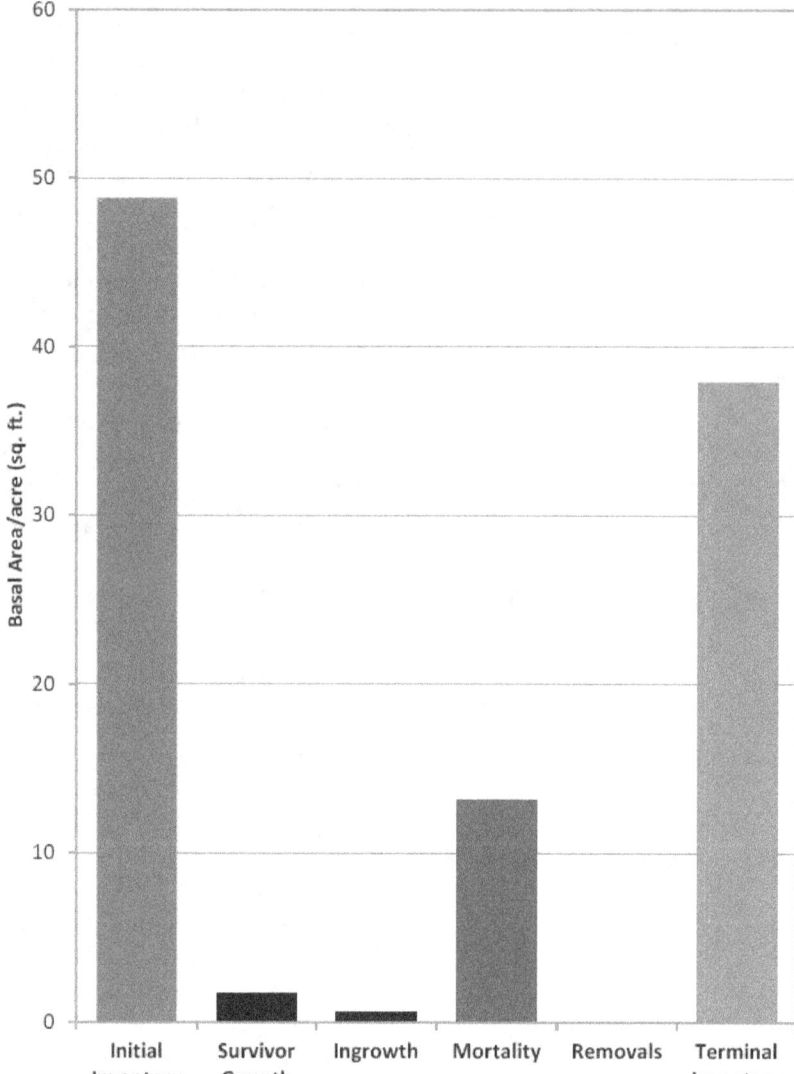

Figure 15—Periodic estimates of initial inventory, terminal inventory, and change components for whitebark pine in Montana expressed as mean basal area per acre for remeasured plots.

pine is a slow-growing tree. Depending on site conditions, the tree can attain small to moderately large size after 250 or more years, but may start producing cones as early as 70 years old.

This analysis underscores the need to use broad-scale inventory data for monitoring trends in whitebark pine. The power to detect significant effects related to whitebark pine mortality and other parameters of interest will increase substantially with estimates derived from the remeasurement (paired) plots that will be available as the IWFIA region begins to accumulate data from remeasured plots.

Fire in Montana Forests

Fire is an important disturbance in Montana forests. In some forest types, like ponderosa pine, fire can maintain open stands and promote grasses and forbs growth in the understory. For other forest types, such as aspen and lodgepole pine, fire plays an important role in stand regeneration. In some areas, a century of fire suppression has led to a buildup of fuels and stand densification. In these areas there can be uncharacteristically intense fires. Some areas that are intensely burned may experience slow regeneration, but others may recover relatively quickly.

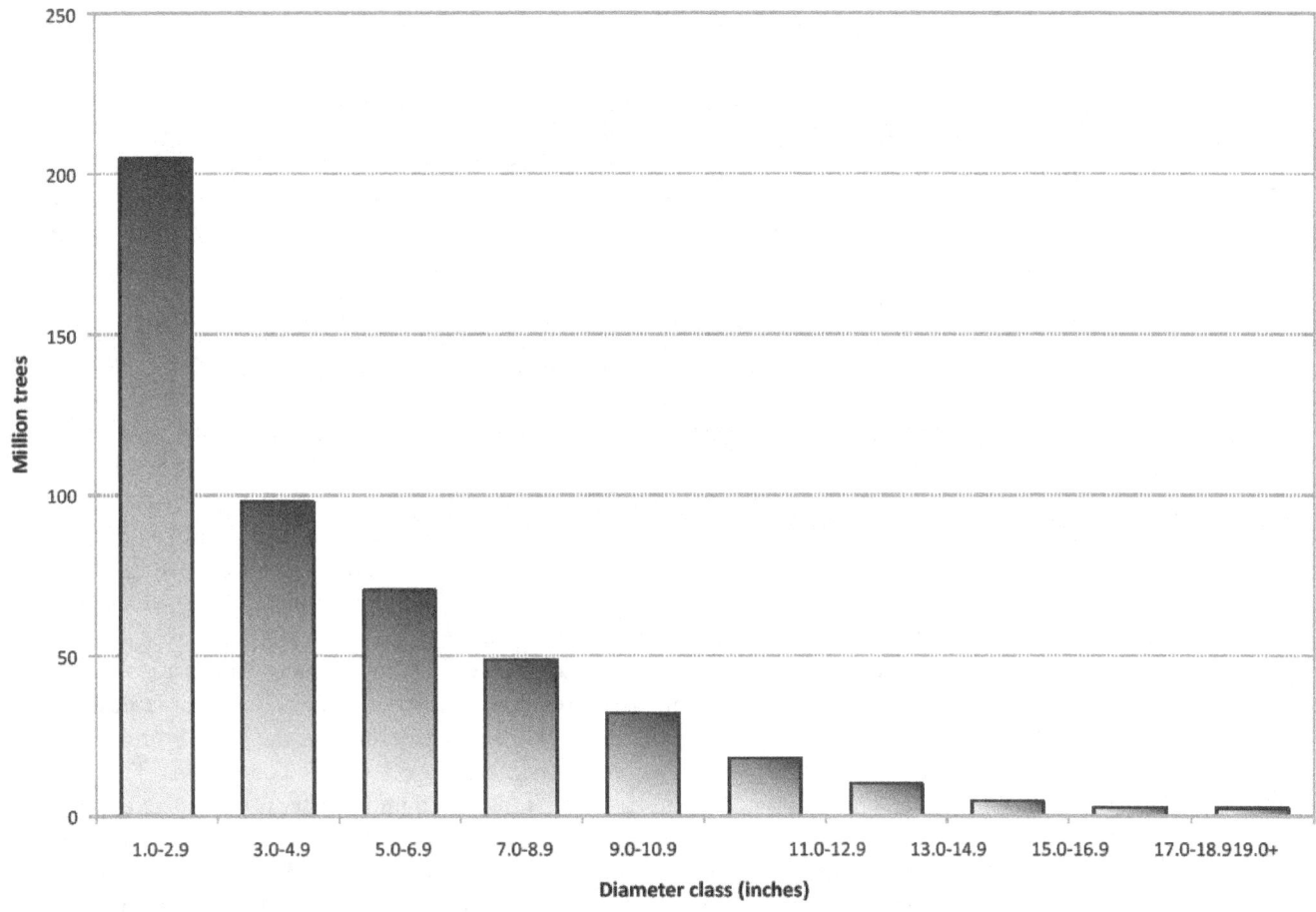

Figure 16—Numbers of live whitebark pines by diameter class in Montana, cycle 2, 2003-2009.

For example, the area inside the boundary of the large 1910 fires in Idaho and Montana (Cohen and Miller 1978; Pyne 2008; Egan 2009) now carries about the same amount of live tree volume per acre as areas outside the fires, although the mean stand age is somewhat lower and the volume is generally distributed among smaller trees (Wilson and others 2010).

Assessment of fire effects without a complete cycle of FIA data is not straightforward. During the period covered by this report there were many fires in Montana. Some FIA plots within fire boundaries were measured before the fire occurred in that area and some were measured after. As a result, within the perimeter of a large fire there may be pre- and post-fire data, or a plot within the perimeter of a small fire may represent only pre-fire conditions. This means that normal data compilation methods cannot be used without introducing some element of temporal bias—that is, plots measured earlier in the inventory will tend to underestimate the effect of fire because they might have been affected by fire after they were measured. These limitations on analysis will be reduced as the current inventory cycle is completed and remeasurement data are acquired during the next cycle. However, there are some general analyses that can be conducted with the current data. These results should be considered preliminary.

We used data from the Monitoring Trends in Burn Severity (MTBS) project, which is an interagency effort being conducted and maintained by the USDA Forest Service Remote Sensing Applications Center and the U.S. Geological Survey National Center for Earth Resources Observation and Science (EROS).

The purpose of the MTBS project is to consistently map the burn perimeters and severity of fires across all lands of the United States. The multi-year project was designed to "assesses the frequency, extent, and magnitude (size and severity) of all large wildland fires (includes wildfire, wildland fire use, and prescribed fire) in the conterminous United States (CONUS), Alaska, Hawaii, and Puerto Rico for the period of 1984 through 2010 (Eidenshenk and others 2007). The analysis presented here is based on burned area perimeters of wildland fires identified by the MTBS program between 2003 and 2009 and FIA plot data for the corresponding period in Montana.

MTBS data showed 238 fires and fire complexes (hereafter, fires) burned 2.48 million acres in Montana between 2003 and 2009. The size of these fires ranged from just a few acres to over 200,000 acres, with an average of 10,403 acres. Forested plots measured during the same period occurred within the boundaries of 74 of the fires. The remaining 164 fires encompassed only non-forested plots, encompassed plots that have not yet been measured on the current cycle, or did not encompass an FIA plot location. The largest fire—the Derby Fire, at 201,000 acres—encompassed 12 forested conditions. The area expansion estimated by these conditions is just over 108,000 acres, which indicates that just over half of the Derby Fire burned forested areas. The other four fires that were over 100,000 acres only encompassed two to six forested conditions each, which translates to about 20 to 30 percent of these fires burning forested land. The sixth largest fire (Chippy Creek) covered almost 96,000 acres according to the MTBS fire perimeter, but it encompassed the highest number (13) of forested conditions. The plot-based area estimate for these 13 conditions is slightly higher (103,000 acres) than the MTBS area estimate, illustrating the sampling noise that is inherent in small area estimation. However, the fact that there is less than 10 percent difference suggests that all or most of the Chippy Creek fire involved forested land. The average number of forested plots within a sampled fire boundary was just over 2.5, and about half of the fires that were sampled by FIA plots encompassed only one plot. Although the plot-based and MTBS-based acreage estimates for smaller fires can be similar, it is not appropriate to draw inference about the mixture of forest and nonforest for small, individual fires. At this point in the inventory, the scaling factor for a single plot is approximately 10,000 acres, which is larger than most of the fires in the MTBS database. As a result, the proportion of burned area in forest vs. nonforest must be done by aggregating a large number of plots and burned area.

Given that population-scale estimates are difficult to produce with a partial inventory, another way to look at the data is to examine per-acre estimates. There were 2482 forested conditions measured in Montana between 2003 and 2009. Of these, 2262 were located outside the MTBS fire boundaries and 220 were located inside (fig. 17). Of the 220 located inside, 117 were measured prior to the fire in which they were located and 103 were measured after the fire. Conditions located outside the burned areas had an average of 119 square feet of basal area per acre in live and dead trees, with 97 square feet of that in live trees. Conditions within the burned areas that were measured before the fires occurred averaged 116 square feet of total basal area per acre and 89 square feet per acre of live trees. While the unburned conditions within the fires appear to have slightly less basal area than conditions outside the burned areas, the ratio of live basal area to total basal area (live + dead) was similar for both groups (81 percent and 77 percent respectively). This would suggest that the burned areas did not have extraordinarily large amounts of standing dead trees prior to the fires, but the lower standing basal area

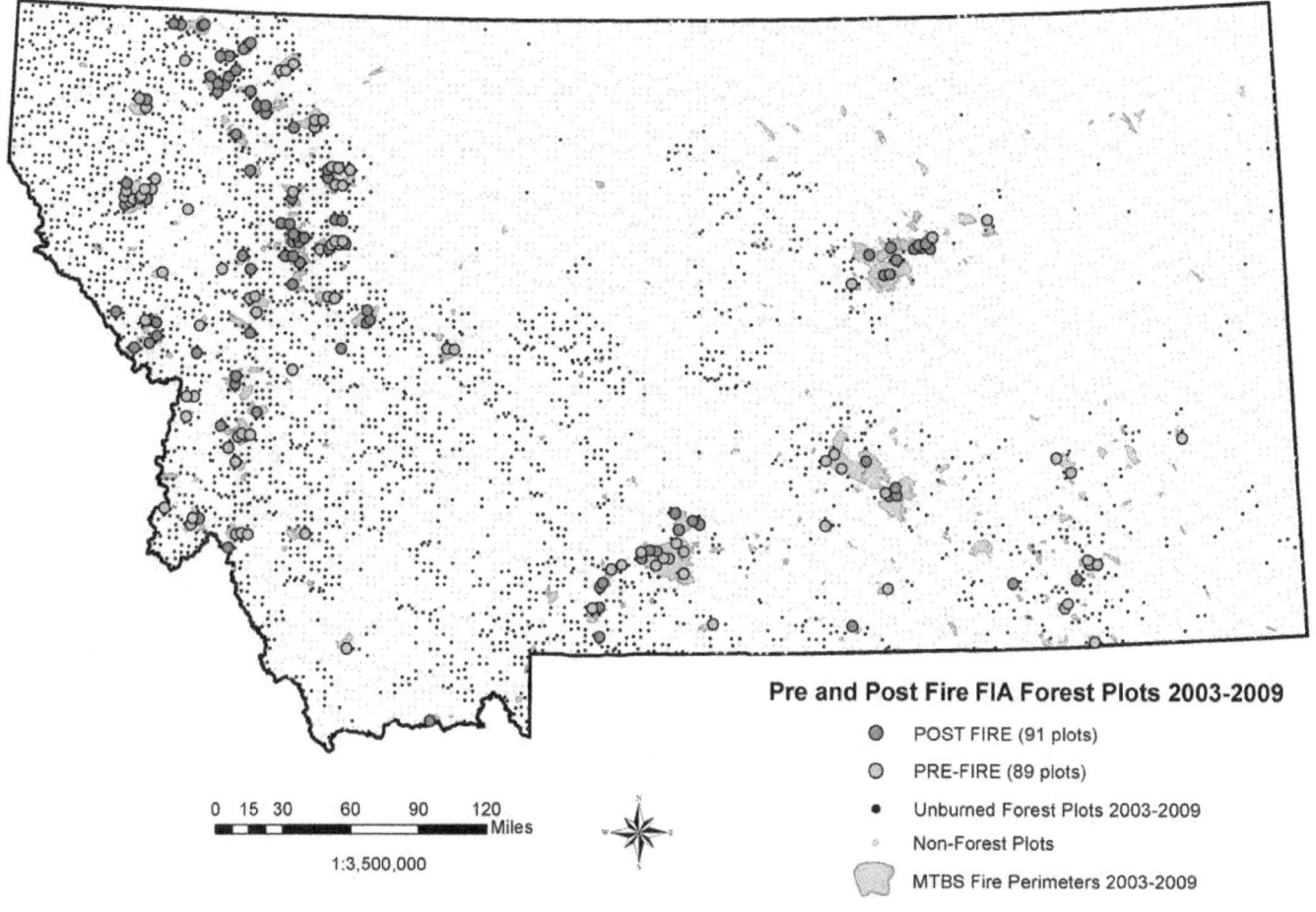

Figure 17—FIA plot locations and MTBS fire perimeters, showing plot status and measurement relative to the time of fires for plots inside fire perimeters, Montana, cycle 2, 2003-2009. Note: plot locations are approximate and some on private land are randomly swapped. Forested plots may include multiple forest conditions or nonforest conditions.

might indicate that the stands were more open or that there was more down wood in these stands.

When comparing within-fire pre-burn conditions to within-fire post-burn conditions, it is possible to estimate the proportion of trees killed within burned areas. Conditions located within fire boundaries and measured after the fires averaged 104 total square feet of basal area per acre, with only 40 square feet of basal area remaining in live trees. The lower average total basal area found in within-fire post-burn conditions as compared to within-fire pre-burn conditions (104 vs. 116 sq. ft. per acre) is consistent with the expectation that fire would result in some basal area being consumed and/or falling down. Likewise, the lower ratio of live to total basal area (39 percent) is consistent with the expectation that only partial mortality of trees located within the fire boundaries would occur. If it is assumed that the pre-burn conditions are representative of the post-burn conditions, then it would appear that the average fire-caused mortality was about 50 square feet per acre, or about 55 percent of the pre-fire live basal area.

One of the potential beneficial effects of fire is the stimulation of aspen regeneration. Although there are only about 708,000 acres of the aspen forest type in Montana, approximately 1.5 million acres have some aspen component (see "Aspen Mortality" in Section V). Of the 191 conditions measured with some

USDA Forest Service Resour. Bull. RMRS-RB-15. 2012

37

aspen component, only six were located within MTBS fire boundaries and only one was measured after the fire had burned. Although this sample is very small, it suggests that the number of potentially fire-disturbed acres with aspen present is around 51,000 acres, or about 3.3 percent of all acres with an aspen component. Converting this figure to an annual rate and assuming that fire will be evenly distributed over time and area, it implies that it would take approximately 210 years for all acres with aspen present to be disturbed by fire. This rate may be lower than would be necessary to maintain aspen across the Montana landscape, but it will only be possible to establish long-term trend with continued monitoring.

The analysis in this section should be considered only a first approximation of fire effects on Montana forests. Although the results are generally consistent with expectations, the magnitude of fire-related mortality cannot be stated with precision at this point in the inventory. However, the data confirm that within fire boundaries there has been only partial mortality. Additional data and analysis will be required to determine whether, for example, mortality is more-or-less evenly distributed among plots within the burned areas or mortality tends to be all-or-none at the plot scale. Remeasurement data will be necessary to confirm the portions of standing live and dead trees that are consumed by fire and converted to the down woody material pool. Also, given the short time period over which the estimate of aspen stand disturbance has been made, it should be considered with a great deal of caution. However, future measurements will not only enable analysis of fires effects on aspen, they will also provide important information on the amount and rate of recovery in all burned areas over time.

Old Growth Forests

An important aspect in managing for ecologically sustainable and diverse ecosystems is the maintenance of forest stands representing the full range of forest succession. The oldest stages of this range are of particular interest to forest managers. Historically, these last stages of forest growth have been difficult to define or describe. The terminology has included late seral, climax, mature, overmature, and old growth, among others. Generally, at issue is that stand structure changes in ways that are important to ecological and habitat function as forests mature. Standardized definitions are difficult because the final structure and age of a given forest stand depends on many biological and physical components: climate and geology, dominant tree species, fire regimes, and others (Kaufman and others 2007; Vosick and others 2007). In addition, the characteristics of old growth can change with the scale of observation, from patches to stands and landscapes (Kaufman and others 2007).

Responding to the Chief's Directive of 1984, all USDA Forest Service Regions developed old growth definitions. The Northern Region has defined old growth for twenty different forest regimes, or potential old growth types, in Montana (Green and others 1992). Potential old growth types are determined based on whether the forest is east or west of the continental divide (12 types on the east side and 8 on the west), on large-tree species dominance, and on habitat type groupings. Each type has minimum old growth screening criteria, including trees per acre with a minimum age and diameter, and minimum live basal area per acre. Depending on the biophysical environment, trees per acre minima range from 4 to 30 trees per acre, ages range from 120 to 200 years, diameters are from 9 to 21 inches, and basal areas range from 40 to 80 square feet per acre; all depend on the potential old growth type. For instance, a stand west of the Continental Divide, with ponderosa pines as the predominant large trees, and a ponderosa pine/Idaho fescue habitat type would require eight trees per acre at least 170 years old and 21 inches diameter, and at least 60 square feet per acre of basal area in order to be considered old growth. A stand east of the Continental Divide, with Engelmann spruce and subalpine firs as the predominant large trees, and a whitebark pine/subalpine fir habitat type would require eight trees per acre at least 135 years old and 13 inches diameter, and at least 40 square feet per acre of basal area.

The old growth types in Green and others (1992) are all based on timber type conifers, so woodland types and hardwoods do not have defined types. This analysis applies the Forest Service Northern Region old growth minimum criteria to all ownerships of forest land in Montana. Although the analysis is based on criteria used by the Northern Region, it was not conducted using the same database structure or specific programming algorithms used internally by the Northern Region, so result may vary.

Fourteen percent, or 3.6 million acres, of Montana's forest land meet the old growth criteria. Nearly 3.0 million acres of that occur on National Forests, accounting for over 19 percent of the National Forest's forest land (fig. 18). Privately owned forests contain over 0.2 million acres of old growth, while just less than 0.2 million acres of old growth are on National Park Service land. The proportion of private forest land that meets old growth criteria is less than 4 percent, while the

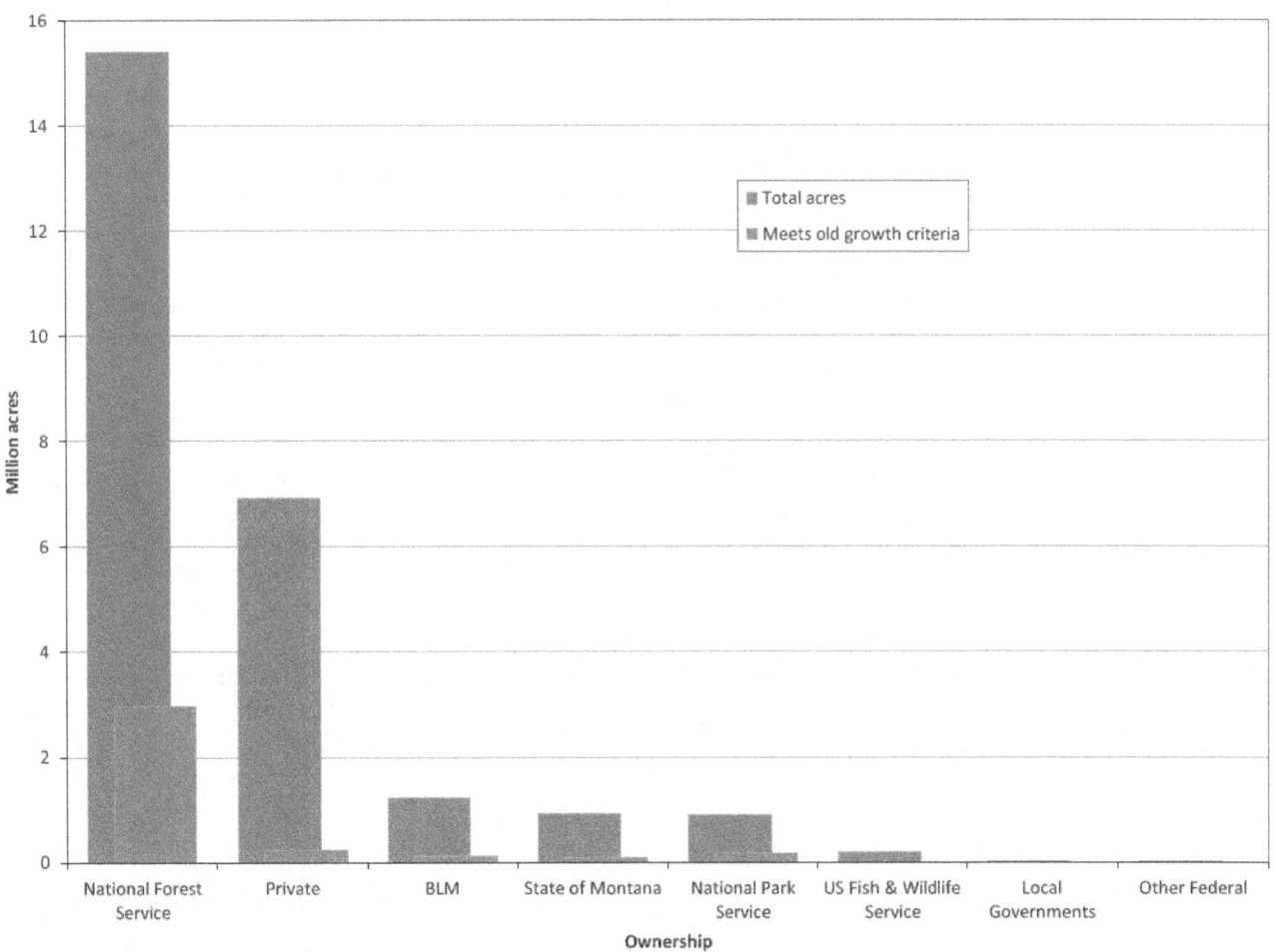

Figure 18—Total area of forest land and area meeting old growth criteria by ownership, Montana, cycle 2, 2003-2009.

National Park Service proportion is 19 percent, similar to National Forests. The proportion of old growth that is reserved is over 20 percent, compared to 13 percent for non-reserved forests.

Of the forest land meeting old growth criteria, one third (1.2 million acres) occurred west of the Continental Divide, while two thirds (2.4 million acres) is located on the east side. Old growth is most common in Montana's southwestern forest survey unit, where 32 percent of the forest land met old growth criteria. Other survey units' proportions of old growth were: west central, 15 percent; western, 10 percent; northwestern, 9 percent; and eastern, 8 percent. See Appendix E, tables 31-37 for counties included in forest survey units, and figure 28 in "Down Woody Material" in Section VI for a map of forest survey units.

The forest types with the most acres meeting the old growth criteria are lodgepole pine and Douglas-fir, each with over 0.8 million acres (fig. 19). These are also the two most common forest types. The forest types with the highest percentage of their area meeting old growth criteria are whitebark pine, at 45 percent, and Engelmann spruce-subalpine fir, at 38 percent. Common forest types with relatively low percentages of area meeting old growth criteria are ponderosa pine (7 percent), western larch (10 percent), grand fir (4 percent), and western redcedar (6 percent). Although the old growth criteria are based on timber type conifers, a few acres designated by FIA as woodland (Rocky Mountain juniper) or hardwoods (Cottonwood) met the old growth criteria, based on the presence of large old timber type conifers in the overstory.

In addition to area, the amount and proportions of aboveground biomass in old growth can also be assessed. Biomass in this analysis uses IWFIA regional equations (see "Volume and Biomass" in Section IV). As might be expected from criteria based on large-diameter trees and with minimum basal area requirements, proportions of live biomass occurring in forests that meet the old growth criteria are larger than proportions for acres. Over 25 percent of Montana's aboveground live biomass, 221 million tons, occurs in forests meeting old growth criteria. Similar to area, the Douglas-fir and lodgepole pine forest types have the most biomass in stands meeting old growth criteria with 52 million tons and 48 million tons, respectively. Forest types with high proportions of their total biomass occurring in old growth stands are whitebark pine (59 percent) and Engelmann spruce-subalpine fir (50 percent). Common forest types with low proportions of their total biomass occurring in old growth stands are ponderosa pine (16 percent), grand fir (13 percent) and western redcedar (8 percent).

Another measure to evaluate the old growth stands selected in this analysis could be the number of snags per acre. Higher than average densities of snags larger than about 9 inches is used as a secondary characteristic of old growth by Green and others (1992), and as a structural feature or indicator of old growth by both Fiedler and others (2007) and Kaufmann and others (2007). Density of standing dead trees at least 9 inches diameter is 14.1 snags per acre for all forest land in Montana, 13.0 snags per acre for conditions not meeting old growth criteria, and 23.4 snags per acre for old growth conditions. Figure 20 shows the number of snags per acre for the eight forest types with the most acres meeting old growth criteria along with estimates for all forest types combined, for both old growth and non-old growth conditions. In all cases, snags per acre are approximately 20 to 80 percent higher in old growth than in non-old growth.

As discussed in Section IV ("Quality Assurance Analysis") tree age and habitat type are two of the FIA variables that are most difficult to collect accurately and consistently. This analysis depends heavily on those variables, so some caution

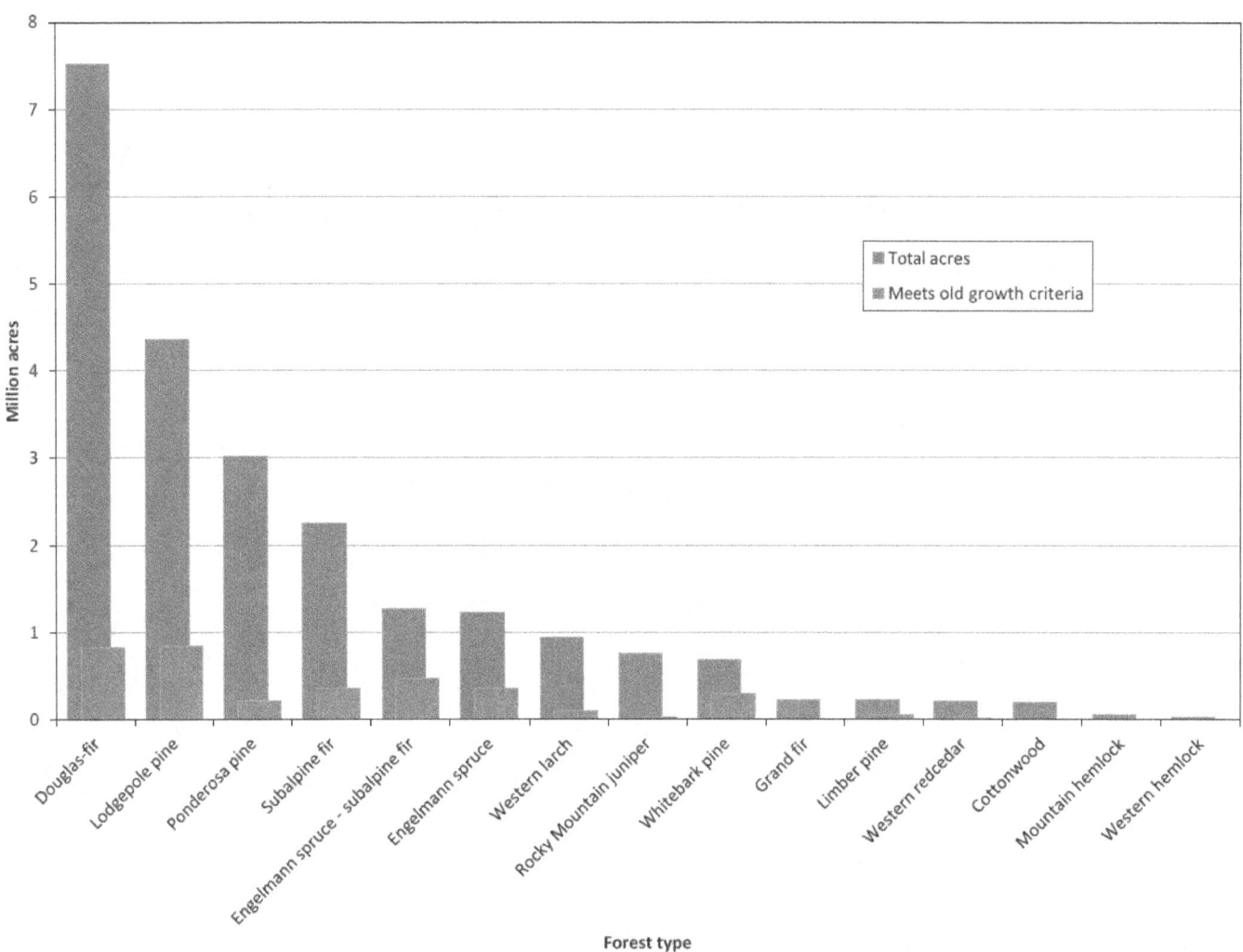

Figure 19—Total area of forest land and area meeting old growth criteria by forest type (showing only forest types with acreage meeting old growth criteria), Montana, cycle 2, 2003-2009.

must be taken with these results due to the increased possibility of measurement error. The use of habitat type groups in this analysis to assess site potential presents the possibility that the compliance rate for habitat type could be improved. That is, although two FIA field crews may disagree on the specific habitat type for a site, the two preferred types may be similar enough that they would both be in the same group. However, many plot conditions either met or did not meet old growth criteria based on tree ages within a few tolerance levels of the minimum tree age. While the old growth criteria presented by Green and others (1992) were developed to be compatible with inventory data, future research could focus on methods to improve the utility of FIA data for assessing old growth criteria. Options include improving data collection methods to increase repeatability, identifying possible surrogate measurements, and collection of additional field attributes to increase the reliability of habitat type assignment. Also, for areas of the country and for forest types where old growth characteristics are not as well defined as they are in Montana, the FIA database could be used to help quantify potential tree and stand characteristics to be used for defining the minimum criteria of old growth.

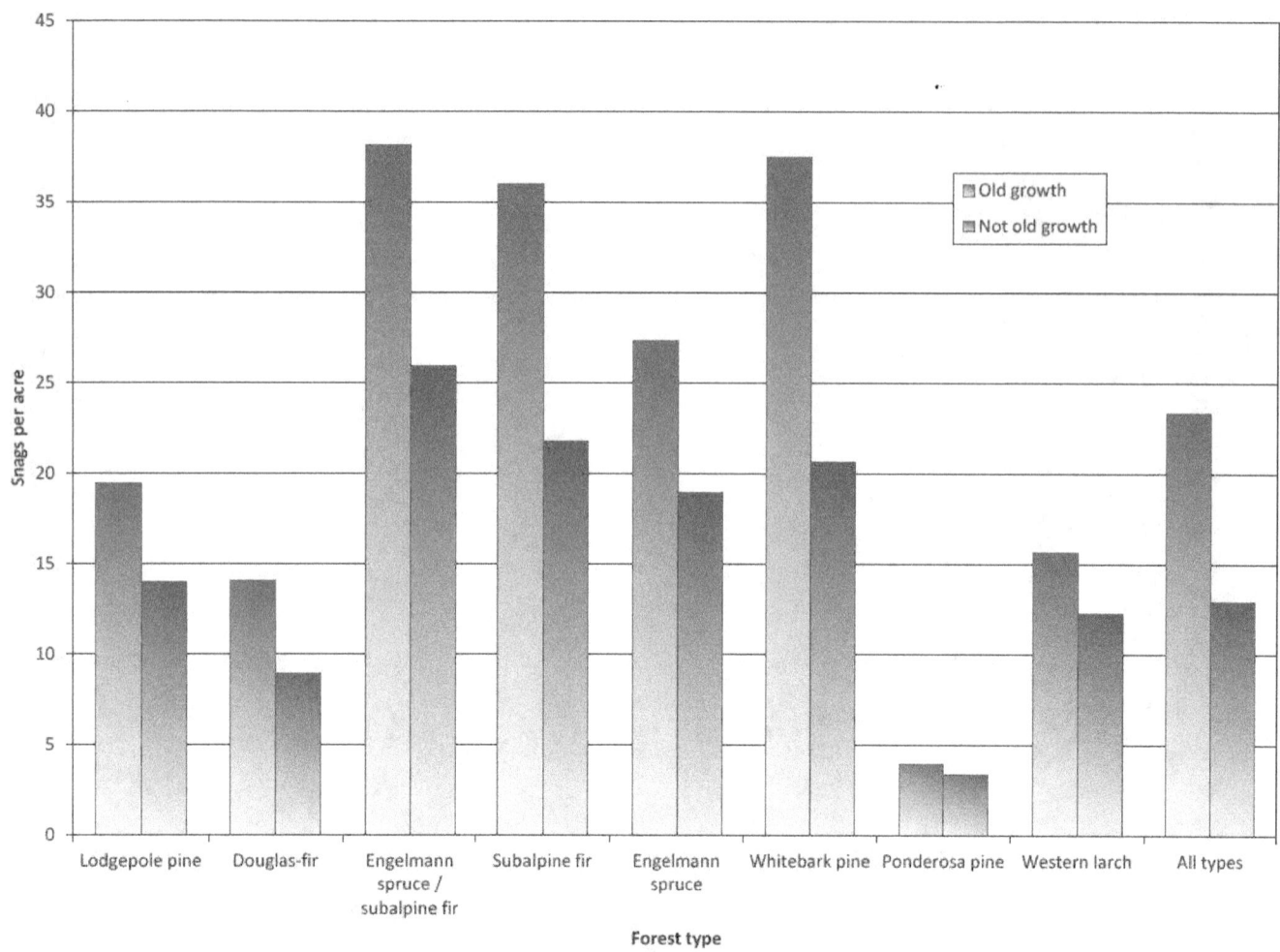

Figure 20—Snags per acre by old growth and non-old growth for the eight forest types with the most area meeting old growth criteria, and for all forest types combined, Montana, cycle 2, 2003-2009.

Noxious Weeds

Noxious plant species can have many negative effects on forest communities. Noxious species can displace native flora, alter fire regimes, reduce diversity in the plant and pollinator communities, and generally reduce the diversity and resiliency of forest ecosystems. FIA field crews record any instance where a noxious weed is found on a plot that contains a forested condition. This allows the spatial and temporal extent of these species to be documented as plots are revisited. A total of 3,382 sampled conditions were used to assess the occurrence of noxious plants in Montana. These samples represent plots that had a forested condition recorded somewhere within the boundaries of the four subplots.

Twenty-four different species were documented on forested plots in Montana, with one or more found on 555 (16 percent) of the sampled plots. Spotted knap-weed (*Centaurea diffusa*), Canada thistle (*Cirsium arvence*), and gypsyflower (*Cynoglossum officinale)* were the most common species by a large margin. These three species accounted for 77 percent of the weed occurrences (fig. 21). It appears that Montana's hardwood forest types are most prone to noxious plant infestation. This may be due to one or more factors, including soil conditions, accessibility

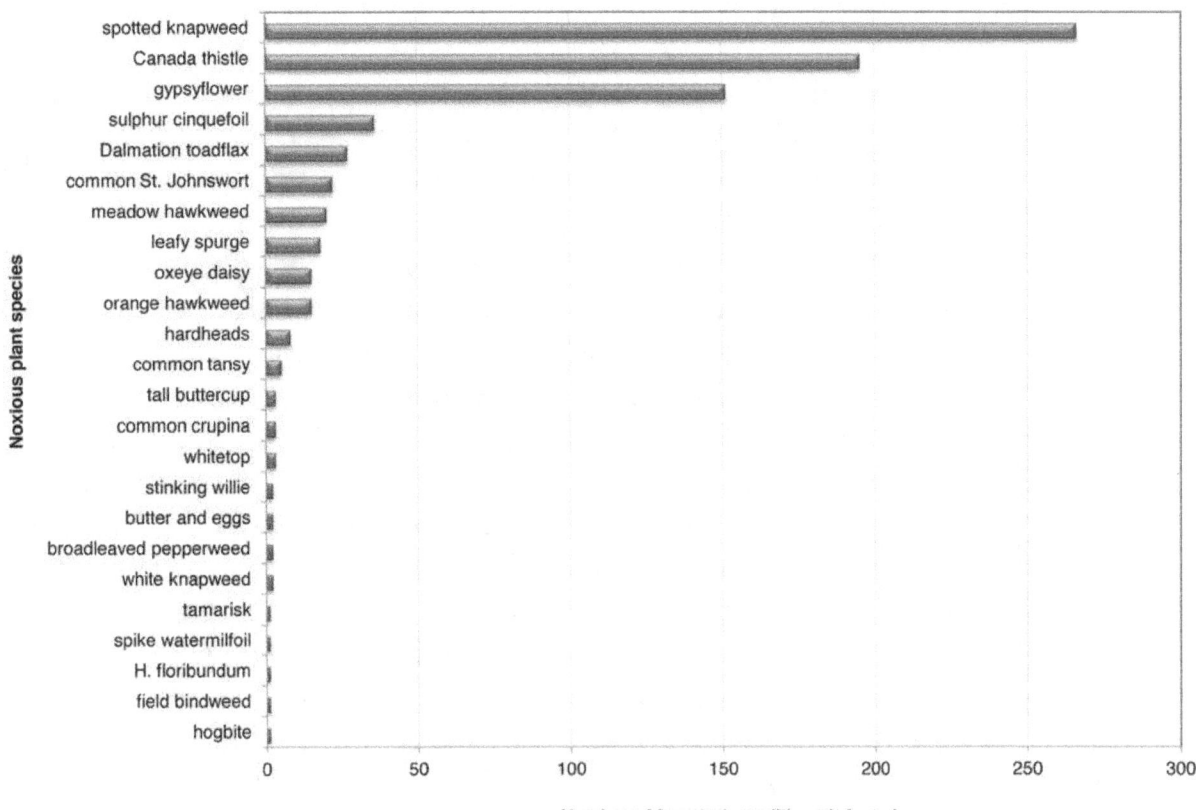

Figure 21—Number of forested conditions infested by each State-listed noxious plant, Montana, cycle 2, 2003-2009.

to livestock grazing, road and foot traffic, and/or high frequency of both natural and man-induced disturbance. Of the forest types having more than one condition sampled, the sugarberry-hackberry-elm-green ash forest type has the highest percentage of its area infested with at least one noxious species (fig. 22). However, a low sample size (n = 5) needs to be considered in this instance. Conversely, the Limber pine type had the smallest proportion of infested locations (2.0 percent). Nineteen percent of all sampled plots in Montana had multiple conditions.

Multiple conditions on a plot indicate transition zones between forest types and between forest and non-forest conditions. These "edge" areas are often dynamic in terms of site occupation, utilization, and species composition. This makes them more susceptible to occupation by noxious plants than the more stable interior of the stands. Locations that had more than one condition (more than one forest type or a portion of the plot was non-forest) had almost twice the occurrence of noxious species than did those locations where only a single forested condition represented the entire plot (24 percent and 13 percent respectively).

Snags as Wildlife Habitat

Standing dead trees (snags) provide important habitat in the forested ecosystems of Montana. There are many organisms that utilize snags at some point in their life history. These include, but are not limited to, bacteria, fungi, insects, rodents, cavity-nesting birds, bats, raptors, mustelids, and black bears. The diameters of standing dead trees are important variables to species that consider the utility

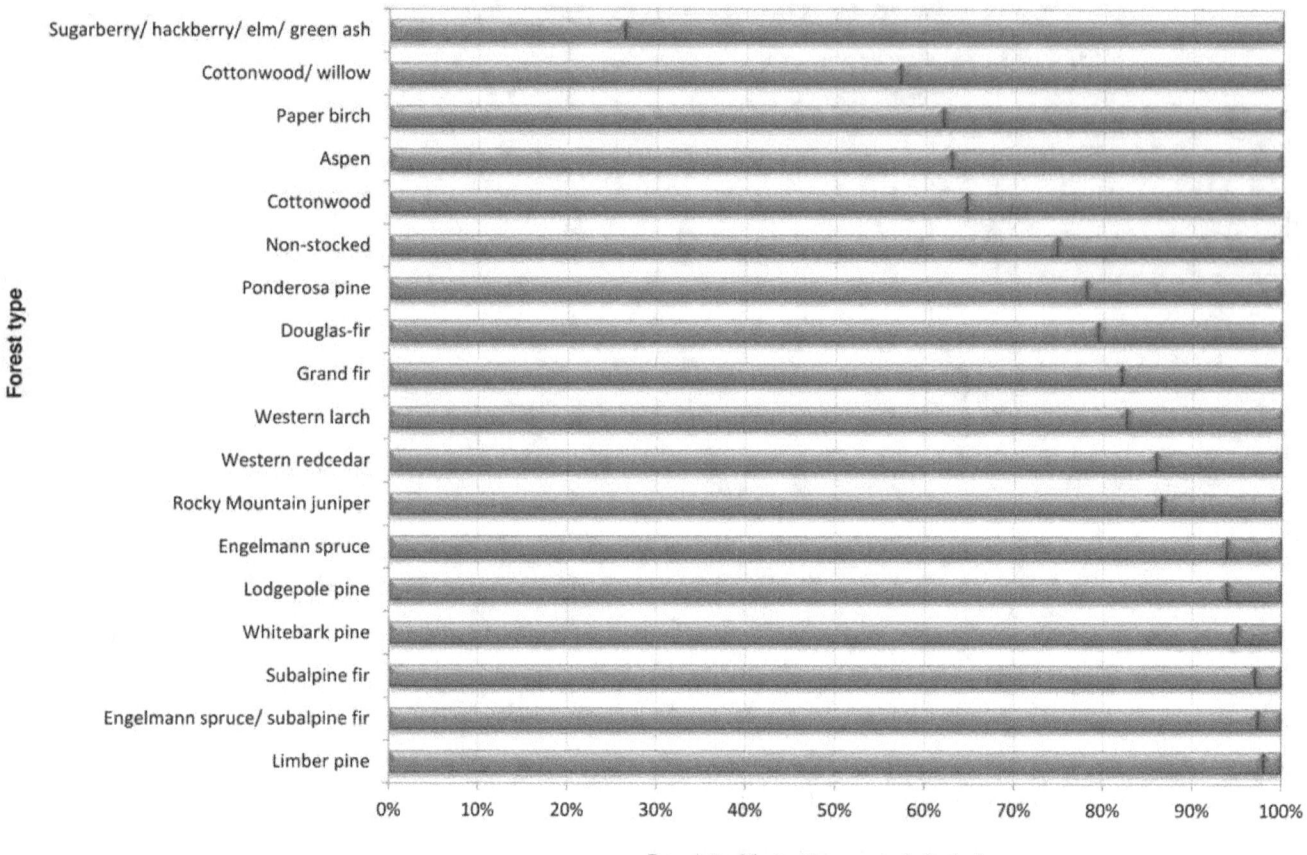

Figure 22—Percentage of area infested with noxious plant species by forest type, Montana, cycle 2, 2003-2009.

of snags as a nesting, roosting, or den site. Individual tree data collected by FIA field crews allow for population level analysis of the availability and quality of individual snags that meet criteria important to wildlife.

Cavity-nesting birds in Montana are especially dependent on snags for both nesting and foraging activities. There are a handful of bird species that act as primary excavators of nest sites. These birds create a cavity during one breeding season, but often abandon it and create a new cavity the following year. The old cavities are then occupied by secondary cavity-nesting birds. Secondary cavity-nesters do not excavate their own nest sites and are dependent on primary excavators for their cavities. The suitability of an old cavity for a secondary nester often depends on the species of primary excavator that created it. Here we present data reflecting the number of snags in Montana that are suitable for three important primary excavators that provide the bulk of cavities for secondary nesters. The hairy woodpecker (*Picoides villosus*), red-naped sapsucker (*Sphyrapicus nuchalis*), and northern flicker (*Colaptes auratus*) create different sized openings and cavities and are also relatively abundant and widespread throughout the different forest types of Montana; therefore, they provide suitable nest sites for a wide variety of secondary nesting species. The distribution of suitable snags by stand age is also presented. Suitability is based on mean diameters found to be used by these birds (Flack 1976; McClelland and others 1979; Dobkin and others 1995; Martin and others 2004).

USDA Forest Service Resour. Bull. RMRS-RB-15. 2012

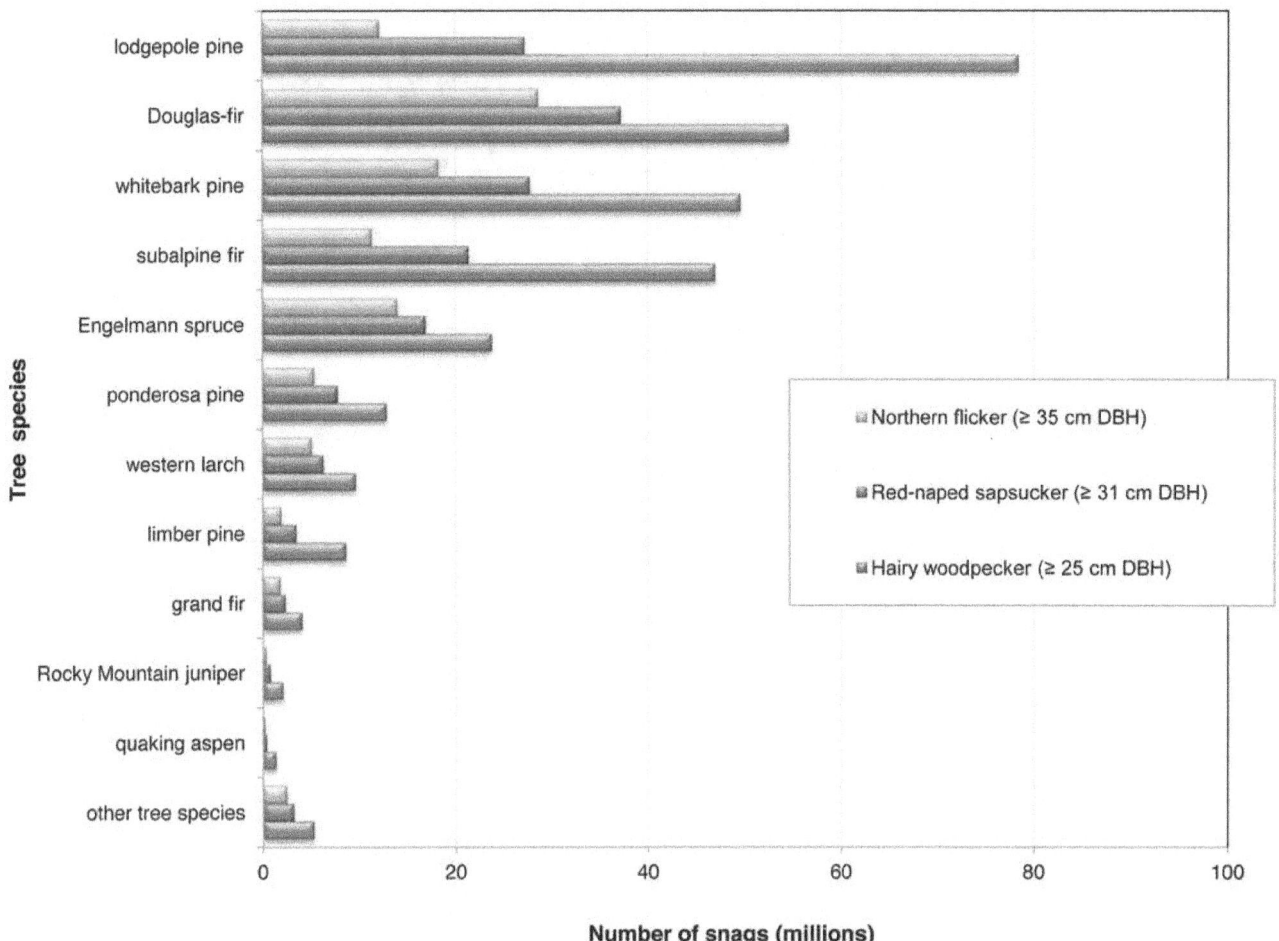

Figure 23—Number of snags meeting the preferences of three important cavity-excavating birds by tree species, Montana, cycle 2, 2003-2009.

There are more than 297 million snags in Montana that meet the size preferences of the hairy woodpecker (≥25cm (9.8 inches) d.b.h.). The most abundant tree species contributing to these bird's nesting sites are lodgepole pine (78.4 million snags), Douglas-fir (54.5 million), and whitebark pine (49.6 million) (fig. 23). These snags are predominately found in the Douglas-fir, lodgepole pine, and subalpine fir forest types. Nearly 155 million snags meet the diameter preferences of the red-naped sapsucker (≥31cm (12.2 inches) d.b.h.). Douglas-fir, whitebark pine, and lodgepole pine species again contribute the majority of these snags at 37.2, 27.7, and 27.3 million snags respectively. The forest types where most of these snags can be found are Douglas-fir, subalpine fir, and nonstocked. Most potential northern flicker snags (≥35cm (13.8 inches) d.b.h.) are also found in the Douglas-fir, subalpine fir, and nonstocked forest types. The tree species that comprise most of the suitable snag population for northern flickers are Douglas-fir (28.6 million), whitebark pine (18.3 million), and Engelmann spruce (14.0 million). The nonstocked forest type often includes areas disturbed by wildfire, disease, and insect infestations. These types of stands account for the high number of snags in this forest type.

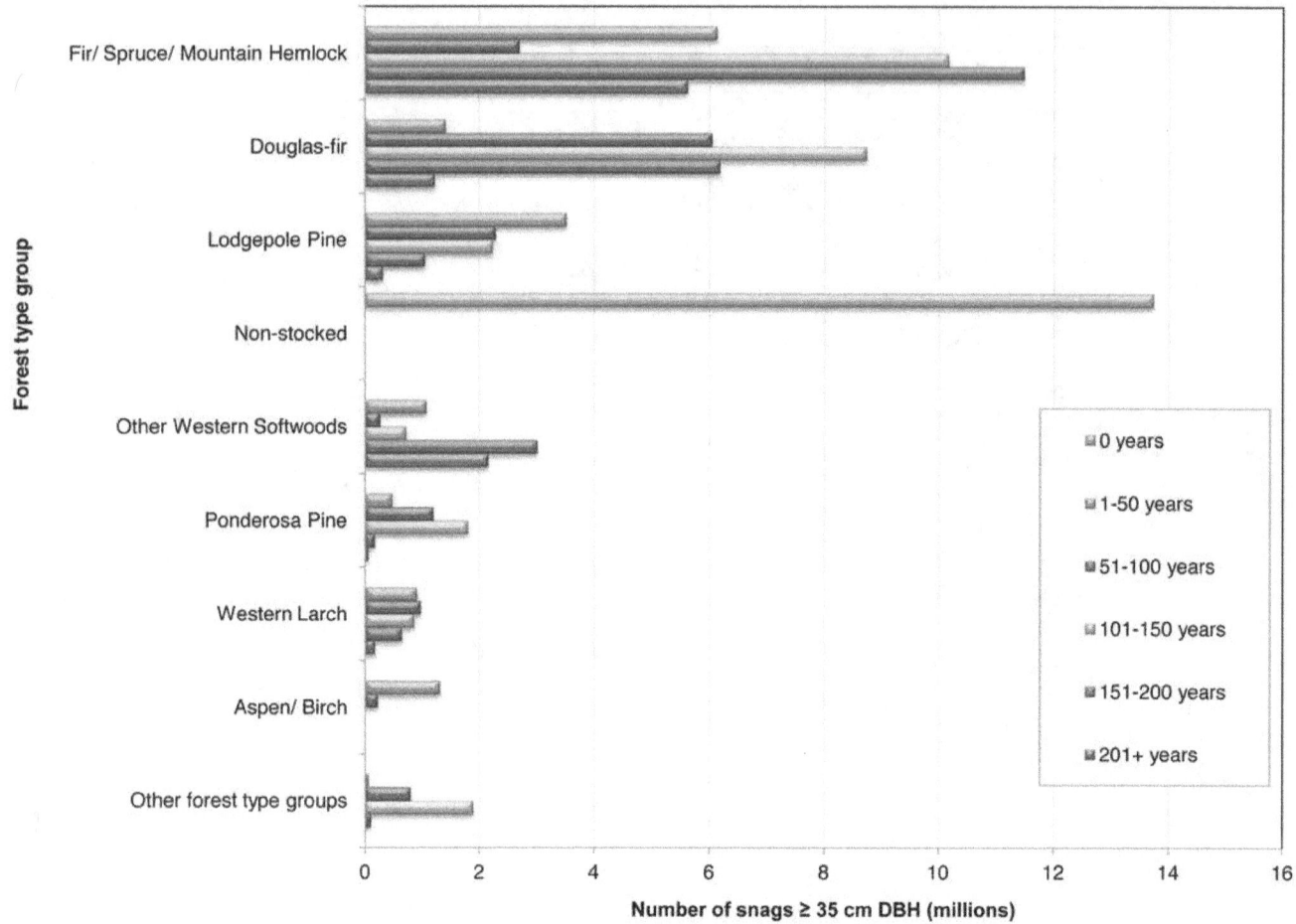

Figure 24—Number of snags meeting the preferences of three important cavity-excavating birds by stand-age class and forest type group, Montana, cycle 2, 2003-2009.

Figure 24 shows the distribution of snags ≥35cm d.b.h by stand-age. These snags are large enough to accommodate all three species of cavity excavators discussed here. The largest percentage of suitable snags for all three birds is found in the 101-150 (26 percent) and the 151-200 (22 percent) age-classes. The zero age-class holds a large amount of suitable snags due to the large amount of disturbed forests in the nonstocked forest type. Another notable forest group is aspen-birch. Aspen forests are particularly important for some primary and secondary nesting birds because of the relationship of diseased aspen, primary excavators, and secondary nesters (Hart and Hart 2001). Diseased trees provide a relatively soft substrate for primary excavators to build their nest cavities in. The secondary nesters then occupy many of these cavities in subsequent years. Because few aspen trees live past 100 years in Montana and aspen snag retention time is short, the majority (83 percent) of snags in aspen forests are found in the 1- to 50-year age-class.

Variables other than snag dimensions and numbers need to be considered when predicting suitable wildlife habitat for forest-dwelling species. Proximity to forest edge and stand density of live trees is important to many cavity-nesting birds. The state of decay of a tree and its distance to foraging also plays a role in nest site suitability. FIA data can address many of these factors and there are current efforts to build predictive models for these species using data collected by our crews. These models can be valuable tools for Federal and State land managers, as most of the forests containing suitable snags occur on public lands.

VI. FIA Indicators

Forest Soil Resources

Soils on the landscape are the product of five interacting soil forming factors. These are parent material, climate, landscape position (topography), organisms (vegetation, microbes, other soil organisms), and time (Jenny 1994). Many external forces can have a profound influence on forest soil condition and hence forest health. These include agents of change or disturbances to apparent steady-state conditions such as shifts in climate, fire, insect and disease activities, land use activities, and land management actions.

The Soil Indicator of forest health was developed to assess the status and trend of forest soil resources in the United States across all ecoregions, forest types, and land ownership categories. For this report, data were analyzed and are being reported by forest type groups. This forest type stratification not only reflects the influence of forest vegetation on soil properties, but also the interaction of parent material, climate, landscape position, and time with forest vegetation and soil organisms. A complete listing of mean soil properties in Montana, organized by forest type, is in the Soil Indicator core tables in Appendix F ("Tables of Mean Soil Properties"). Some plots had a repeat visit so the data are summarized by visit number (1 or 2) and by forest type. Plots visited for the first Soil Indicator measurements were sampled in 2003 through 2007. Only a small subset of plots have been re-visited thus far in 2008 and 2009 so there is not yet enough data to run a valid repeated measures analysis. Nevertheless, we report the data for the re-visited plots summarized by forest type in the Soil Indicator core tables. Some of the key soil properties were graphed by forest type group in Montana and are highlighted in the discussion below.

Generally, soil moisture increases with elevation and latitude (associated with cooler temperatures) and forest types tend to reflect this climatic gradient. When expressed in terms of megagrams of C per hectare of forest area, C stocks generally increase with elevation and/or soil moisture storage (fig. 25). In Montana, spruce-fir forests tend to store the most C in terms of forest floor mass and belowground in mineral soil compared to other forest types. Soil N stocks in spruce-fir forests in Montana also tend to be higher than those in other forest types. This is in contrast to States such as Utah and Colorado where higher amounts of N are stored in aspen-dominated landscapes (DeBlander and others 2010; Thompson and others 2010). However, the cottonwood-aspen-birch group in Montana is represented by only seven plots and only three of those are dominated by aspen. This is far too small a sampling to generalize findings for this forest type across the State as a whole.

Soils in drier areas such as soils under Rocky Mountain juniper and ponderosa pine tend to be less weathered and have higher amounts of exchangeable base cations such as sodium, potassium, magnesium, and calcium (fig. 26). Acidic soils, many of which are found in wetter, higher elevation environments (e.g., spruce-fir), tend to have lower levels of exchangeable base cations and have measureable levels of exchangeable aluminum. In none of the plots sampled are soil exchangeable aluminum levels high enough to pose a toxicity risk to tree roots given the ample supply of exchangeable calcium.

USDA Forest Service Resour. Bull. RMRS-RB-15. 2012

47

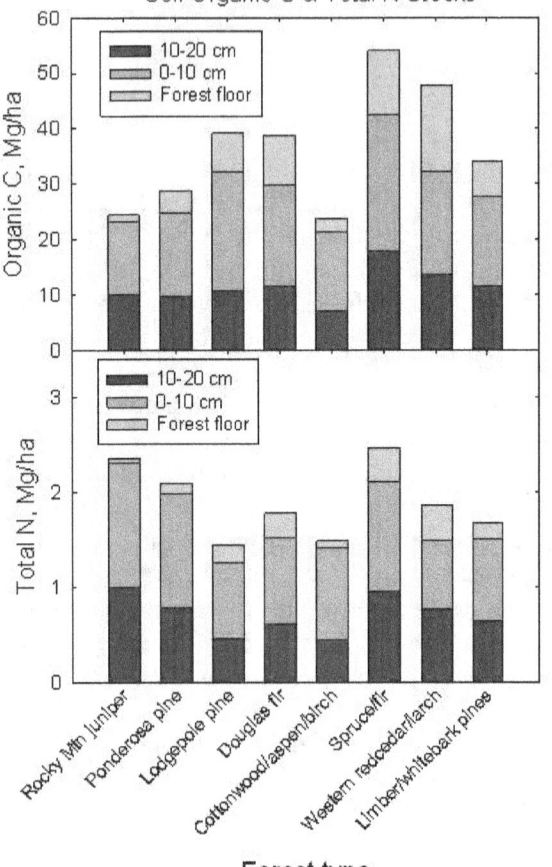

2003-07 Montana FIA Forest Health Monitoring Plots
Soil Organic C & Total N Stocks

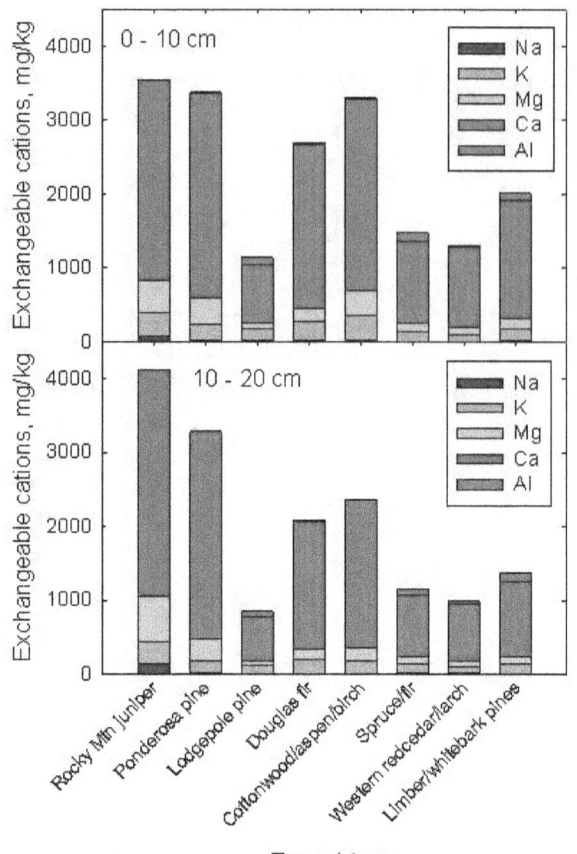

2003-07 Montana FIA Forest Health Monitoring Plots
Exchangeable cations

Figure 25—Soil organic carbon (top) and total nitrogen (bottom) stocks (Mg/ha) in the forest floor and 0-10 and 10-20 cm soil layers arranged by forest type groups in Montana. The forest type groups are arranged left to right in order of increasing latitude, elevation, and precipitation with some overlap among forest types. The spruce/fir group in MT includes grand fir, Engelmann spruce, subalpine fir, and mixed Engelmann spruce/subalpine fir.

Figure 26—Exchangeable cations (sodium, potassium, magnesium, calcium, and aluminum) in the 0-10 and 10-20 cm soil layers arranged by forest type groups in Montana.

Soil pH in drier calcareous soils tends to be near-neutral to alkaline (fig. 27 top) and such soils are found under Rocky Mountain juniper and ponderosa pine in Montana. The lowest pH soils are found under lodgepole pine and spruce-fir forests and these tend to be only moderately acid as a whole in Montana. Moderately acid soils often have elevated levels of extractable manganese (fig. 27 middle). Although elevated levels of manganese present some toxicity risk to sensitive species, potentially toxic levels of extractable manganese have yet to be established for most forest plant species. In general, only about 3.4 percent of the 0-10 cm forest soil layers in the Interior West contain extractable Mn levels greater than 100 mg/kg (Amacher and Perry 2011). In Montana, most of the forest soils with elevated levels of extractable Mn are found under lodgepole pine (mean extractable Mn = 40 mg/kg in 0-10 cm layer).

The lowest levels of extractable phosphorus by the Olsen method were found in soils under Rocky Mountain juniper and Ponderosa pine forests, whereas the highest were found under Douglas-fir (fig. 27 bottom). The lower levels of extractable

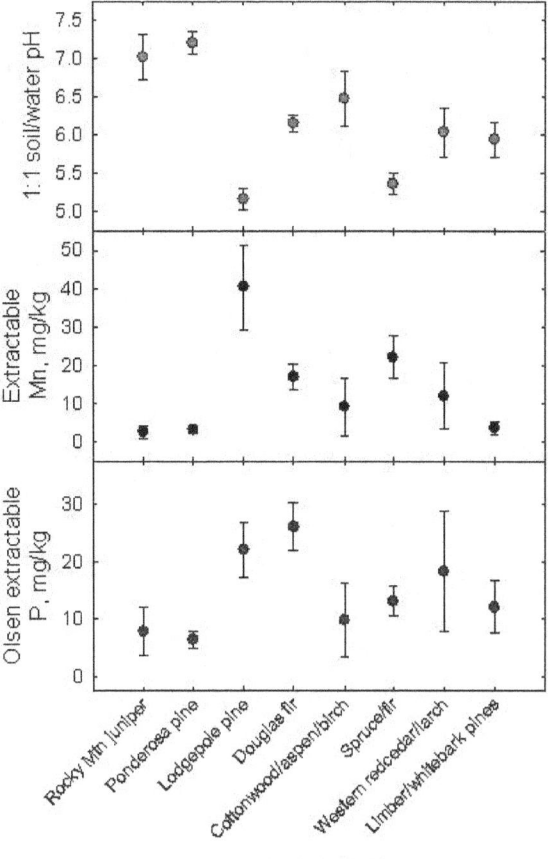

Figure 27—Averages, with standard errors, of soil pH, 1 M NH$_4$Cl-extractable manganese, and Olsen (pH 8.5 0.5 M NaHCO$_3$)-extractable phosphorus in the 0-10 cm soil layer arranged by forest type groups in Montana.

P in the calcareous soils reflects strong attenuation of plant-available P by the abundant calcium minerals in these soils.

Overall, soils under lodgepole pine in Montana tended to have the least nitrogen stocks, the lowest levels of exchangeable bases, and the lowest pH. This probably reflects the ability of the widely distributed lodgepole species to occupy lower fertility soils, whereas many other species prefer richer deeper soils. Throughout the Interior West as a whole, aspen, for example, tends to occupy deeper, richer, wetter soils and is associated with sites with higher nitrogen and potassium reserves, near-neutral pH levels, and a general absence of exchangeable aluminum (DeBlander and others 2010).

Down Woody Material

Down woody material (DWM) is an important component of forests that greatly impacts fire behavior, wildlife habitat, soil stabilization, and carbon sources. Some examples of DWM are fallen trees, branches, and leaf litter commonly found within forests in various stages of decay. The main components of DWM include fine woody debris (FWD), coarse woody debris (CWD), litter, and duff. FWD comprises the small diameter (1- to 3-inch) fire-related fuel classes (1-hr, 10-hr, 100-hr), and CWD comprises the large diameter (3-inch +) 1000-hr fuels.

USDA Forest Service Resour. Bull. RMRS-RB-15. 2012

49

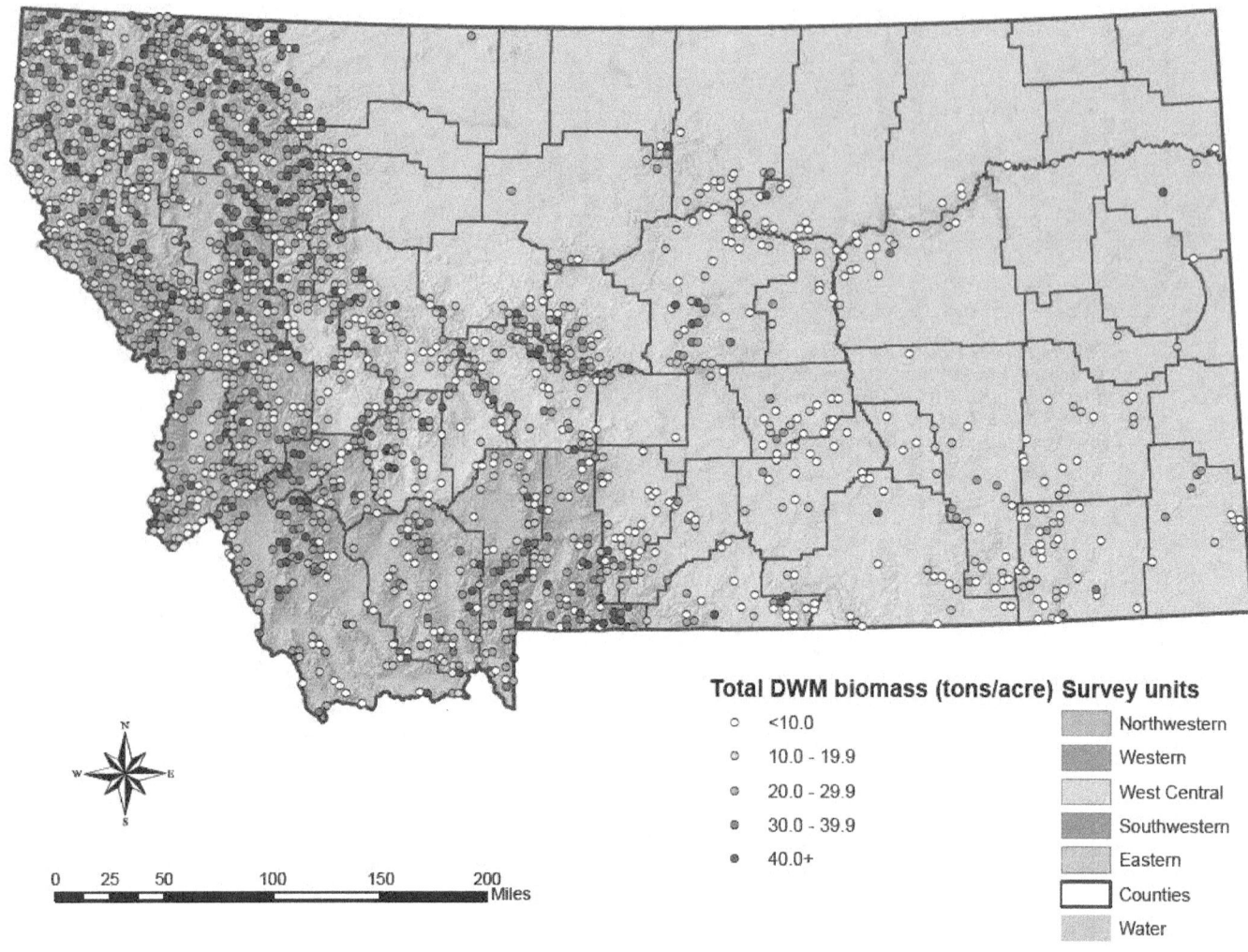

Total DWM biomass (tons/acre)

○ <10.0
◎ 10.0 - 19.9
◉ 20.0 - 29.9
● 30.0 - 39.9
● 40.0+

Survey units

Northwestern
Western
West Central
Southwestern
Eastern
Counties
Water

0 25 50 100 150 200 Miles

Figure 28—Plot distribution of total DWM biomass (tons per acre) by FIA survey unit, Montana, cycle 2, subcycles 4-7, 2006-2009.

Nationally, DWM is measured on Phase 3 (P3) plots. In 2006, due to the increasing need for more intensive DWM information, IWFIA initiated a Phase 2 (P2) DWM inventory in all its annual States. This DWM analysis used regional P2 protocols (USDA 2006-2009) for data collected from 2006 to 2009. Due to the presence of snow or other hazardous conditions, not all DWM components were able to be sampled on all plots. Only plots that sampled all six DWM components were included.

The random distribution of four annual subcycles of P2 DWM plots is displayed in figure 28. This shows the total DWM biomass (tons per acre) by FIA survey unit for 1,860 plot/conditions in Montana. In general, DWM biomass is highest in the northwestern and southwestern parts of the State; this distribution reflects the distribution of forest types. Moist, northwestern forest types, such as western larch, have high DWM biomass estimates, as do high-elevation types common in the southwest, like Engelmann spruce-subalpine fir; while Rocky Mountain juniper, a dryer forest type common in the eastern survey unit, has relatively low DWM biomass estimates.

Table 6 shows the mean biomass (tons per acre) by DWM component, number of plot/conditions sampled, and average elevation, for FIA survey units. The northwestern survey unit has the highest mean DWM, at 28.2 tons/acre, followed by

Table 6—Average elevation and DWM loadings by FIA survey unit with number of plots. Montana, cycle 2, subcycles 4-7, 2006-2009.

FIA survey unit	Number of plots	Elevation	CWD	FWD large	FWD medium	FWD small	Duff	Litter	Total DWM
Northwestern	512	4,686	9.4	2.0	0.5	0.2	12.5	3.6	28.2
Western	305	5,626	6.1	1.5	0.5	0.2	9.2	2.7	20.0
West Central	318	6,084	4.9	1.4	0.4	0.2	10.3	2.8	20.1
Southwestern	340	7,441	7.9	1.4	0.4	0.1	10.7	3.1	23.7
Eastern	385	4,369	2.1	0.9	0.3	0.1	7.1	3.7	14.2
All types	**1,860**	**5,517**	**6.3**	**1.5**	**0.4**	**0.2**	**10.2**	**3.3**	**21.8**

the southwestern at 23.7 tons/acre. The eastern survey unit has the lowest, at 14.2 tons/acre. The mean DWM for the entire State is 21.8 tons/acre. Specific DWM components mostly show a similar pattern. The exception is the litter component, where the eastern survey unit has the highest mean tons/acre. Table 7 shows the mean biomass (tons per acre) by DWM component, number of plot/conditions sampled, and average elevation for forest type groups and forest types. Western larch has the highest mean DWM, at least for forest types with more than a few plot/conditions, at 40.5 tons/acre; and the lowest is 6.8 tons/acre for juniper types in the pinyon-juniper group. Some of the forest types in this analysis may not be representative due to small sample sizes.

Fuel loadings by DWM component are essential for predicting fire behavior. Table 7 also shows that the duff DWM component has the highest mean fuel loadings over all, followed by the CWD component and then the litter component. Several forest types show some variation from this general trend. Also, fuel loading variation among forest types in the three FWD classes is not as great as in the CWD, duff, and litter classes.

Surface fuel classifications of duff, litter, FWD, and CWD for estimating fire effects were compiled from a wide variety of recent fuel sampling projects conducted across the contiguous United States (Lutes and others 2009). For each FIA plot/condition, fuel loading ranges from these four classes were used to identify one of 21 potential fuel loading models (FLM) described by Lutes and others (2009). Figure 29 displays the number of plot/conditions identified by FLM class for the five survey units in Montana. This shows that for this DWM dataset all of the 21 possible FLM's were identified, and the largest proportion of all the plot/conditions (249) occurred in the class 31 FLM, followed by classes 21 (171 plot/conditions) and 11 (170 plot/conditions). Class 31 was the most common FLM for all of the survey units except the eastern unit, where class 11 was the most common. Although these plot classifications are currently under review, once they are objectively classified they can be used as inputs to fire effects models to compute smoke emissions, fuel consumption, and carbon released to the atmosphere.

Structural diversity in terms of CWD diameters and decay classes are important criteria for wildlife habitat. IWFIA field crews identify one of five large-end diameter classes for each P2 CWD piece tallied. This information may be critical for wildlife species that use large-diameter logs for habitat. Figure 30 displays the percentage of CWD pieces for decay classes 1 through 4 in each large-end diameter class by forest type. Although they contribute to biomass and carbon pools, large-end diameter class is not recorded for decay class 5 pieces due to their degree of decomposition. At over 3 percent, the fir-spruce-mountain hemlock group (consisting of the Engelmann spruce, Engelmann spruce-subalpine fir, subalpine fir, grand fir and mountain hemlock forest types) has the highest percentage of CWD pieces in the 21.0-inch and greater class. Three other groups also have close to 3 percent in the 21.0-inch and greater class: the other western softwoods forest type group (consisting of the

Table 7—Average elevation and DWM loadings by forest type group and forest type with number of plots. Montana, cycle 2, subcycles 4-7, 2006-2009.

Forest type group and forest type	Number of plots	Elevation	CWD	FWD large	FWD medium	FWD small	Duff	Litter	Total DWM
Pinyon-juniper group									
Rocky Mountain juniper	70	3,887	0.4	0.5	0.2	0.1	3.3	2.7	7.2
Juniper woodland	5	5,283	0.1	0.1	0.1	0.0	0.3	1.0	1.6
Total	75	3,980	0.4	0.4	0.2	0.1	3.1	2.6	6.8
Douglas-fir group									
Douglas-fir	525	5,341	4.3	1.8	0.5	0.2	7.6	2.4	16.9
Total	525	5,341	4.3	1.8	0.5	0.2	7.6	2.4	16.9
Ponderosa pine group									
Ponderosa pine	203	3,883	1.7	0.8	0.3	0.1	6.4	4.3	13.5
Total	203	3,883	1.7	0.8	0.3	0.1	6.4	4.3	13.5
Fir-spruce-mountain hemlock group									
Engelmann spruce	93	6,423	11.8	1.5	0.4	0.2	12.1	2.3	28.4
Engelmann spruce / subalpine fir	84	6,538	12.8	1.5	0.5	0.2	13.6	2.8	31.4
Grand fir	13	3,765	10.6	1.9	0.7	0.2	14.7	4.0	32.2
Subalpine fir	171	6,712	10.8	1.3	0.4	0.2	10.9	2.1	25.7
Mountain hemlock	4	5,667	5.2	1.2	0.1	0.1	4.2	2.5	13.2
Total	365	6,482	11.4	1.4	0.4	0.2	11.9	2.4	27.8
Lodgepole pine group									
Lodgepole pine	298	6,464	9.0	1.6	0.3	0.1	14.4	4.2	29.7
Total	298	6,464	9.0	1.6	0.3	0.1	14.4	4.2	29.7
Hemlock-Sitka spruce group									
Western hemlock	2	4,173	14.9	2.2	0.5	0.2	13.5	2.5	33.8
Western redcedar	12	3,840	15.2	2.3	0.5	0.3	11.5	3.0	32.7
Total	14	3,887	15.1	2.3	0.5	0.3	11.8	2.9	32.9
Western larch group									
Western larch	74	4,488	12.6	2.8	0.6	0.2	18.2	6.1	40.5
Total	74	4,488	12.6	2.8	0.6	0.2	18.2	6.1	40.5
Other western softwoods group									
Limber pine	19	6,468	1.5	0.8	0.2	0.1	7.8	3.7	14.1
Whitebark pine	45	8,504	4.7	0.8	0.3	0.1	13.5	3.3	22.7
Miscellaneous western softwoods	4	7,784	0.5	0.5	0.2	0.1	5.4	2.0	8.5
Total	68	7,893	3.6	0.8	0.3	0.1	11.4	3.4	19.5

Oak-hickory group									
Elm / ash / black locust	1	2,667	0.2	1.2	0.6	0.1	24.5	17.1	43.7
Total	1	2,667	0.2	1.2	0.6	0.1	24.5	17.1	43.7
Elm-ash-cottonwood group									
Cottonwood	16	3,418	2.3	2.9	0.8	0.2	19.9	4.4	30.4
Sugarberry / hackberry / elm / green ash	1	3,093	5.9	0.0	0.0	0.1	15.7	7.8	29.5
Cottonwood / willow	2	3,512	5.0	7.5	0.4	0.1	10.5	8.6	32.1
Total	19	3,411	2.7	3.2	0.7	0.2	18.7	5.0	30.5
Aspen-birch group									
Aspen	36	5,431	4.6	1.7	0.3	0.1	20.2	5.6	32.5
Paper birch	2	3,732	4.1	3.2	0.5	0.2	37.5	11.5	57.0
Total	38	5,342	4.6	1.8	0.3	0.1	21.1	5.9	33.8
Alder-maple group									
Red alder	1	3,338	5.5	1.4	0.7	0.3	44.9	2.4	55.2
Total	1	3,338	5.5	1.4	0.7	0.3	44.9	2.4	55.2
Woodland hardwoods group									
Cercocarpus (mountain brush) woodland	1	5,975	0.8	0.0	0.2	0.0	8.4	1.6	11.1
Total	1	5,975	0.8	0.0	0.2	0.0	8.4	1.6	11.1
Nonstocked									
Nonstocked	178	4,920	3.5	1.1	0.2	0.1	6.7	3.0	14.6
Total	178	4,920	3.5	1.1	0.2	0.1	6.7	3.0	14.6
All types	1,860	5,517	6.3	1.5	0.4	0.2	10.2	3.3	21.8

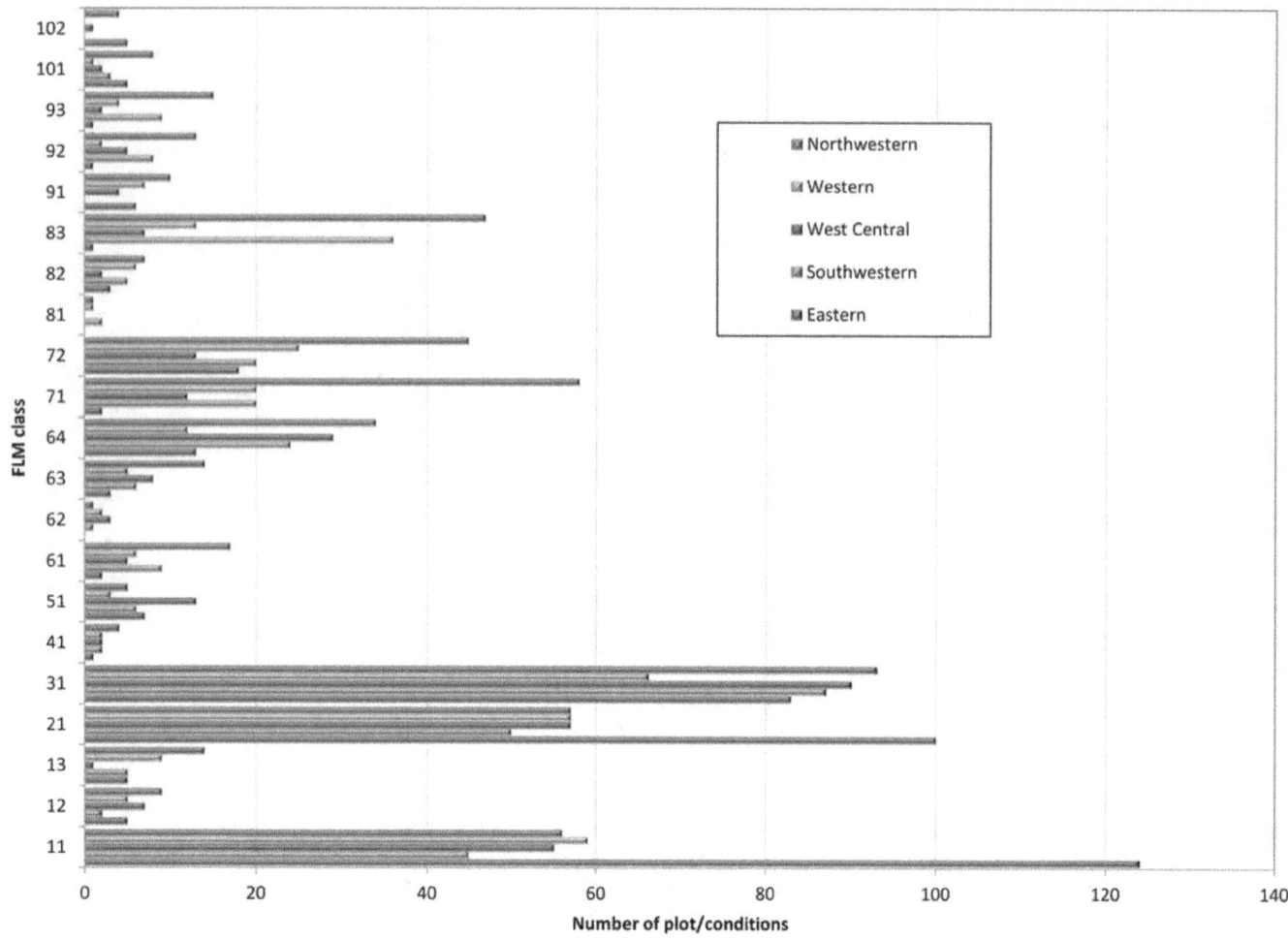

Figure 29—Number of plot/conditions by fuel loading model (FLM) class and FIA survey unit, Montana, cycle 2, subcycles 4-7, 2006-2009.

whitebark pine, limber pine, and miscellaneous western softwoods forest types), the aspen-birch group (aspen and paper birch forest types), and the western larch type/ group. At 15.0 to 20.9 inches large-end diameter, the hemlock-Sitka spruce forest type group (consisting of the western redcedar and western hemlock forest types) has the most at 12 percent, followed by the fir-spruce-mountain hemlock group (consisting of Engelmann spruce, subalpine fir, Engelmann spruce-subalpine fir, grand fir, and mountain hemlock forest types) and the pinyon-juniper group (Rocky Mountain juniper and juniper woodland forest types), each with 10 percent.

Another consideration other than size is the degree of decay of individual logs. Decay classes can range from class 1, which are newly fallen trees with no decay, to class 5, which still resemble a log but often blend into the duff and litter layers. Figure 31 shows the percentage of CWD pieces by forest type and decay class. In general, the wetter types have a higher percentage of CWD pieces in the advanced decomposition classes, while drier types have a lower percentage.

The annual FIA system supports live and standing dead tree inventories but does not include down dead trees as did some past periodic inventories. The current P3 DWM protocols and estimation procedures (Woodall and Monleon 2008) include improvements such as population estimation, and are designed to capture some important aspects that serve as a better surrogate for answering relevant questions about the various components of down woody materials in forests. However, as

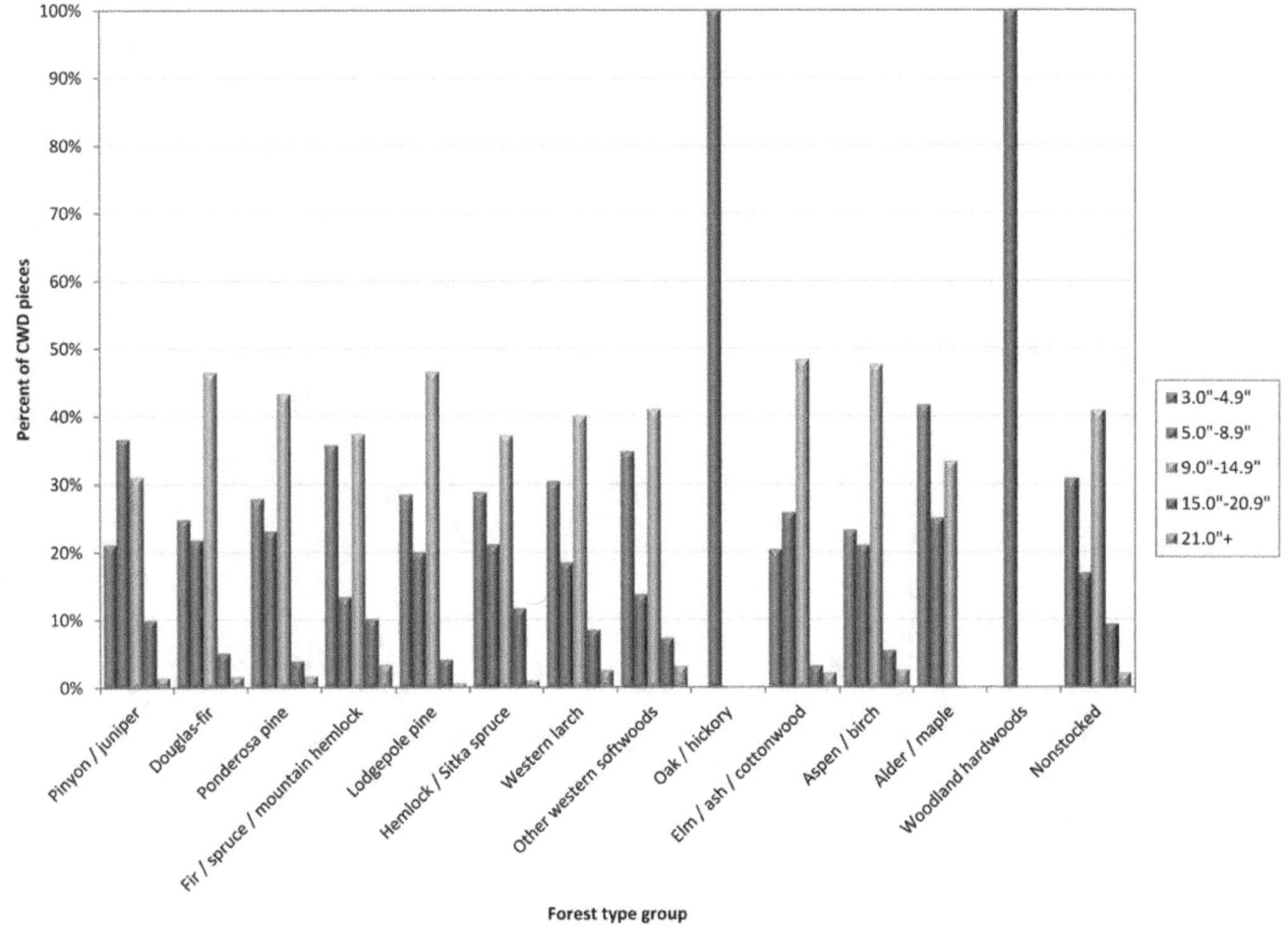

Figure 30—Percentage distribution of CWD pieces by large-end diameter class and forest type group, Montana, cycle 2, subcycles 4-7, 2006-2009.

discussed in Section II, P3 is a 1/16th sample of P2, and although it may be adequate at the regional or national level, it is often inadequate for many DWM applications at the State level.

Although this analysis included only plot-level per acre estimates and analysis, soon IWFIA will have population estimate capabilities for its regional P2 DWM database. This will allow analyses of the impacts and implications of expanding plot level information to the State.

For example, table 7 showed that although the western larch forest type in Montana has three times the total per acre DWM biomass of the ponderosa pine type, the area of the ponderosa pine type is over three times that of the western larch type (Appendix E, table 3). Once population estimates are factored in, the ponderosa pine type could contain more total DWM biomass and carbon than the western larch type.

Furthermore, the Pacific Northwest FIA and IWFIA are jointly investigating a national P2 inventory version of DWM to support a more robust dataset for future fire fuel, wildlife structure, and carbon assessments. These protocols should be complementary and compatible with the current regional P2 variations. As estimates of DWM are improved and refined, along with FIA's understory vegetation and standing tree inventory, FIA will be better positioned for addressing estimates of total forest biomass.

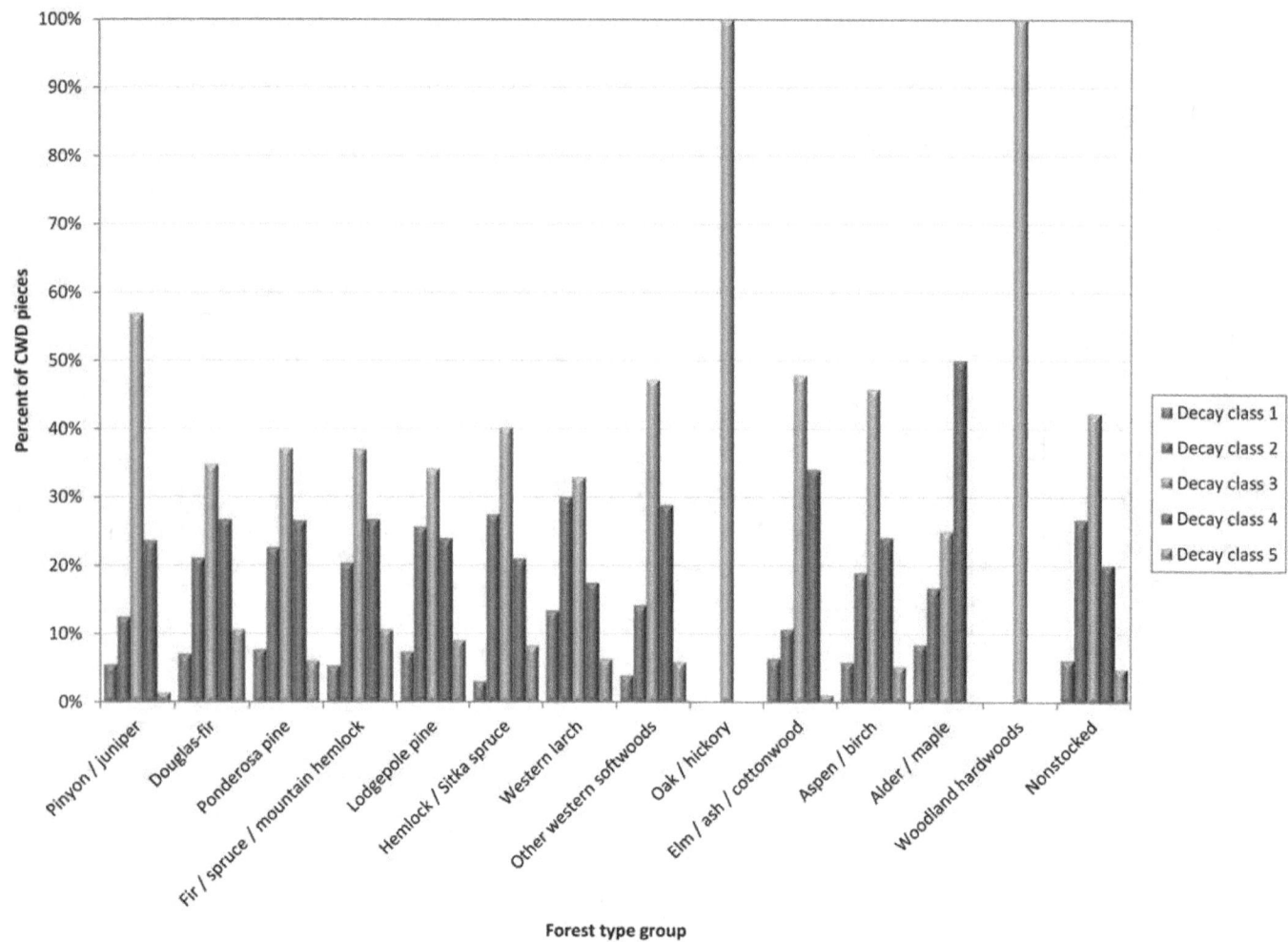

Figure 31—Percentage distribution of CWD pieces by decay class and forest type group, Montana, cycle 2, subcycles 4-7, 2006-2009.

Damage to Live Trees

The Interior West FIA program has used a regionally defined damage protocol for most of the periodic and annual inventories since 1981. Throughout this time, the protocol has remained consistent, with only a few modifications to the damage categories. Damages are assigned only to live trees, in contrast to mortality agents, which are only assigned to recently dead trees. Not all damaging agents are potential mortality agents, so there is only partial overlap in the two agent lists.

There are currently 50 damage codes representing a wide range of biotic, abiotic, and anthropogenic agents. Up to three damage agents may be assigned to a tree. However, less than a third of damaged trees have more than one agent assigned, and less than 25 percent of trees with two damage agents will have a third agent assigned.

The protocol is based on a threshold system, where damage is only recorded if it is considered "serious." Although this is somewhat subjective, the general rules are that damage should be recorded when it will cause one of the following:

• Prevent the tree from living to maturity, or surviving 10 more years if already mature;

• Prevent the tree from producing marketable products;

• Reduce (or has seriously reduced) the quality of the tree's potential products.

These rules roughly correspond to two main categories of damaging agents. Agents that are likely to prevent a tree from living to maturity or surviving for 10 years after the inventory date tend to be those related to insects, disease, fire, and atmospheric effects (drought, flooding, wind, etc.), whereas agents that preclude or reduce a tree's merchantability are more likely to be problems with form, such as forks, broken tops, or logging scars. The latter group may or may not affect trees with respect to survival. Therefore, not all trees with damages recorded are expected to die, and some of those with poor merchantability may live to typical upper ages for their species.

A nationally consistent protocol for non-lethal damage to trees is scheduled to be implemented by the FIA program in 2013. A majority of the damage categories used in the national protocol crosswalk directly with the Interior West regional categories, ensuring that it will be possible to track trends in damaging agents over time.

Because earlier inventories of Montana were done under the periodic system and parts of those inventories were spread over a wide range of years, it is difficult to compare earlier results to the current annual inventory. In order to keep the data as comparable as possible, damages are described as proportions of the trees tallied during the different time periods, that is, they are not expanded to make population-scale estimates.

There were 79,037 live trees tallied during the Montana periodic inventory years (1988 to 2001), and 89,068 live trees tallied during the first 7 years of annual inventory (2003-2009). During the periodic inventories, 36.8 percent of trees were assigned one damage agent, 8.4 percent had two agents, and 1.8 percent had three. During the annual inventory, nearly the same proportion of trees (37.6 percent) were assigned one damage agent, although the proportions of trees with secondary (12.8 percent) and tertiary (3.3 percent) damage agents appeared to increase. Although the overall frequency of primary damage was the same between periodic and annual inventories, the change in frequency was mixed among damage agent groups. The insects, fire, and form categories showed increases, with the remainder of groups showing decreases (table 8).

Damage agents related to merchantability accounted for the majority of primary damage agents (table 8). The next most frequent damage category was diseases, with the most frequently recorded agents within this category being stem and butt rots, cankers, stem rusts, and dwarf mistletoes. It should be noted that dwarf mistletoe is recorded for all infected trees using a separate variable, but only trees with a dwarf mistletoe rating (DMR; Hawksworth 1977) of 4 to 6 are considered as "serious" for the purpose of damage agent assignment. Notable damage agents within the insect category were bark beetles (0.22 percent in periodic and 0.82 percent in annual) and defoliators (0.20 percent in periodic and 1.12 percent in annual). Within the animal category, the majority of damage was caused by porcupines (0.55 percent in periodic and 0.46 percent in annual); within the atmosphere category, the most common sources of damage were frost (0.24 percent in periodic and 0.34 percent in annual), wind (0.17 percent in periodic and 0.07 percent in annual), snow (0.15 percent in periodic and 0.04 percent in annual), and lightening (0.12 percent in periodic and 0.03 percent in annual).

While it is difficult to compare changes in damage rates between periodic and annual inventories with statistical certainty, it is possible to consider some of the expected patterns in comparison to the data. For example, it may seem reasonable that the decreases in suppression and disease damages could be the result of fuel

Table 8—Distribution of primary damage agents by agent group, Montana periodic (1988-2001) and annual (2003-2009) inventories.

Damage agent group	Periodic	Annual
	Percent	
No damage (0)	63.20	62.40
Insects (10-16)	0.70	2.70
Diseases (20-29)	7.50	5.40
Fire (30-31)	0.30	0.40
Animals (40-48)	0.80	0.70
Atmosphere (50-59)	0.80	0.50
Suppression (61)	2.30	0.40
Form (71-79)	23.50	27.20
Human (80-85)	0.30	0.10
Unknown / Unidentified (70)	0.60	0.20
All agents	100.00	100.00

reduction and other silvicultural activities, which would tend to target trees in these categories disproportionally. In this respect, the apparent increase in form-damage trees is unexpected, because these trees would be targeted by silvicultural activities as well. However, the effect of management on the proportion of form-damage trees cannot be known with certainty until remeasurement occurs under the annual inventory system. On the other hand, the apparent increases in the insect categories of bark beetles and defoliators are consistent with aerial surveys and other information sources that show these agents have been on the increase in recent years. Damage from bark beetles shows a moderate increase compared to the known increase in mortality in many conifers (see "Forest Growth and Mortality" in Section IV), but this is not surprising given that FIA crews are more likely to encounter a bark beetle-infested tree when it is dead, and not during the brief period when it is live and heavily infested. In the typical situation, bark beetles would be assigned as the mortality agent of a dead tree as opposed to the damaging agent of a live tree.

The comparison of damage frequency over time also illustrated a key difference between periodic and annual inventory data. Periodic data are intended to be taken together as a whole inventory, even though the plots may be spread out over several years. During a periodic inventory, it is not uncommon for the plots done in a given year to be concentrated in a particular part of the State. As a result, there is geographic bias when measurement years are considered separately. Under annual inventory, the plots are geographically distributed every year and there is no geographic bias. The end result is that apparent trend within the periodic inventory may actually be the result of geographic bias. Under annual inventory, any trend over time may be more reliably interpreted as real. This is apparent when total damage frequency is plotted by measurement year (fig. 32). Note that the proportion of damaged trees varies widely over the periodic inventory years (1988-2002), but remains relatively consistent (but with a slightly declining trend) over the annual inventory years (2003-2009). The variation among periodic years is likely due to plots being located in areas of relatively high or low damage (e.g., recent fires, areas with snow damage, or localized insect outbreaks) in any given year.

As noted above, assignment of damage does not necessarily imply impending death of a tree. The types of form damages most frequently recorded—lean, forks

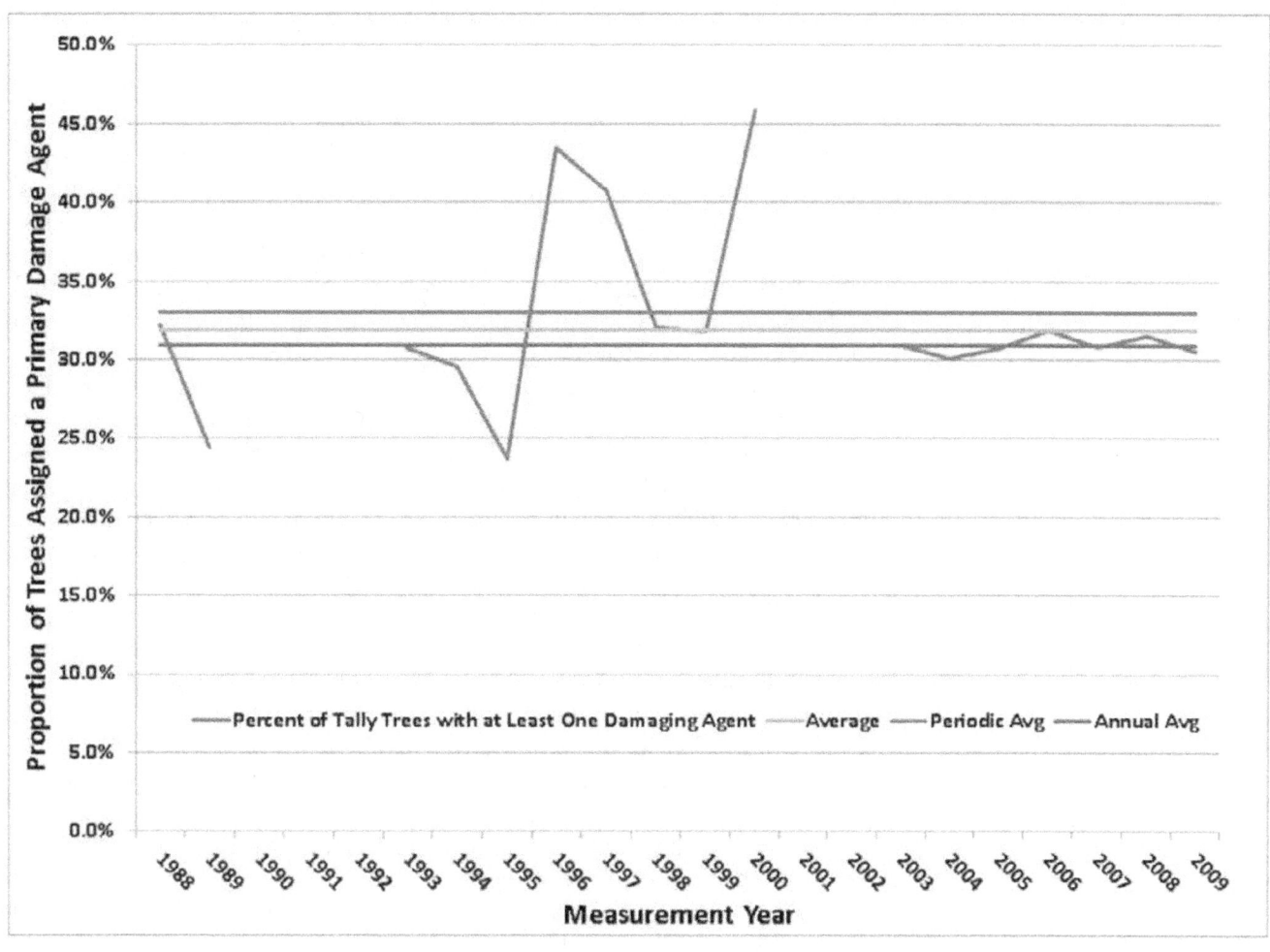

Figure 32—Variation of proportion of damage trees recorded by measurement year, 1988-2009. Years 1988 to 2001 were part of the Montana periodic inventory; 2003 to 2009 were measured as part of the annual inventory system.

below or above merchantable top, broken or dead tops, and crook/sweep/taper—are unlikely to result in mortality, so few of those in the form damage group should be expected to die. If we assume that the form damage group is considered non-lethal and all other agents combined are considered as potentially lethal within a 10-year window, the numbers are probably within what would be expected for normal stand development. For example, form-damaged and undamaged trees account for 89.6 percent of all tally trees. If the remaining trees are assumed to be at risk of mortality, the expected mortality rate can be approximated. Over a 10-year window, this equates to just over 1 percent on an annual basis, which can easily be accounted for under normal stand dynamics. Of course, the damaged trees that are expected to die are in addition to the mortality trees encountered during the most recent plot visits, and mortality is elevated in many species. This may suggest that damage frequencies are not greatly affected by periodically elevated mortality rates, because for many agents the transition from "healthy" to dead may occur relatively quickly. It is possible that elevated mortality could partly explain the apparent decrease in many agent categories, because, as the damage variables are intended, they identify trees that are predisposed to early mortality. Although this is the underlying assumption, it will not be conclusively demonstrable until annual remeasurement occurs.

USDA Forest Service Resour. Bull. RMRS-RB-15. 2012

59

VII. Montana Timber Harvest and Forest Products Industry Summary

The University of Montana Bureau of Business and Economic Research (BBER), in cooperation with the Interior West Forest Inventory and Analysis program, conducts periodic censuses of Montana's timber processing facilities. The BBER conducted a statewide census of primary forest products facilities in Montana for calendar year 2004 (Spoelma and others 2008) and is now completing the 2009 census. This section reports key aspects of the 2009 census and updates based on annual assessments done in conjunction with the BBER's annual Economic Outlook Seminar series.

Primary forest products facilities are firms that process timber into manufactured products such as lumber, and facilities such as pulp and paper mills and particleboard plants that use wood fiber residue directly from timber processors. A total of 119 primary forest products plants were identified as active in Montana during 2009, including 35 sawmills; 32 log home facilities; 27 post, pole, and log furniture manufacturers; 17 residue-related products facilities; 2 plywood/veneer plants; and 6 other miscellaneous facilities (fig. 33).

When the previous Montana census of primary timber processors was conducted for calendar year 2004, annual U.S. housing starts were surging towards 2 million, topping out at 2.1 million in 2005. However, with the housing market downturn beginning in 2006, the official recession starting in 2007, and the 2008 global financial crisis, housing starts fell to a post-World War II record low of 554,000. Housing starts only rebounded slightly in 2010, and are unlikely to increase significantly until 2013 or beyond. Several large mills and numerous smaller mills in the State have either curtailed operations or permanently closed in response to these operating conditions. The State's largest single forest products employer and largest user of wood fiber was lost when the Smurfit-Stone Container linerboard facility permanently closed in January 2010.

The capacity to process timber at Montana mills dropped 33 percent between 2004 and 2009 and dropped another 25 percent from 2009 to 2010. Capacity was over 1 billion board feet (Scribner) in 2000, but had fallen to 485 million board feet (MMBF) by 2010. Utilization of timber-processing capacity is an important indicator of the ability of the industry to quickly respond to increased demand for wood products when markets recover after an economic downturn. While capacity utilization was above 80 percent in 1986 and 1996, it fell to 76 percent in 2003, 70 percent in 2005, and 59 percent during 2010.

The sales value of Montana's wood and paper products was down from $1.3 billion in 2004, to $550 million in 2009, and $325 million in 2010. Total forest industry employment decreased from 9,875 workers in 2004, to 7,051 in 2009, and 6,743 in 2010. Production of lumber, the major output of Montana's wood products industry, fell from 917 MMBF, lumber tally in 2004 to a low of 418 MMBF in 2009, before a slight increase to 480 MMBF in 2010 (fig. 34).

Timber harvest for 2010 was 321 MMBF, approximately 12 percent higher than the 2009 harvest, but still less than half of the 2004 level of 751 MMBF. As shown in figure 35, the harvest totals from 2009 and 2010 are the lowest on record since 1945. In 2010, 54 percent of the harvest volume came from private lands, 24 percent from National Forest lands, and the remaining 22 percent came from other ownerships including State, BLM, and tribal lands.

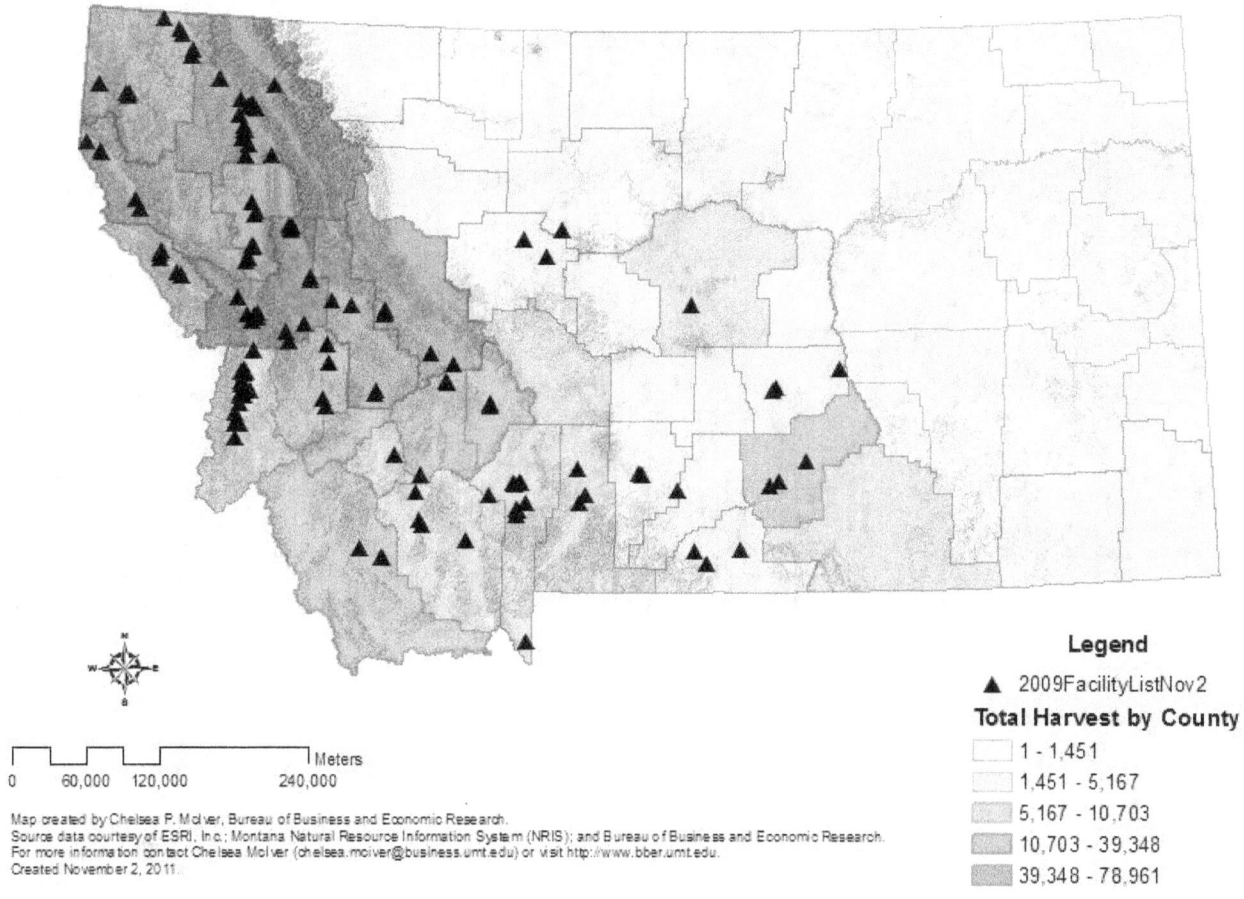

Legend

▲ 2009FacilityListNov2

Total Harvest by County

- [ ] 1 - 1,451
- [ ] 1,451 - 5,167
- [ ] 5,167 - 10,703
- [ ] 10,703 - 39,348
- [ ] 39,348 - 78,961

Map created by Chelsea P. McIver, Bureau of Business and Economic Research.
Source data courtesy of ESRI, Inc.; Montana Natural Resource Information System (NRIS); and Bureau of Business and Economic Research.
For more information contact Chelsea McIver (chelsea.mciver@business.umt.edu) or visit http://www.bber.umt.edu.
Created November 2, 2011.

Figure 33—Montana's primary timber processing facilities and timber harvest by county, 2009.

Markets for Montana wood products have improved little in 2011. Although modest improvements are expected in 2012, significant improvements are unlikely until 2013 or later, as U.S. home building recovers. However, with approximately 40 percent of the State's timber-processing capacity unutilized, Montana mills could quickly increase production in response to increased demand, depending on the timing of economic recovery and any resurgence in new home construction.

Figure 34—Montana lumber production (million board feet, Scribner rule), 1945-2010.

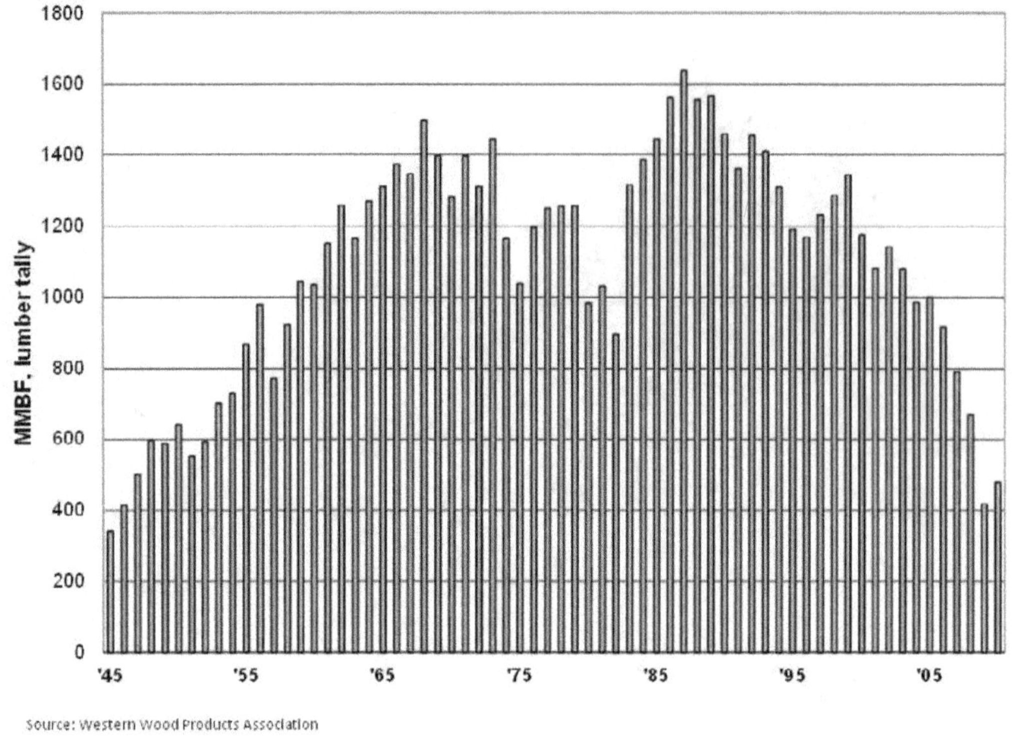

Source: Western Wood Products Association

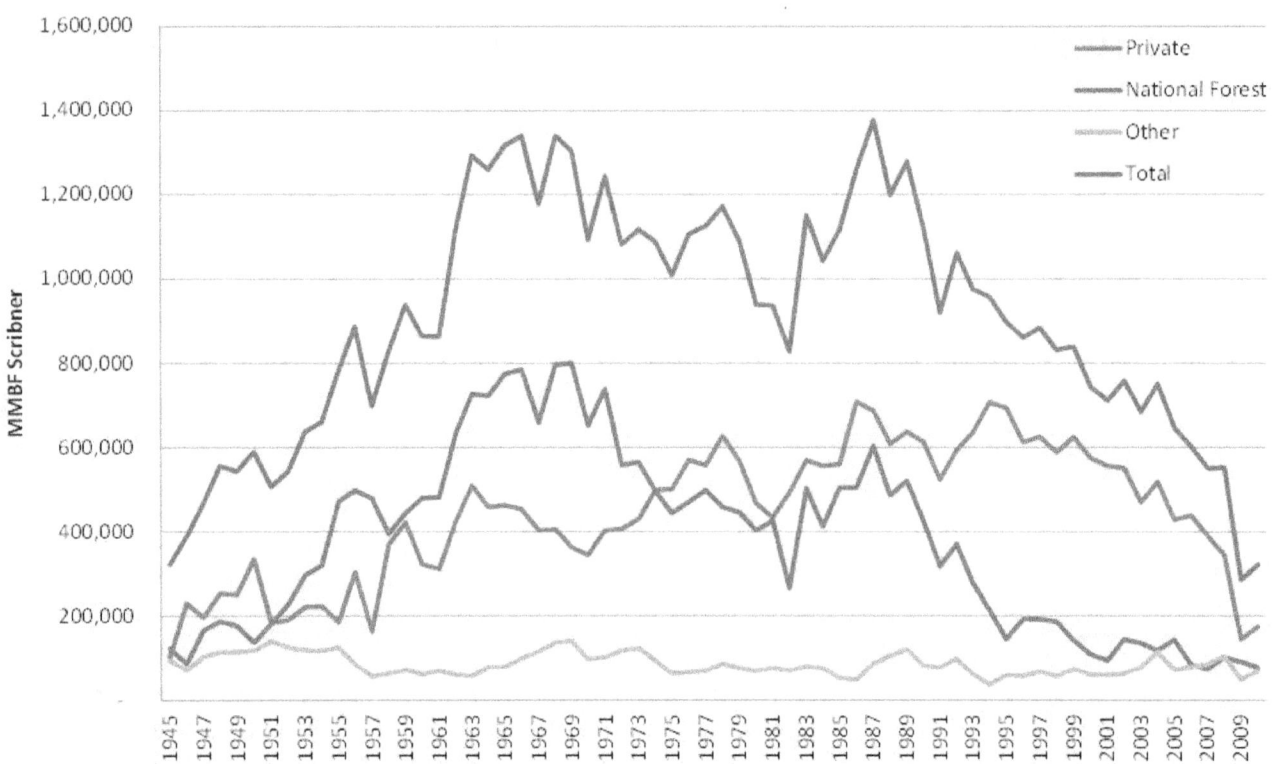

Source: USDA Forest Service, Region One, Missoula, MT.

Figure 35—Montana timber harvest (million board feet, Scribner rule) by ownership, 1945-2010.

USDA Forest Service Resour. Bull. RMRS-RB-15. 2012

VIII. Conclusions

Montana's nearly 26 million acres of forest land is diverse in the context of Intermountain West forest. It encompasses 28 individual FIA forest tree species, which in different combinations compose 25 different forest types. These occur across a wide range of elevation and climatic regimes, from forests dominated by ponderosa pine and Rocky Mountain juniper in the hills and break lands in the eastern half of the State, to high mountain forests typical of those found throughout the mountains of the Interior West in the southwestern portion of the State, to the dense and moist larch, hemlock, and redcedar dominated forests in the northwestern part of the State. These forests provide an abundance of services, including timber products, recreational opportunities, air and water quality, wildlife habitat, and scenic beauty. Major forest type groups include Douglas-fir, spruce-fir-mountain hemlock, lodgepole pine, and ponderosa pine. Major species groups are the main components of these forest types: true firs, Douglas-fir, lodgepole pine, Engelmann spruce, and ponderosa pine.

Seventy-three percent of these forests are in the public domain, with 60 percent managed by the National Forest Service. The Bureau of Land Management and the National Park Service are the other major public forest managers, but neither encompasses as much forest land as is owned by various private and tribal entities in Montana.

Currently in Montana, there are several factors leading to higher than average mortality rates. During the 2003-2009 FIA inventory period, forest tree mortality rates have begun to outpace growth rates in lodgepole pine, Douglas-fir, true firs, Engelmann spruce, and particularly in whitebark pine. The alarming rate of loss of whitebark pine can be further demonstrated and quantified using remeasurement data from previous inventory plots. Even though many small, young whitebark pines are present in the inventory, the long term reproductive success and sustainability of whitebark pine remains in question.

Quaking aspen is another tree species that has generated concern regarding forest health and sustainability. The current inventory, and comparisons to past inventory data, does not provide clear evidence of impending threats to Montana's aspen. However, assessments of trends in all tree species populations and forest dynamics will be greatly facilitated as annual plots come under full remeasurement of all inventory plots beginning in 2013 in Montana.

Montana's wood production and timber harvest have been declining over the past thirty years, but the recent recession and housing market bust have been especially devastating. Wood product processing facilities' production capacity has fallen off sharply over the past 5 years. Even at that, the utilization of those facilities is estimated at about 60 percent. The result is a loss of income and employment in Montana's economy. The extra wood processing capacity due to under utilization means, however, that the wood products industry could respond if demand were to increase in the near future.

Many of the analyses performed for this report demonstrate both the utility of FIA data as an analysis tool and the potential for further, more in-depth analysis of a wide range of topics. Data from FIA's annualized inventory will continue to provide valuable information to resource managers and researchers who are interested in the health, status, and quantity of resources provided by Montana's forests.

IX. Standard Forest Inventory and Analysis Terminology

Average annual mortality—The average annual volume of trees 5.0 inches d.b.h./d.r.c. and larger that died from natural causes.

Average net annual growth—Average annual net change in volume of trees 5.0 inches d.b.h./d.r.c. and larger in the absence of cutting (average annual gross growth minus average annual mortality).

Basal area (BA)—The cross-sectional area of a tree stem/bole (trunk) at the point where diameter is measured, inclusive of bark. BA is calculated for trees 1.0 inch and larger in diameter, and is expressed in square feet. For timber species, the calculation is based on diameter at breast height (d.b.h.); for woodland species, it is based on diameter at root collar (d.r.c.).

Biomass—The quantity of wood fiber, for trees 1.0 inch d.b.h./d.r.c. and larger, expressed in terms of oven-dry weight. It includes above-ground portions of trees: bole/stem (trunk), bark, and branches. Biomass estimates can be computed for live and/or dead trees.

Board-foot volume—A board-foot is a unit of measure indicating the amount of wood contained in an unfinished board 1 foot wide, 1 foot long, and 1 inch thick. Board-foot volume is computed for the sawlog portion of a sawtimber-size tree; the sawlog portion includes the part of the bole on sawtimber-size tree from a 1-foot stump to a minimum sawlog top of 7 inches diameter outside bark (d.o.b.) for softwoods, or 9 inches d.o.b. for hardwoods. Net board-foot volume is calculated as the gross board-foot volume in the sawlog portion of a sawtimber-size tree, less deductions for cull (note: board-foot cull deductions are limited to rotten/missing material and form defect—referred to as the merchantability factor—board-foot). Board-foot volume estimates are computed in both Scribner and International ¼-inch rule, and can be calculated for live and/or dead (standing or down) trees.

Census water—Streams, sloughs, estuaries, canals, and other moving bodies of water 200 feet wide and greater, and lakes, reservoirs, ponds, and other permanent bodies of water 4.5 acres in area and greater.

Coarse woody debris—Down pieces of wood leaning more than 45 degrees from vertical with a diameter of at least 3.0 inches and a length of at least 3.0 feet.

Condition class—The combination of discrete landscape and forest attributes that identify, define, and stratify the area associated with a plot. Examples of such attributes include condition status, forest type, stand origin, stand size, owner group, and stand density.

Crown class—A classification of trees based on dominance in relation to adjacent trees in the stand as indicated by crown development and amount of sunlight received from above and the sides.

Crown cover (Canopy cover)—The percentage of the ground surface area covered by a vertical projection of plant crowns. Tree crown cover for a sample site includes the combined cover of timber and woodland trees 1.0 inch d.b.h./d.r.c. and larger. Maximum crown cover for a site is 100 percent; overlapping cover is not double counted.

Cubic-foot volume (merchantable)—A cubic-foot is a unit of measure indicating the amount of wood contained in a cube 1-by-1-by-1 foot. Cubic-foot volume is computed for the merchantable portion of timber and woodland species; the merchantable portion for timber species includes that part of a bole from a 1-foot stump to a minimum 4-inch top d.o.b, or above the place(s) of diameter measurement for any woodland tree with a single 5.0-inch stem or larger or a cumulative (calculated) d.r.c. of at least 5.0 inches to the 1.5-inch ends of all branches. **Net cubic-foot volume** is calculated as the gross cubic-foot volume in the merchantable portion of a tree, less deductions for cull.

Diameter at breast height (d.b.h.)—The diameter of a tree bole/stem (trunk) measured at breast height (4.5 feet above ground), measured outside the bark. The point of diameter measurement may vary for abnormally formed trees.

Diameter at root collar (d.r.c.)—The diameter of a tree stem(s) measured at root collar or at the point nearest the ground line (whichever is higher) that represents the basal area of the tree, measured outside the bark. For multistemmed trees, d.r.c. is calculated from an equation that incorporates the individual stem diameter measurements. The point of diameter measurement may vary for woodland trees with stems that are abnormally formed. With the exception of seedlings, woodland stems qualifying for measurement must be at least 1.0 inch in diameter or larger and at least 1.0 foot in length.

Diameter class—A grouping of tree diameters (d.b.h. or d.r.c.) into classes of a specified range. For some diameter classes, the number referenced (e.g., 4", 6", 8") is designated as the midpoint of an individual class range. For example, if 2-inch classes are specified (the range for an individual class) and even numbers are referenced, the 6-inch class would include trees 5.0- to 6.9-inches in diameter.

Diameter outside bark (d.o.b.)—Tree diameter measurement inclusive of the outside perimeter of the tree bark. The d.o.b. measurement may be taken at various points on a tree (e.g., breast height, tree top) or log, and is sometimes estimated.

Field plot/location—A reference to the sample site or plot; an area containing the field location center (LC) and all sample points. A field location consists of four subplots and four microplots.

- **Subplot**—A 1/24-acre fixed-radius area (24-foot horizontal radius) used to sample trees 5.0 inches d.b.h./d.r.c. and larger and understory vegetation.

- **Microplot**—A 1/300-acre fixed-radius plot (6.8-foot radius), located at the center of each subplot, used to inventory seedlings and saplings.

Fixed-radius plot—A circular sample plot of a specified horizontal radius: 1/300 acre = 6.8 foot radius (microplot); 1/24 acre = 24.0 foot radius (subplot).

Forest industry land– Land owned by a company or an individual(s) operating a primary wood-processing plant.

Forest land—Land that has at least 10 percent cover of live tally tree species of any size, or land formerly having such tree cover, and not currently developed for a nonforest use. The minimum area for classification as forest land is 1 acre. Roadside, stream-side, and shelterbelt strips of trees must be at least 120 feet wide to qualify as forest land. Unimproved roads and trails, streams and other bodies of water, or natural clearings in forested areas are classified as forest, if less than 120 feet in width or 1 acre in size. Grazed woodlands, reverting fields, and pastures that are not actively maintained are included if above qualifications are satisfied.

Forest type—A classification of forest land based on the species forming a plurality of live-tree stocking.

Gross growth—The annual increase in volume of trees 5.0 inches d.b.h. and larger in absence of cutting and mortality. Gross growth includes survivor growth, ingrowth, growth on ingrowth, growth on removals before removal, and growth on mortality prior to death.

Growing-stock trees—A live timber species, 5.0 inches d.b.h. or larger, with less than 2/3 (67 percent) of the merchantable volume cull, and containing at least one solid 8-foot section, now or prospectively, reasonably free of form defect, on the merchantable portion of the tree.

Growing-stock volume—the cubic-foot volume of sound wood in growing-stock trees at least 5.0 inches d.b.h. from a 1-foot stump to a minimum 4-inch top d.o.b. to the central stem.

Hardwoods—Dicotyledonous trees, usually broadleaf and deciduous.

Hexagonal grid (Hex)—A hexagonal grid formed from equilateral triangles for the purpose of tessellating the FIA inventory sample. Each hexagon in the base grid has an area of 5,937 acres (2,403.6 ha) and contains one inventory plot. The base grid can be subdivided into smaller hexagons to intensify the sample.

Indian Trust lands—American Indian lands held in fee, or trust, by the Federal Government, but administered for tribal groups or as individual trust allotments.

Land use—The classification of a land condition by use or type.

Litter—The uppermost layer of organic debris on a forest floor; that is, essentially the freshly fallen, or only slightly decomposed material, mainly foliage, but also bark fragments, twigs, flowers, fruits, and so forth. Humus is the organic layer, unrecognizable as to origin, immediately beneath the litter layer from which it is derived. Litter and humus together are often termed duff.

Logging residue/products—

- **Bolt**—A short piece of pulpwood; a short log.

- **Industrial wood**—All commercial roundwood products, excluding fuelwood.

- **Logging residue**—The unused sections within the merchantable portions of sound (growing-stock) trees cut or killed during logging operations.

- **Mill or plant residue**—Wood material from mills or other primary manufacturing plants that is not used for the mill's or plant's primary products. Mill or plant residue includes bark, slabs, edgings, trimmings, miscuts, sawdust, and shavings. Much of the mill and plant residue is used as fuel and as the raw material for such products as pulp, palletized fuel, fiberwood, mulch, and animal bedding. Mill or plant residue includes bark and the following components:

- **Coarse residue**—Wood material suitable for chipping, such as slabs, edgings, and trim.

- **Fine residue**—Wood material unsuitable for chipping, such as sawdust and shavings.

- **Pulpwood**—Roundwood, whole-tree chips, or wood residues that are used for the production of wood pulp.

- **Roundwood**—Logs, bolts, or other round sections cut from trees.

Mapped-plot design—A sampling technique that identifies (maps) and separately classifies distinct "conditions" on the field location sample area. Each condition

66

USDA Forest Service Resour. Bull. RMRS-RB-15. 2012

must meet minimum size requirements. At the most basic level, condition class delineations include forest land, nonforest land, and water. Forest land conditions can be further subdivided into separate condition classes if there are distinct variations in forest type, stand-size class, stand origin, and stand density, given that each distinct area meets minimum size requirements.

Merchantable portion—For trees measured at d.b.h. and 5.0 inches d.b.h. and larger, the merchantable portion (or "merchantable bole") includes the part of the tree bole from a 1-foot stump to a 4.0-inch top (d.o.b.). For trees measured at d.r.c., the merchantable portion includes all qualifying segments above the place(s) of diameter measurement for any tree with a single 5.0-inch stem or larger or a cumulative (calculated) d.r.c. of at least 5.0 inches to the 1.5-inch ends of all branches; sections below the place(s) of diameter measurement are not included. Qualifying segments are stems or branches that are a minimum of 1 foot in length and at least 1.0 inch in diameter; portions of stems or branches smaller than 1.0 inch in diameter, such as branch tips, are not included in the merchantable portion of the tree.

Miscellaneous Federal lands—Public lands administered by Federal agencies other than the Forest Service, U.S. Department of Agriculture, or the Bureau of Land Management, U.S. Department of the Interior.

Mortality tree—All standing or down dead trees 5.0 inches d.b.h./d.r.c. and larger that were alive within the previous 5 years.

National Forest System (NFS) lands—Public lands administered by the Forest Service, U.S. Department of Agriculture, such as National Forests, National Grasslands, and some National Recreation Areas.

National Park lands—Public lands administered by the Park Service, U.S. Department of the Interior, such as National Parks, National Monuments, National Historic Sites (such as National Memorials and National Battlefields), and some National Recreation Areas.

Noncensus water—Portions of rivers, streams, sloughs, estuaries, and canals that are 30 to 200 feet wide and at least 1 acre in size; and lakes, reservoirs, and ponds 1 to 4.5 acres in size. Portions of rivers and streams not meeting the criteria for census water, but at least 30 feet wide and 1 acre in size, are considered noncensus water. Portions of braided streams not meeting the criteria for census water, but at least 30 feet in width and 1 acre in size, and more than 50 percent water at normal high-water level are also considered noncensus water.

Nonforest land—Land that does not support, or has never supported, forests, and lands formerly forested where tree regeneration is precluded by development for other uses. Includes areas used for crops, improved pasture, residential areas, city parks, improved roads of any width and adjoining rights-of-way, power line clearings of any width, and noncensus water. If intermingled in forest areas, unimproved roads and nonforest strips must be more than 120 feet wide, and clearings, etc., more than 1 acre in size, to qualify as nonforest land.

Nonindustrial private lands—Privately owned land excluding forest industry land.

Unreserved forest land—Forest land not withdrawn from management for production of wood products through statute or administrative designation.

Other private lands—Privately owned lands other than forest industry or Indian Trust.

USDA Forest Service Resour. Bull. RMRS-RB-15. 2012

67

Other public lands—Public lands administered by agencies other than the Forest Service, U.S. Department of Agriculture. Includes lands administered by other Federal, State, county, and local government agencies, including lands leased by these agencies for more than 50 years.

Other wooded land—Land that has 5 to 10 percent cover of live tally tree species of any size, or land formerly having such tree cover, and not currently developed for a nonforest use. The minimum area for classification as forest land is 1 acre. Roadside, stream-side, and shelterbelt strips of trees must be at least 120 feet wide to qualify as forest land. Unimproved roads and trails, streams and other bodies of water, or natural clearings in forested areas are classified as forest, if less than 120 feet wide or 1 acre in size. Grazed woodlands, reverting fields, and pastures that are not actively maintained are included if above qualifications are satisfied.

Panel—A set of plots scheduled to be measured and remeasured in the same years. FIA divides each State's plots into five panels that can be used independently, or in combination, to sample the population. Thus, after 5 years all of a State's plots have been sampled, and each plot is remeasured every 5 years. Subpanels can be used to lengthen the measurement cycle to 7 or 10 years.

Poletimber-size trees—For trees measured at d.b.h, softwoods 5.0 to 8.9 inches d.b.h. and hardwoods 5.0 to 10.9 inches d.b.h. For trees measured at d.r.c., all live trees 5.0 to 8.9 inches d.r.c.

Primary wood-processing plants—An industrial plant that processes roundwood products, such as sawlogs, pulpwood bolts, or veneer logs.

Productive forest land—Forest land capable of producing 20 cubic feet per acre per year of wood from trees classified as a timber species (see Appendix A) on forest land classified as a timber forest type (see Appendix B).

Productivity—The potential yield capability of a stand calculated as a function of site index (expressed in terms of cubic-foot growth per acre per year at age of culmination of mean annual increment). Productivity values for forest land provide an indication of biological potential. Timberland stands are classified by the potential net annual growth attainable in fully stocked natural stands. For FIA reporting, Productivity Class is a variable that groups stand productivity values into categories of a specified range. Productivity is sometimes referred to as "Yield" or "Mean annual increment (MAI)."

Removals—The net volume of sound (growing-stock) trees removed from the inventory by harvesting or other cultural operations (such as timber-stand improvement), by land clearing, or by changes in land use (such as a shift to wilderness).

Reserved land—Land withdrawn from management for production of wood products through statute or administrative designation; examples include Wilderness areas and National Parks and Monuments.

Sampling error—A statistical term used to describe the accuracy of the inventory estimates. Expressed on a percentage basis in order to enable comparisons between the precision of different estimates, sampling errors are computed by dividing the estimate into the square root of its variance.

Sapling—A live tree 1.0 to 4.9 inches d.b.h./d.r.c.

Sawlog portion—The part of the bole of sawtimber-size trees between a 1-foot stump and the sawlog top.

Sawlog top—The point on the bole of sawtimber-size trees above which a sawlog cannot be produced. The minimum sawlog top is 7 inches d.o.b. for softwoods, and 9 inches d.o.b. for hardwoods.

Sawtimber-size trees—Softwoods 9.0 inches d.b.h. and larger and hardwoods 11.0 inches and larger.

Sawtimber volume—The growing-stock volume in the saw-log portion of saw-timber-size trees in board feet.

Seedlings—Live trees less than 1.0 inch d.b.h./d.r.c.

Site index—A measure of forest productivity for a timberland tree/stand. Expressed in terms of the expected height (in feet) of trees on the site at an index age of 50 (or 80 years for aspen and cottonwood). Calculated from height-to-age equations.

Site tree—A tree used to provide an index of site quality. Timber species selected for site index calculations must meet specified criteria with regards to age, diameter, crown class, and damage.

Snag—A standing-dead tree.

Softwood trees—Coniferous trees, usually evergreen, having needle- or scale-like leaves.

Stand—A community of trees that can be distinguished from adjacent communities due to similarities and uniformity in tree and site characteristics, such as age-class distribution, species composition, spatial arrangement, structure, etc.

Stand density—A relative measure that quantifies the relationship between trees per acre, stand basal area, average stand diameter, and stocking of a forested stand.

Stand density index (SDI)—A widely used measure developed by Reineke (1933), and is an index that expresses relative stand density based on a comparison of measured stand values with some standard condition; **relative stand density** is the ratio, proportion, or percent of absolute stand density to a reference level defined by some standard level of competition. For FIA reporting, the SDI for a site is usually presented as a percentage of the maximum SDI for the forest type. Site SDI values are sometimes grouped into SDI classes of a specified percentage range. Maximum SDI values vary by species and region.

Standing tree—To qualify as a standing dead tally tree, dead trees must be at least 5.0 inches in diameter, have a bole that has an unbroken actual length of at least 4.5 feet, and lean less than 45 degrees from vertical as measured from the base of the tree to 4.5 feet. Portions of boles on dead trees that are separated greater than 50 percent (either above or below 4.5 feet), are considered severed and are included in Down Woody Material (DWM) if they otherwise meet DWM tally criteria. For western woodland species with multiple stems, a tree is considered down if more than 2/3 of the volume is no longer attached or upright; do not consider cut and removed volume. For western woodland species with single stems to qualify as a standing dead tally tree, dead trees must be at least 5.0 inches in diameter, be at least 1.0 foot in unbroken actual length, and lean less than 45 degrees from vertical.

Stand-size class—A classification of forest land based on the predominant diameter size of live trees presently forming the plurality of live-tree stocking. Classes are defined as follows:

- **Sawtimber stand (Large-tree stand)**—A stand at least 10 percent stocked with live trees, in which half or more of the total stocking is from live trees 5.0-inches or larger in diameter, and with sawtimber (large tree) stocking equal to or greater than poletimber (medium tree) stocking.

- **Poletimber stand (Medium-tree stand)**—A stand at least 10 percent stocked with live trees, in which half or more of the total stocking is from live trees 5.0 inches or larger in diameter, and with poletimber (medium tree) stocking exceeding sawtimber (large tree) stocking.

- **Sapling/seedling stand**—A stand at least 10 percent stocked with live trees, in which half or more of the total stocking is from live trees less than 5.0 inches in diameter.

- **Nonstocked stand**—A formerly stocked stand that currently has less than 10 percent stocking, but has the potential to again become 10 percent stocked. For example, recently harvested, burned, or windthrow-damaged areas.

Stockability (Stockability factor)—An estimate of the stocking potential of a given site; for example, a stockability factor of 0.8 for a given site indicates that the site is capable of supporting only about 80 percent of "normal" stocking as indicated by yield tables. Stockability factors (maximum site value of 1.0) are assigned to sites based on habitat type/plant associations.

Stocking—An expression of the extent to which growing space is effectively utilized by live trees.

Subpanel—A further subdivision of the FIA five-panel system that allows for a 7- or ten-10 remeasurment cycle. Subpanels are used in Western States to establish a 10-year cycle, so that after 10 years all the plots have been sampled, and each plot is remeasured every 10 years. Using subpanels, each year's plots can still be used independently, or in combination, to sample the population.

Timber species—Tally tree species with a typical growth form featuring relatively tall trees with a single stem or bole. This form dictates a separate set of field measurement and assessment protocols (as opposed to woodland species). Most importantly, diameter is measured at breast height (d.b.h.). Although this group includes species traditionally used for industrial wood products, it is not exclusive to them. Additionally, it is not uncommon for some timber species to be found on mixed-species plots that have a woodland forest type.

Timber stand improvement—A term comprising all intermediate cuttings or treatments, such as thinning, pruning, release cutting, girdling, weeding, or poisoning, made to improve the composition, health, and growth of the remaining trees in the stand.

Timberland—Unreserved forest land capable of producing 20 cubic feet per acre per year of wood from trees classified as a timber species (see Appendix A) on forest land designated as a timber forest type (see Appendix B).

Unproductive forest land—Forest land not capable of producing 20 cubic feet per acre per year of wood from trees classified as a timber species (see Appendix A) on forest land designated as a timber forest type and all forest lands designated as a woodland forest type (see Appendix B).

Wilderness area—An area of undeveloped land currently included in the Wilderness System, managed to preserve its natural conditions and retain its primeval character and influence.

Woodland species—Tally tree species with a typical growth form featuring relatively short trees with a variable number of stems. This form dictates a separate set of field measurement and assessment protocols (as opposed to timber species). Most importantly, diameter is measured at the root collar (d.r.c.). These species (examples include pinyon, most junipers, mesquite, curlleaf mountain-mahogany, and most intermountain maples and oaks) are not usually converted into industrial wood products, but may be utilized for specialty wood products (artisanal woods, fuel biomass including firewood, and fenceposts). Woodland species may be found in the understory of mixed-species plots that have a timber forest type.

Note: For the FIA national glossary please go to:
http://socrates.lv-hrc.nevada.edu/fia/ab/issues/pending/glossary.html.

USDA Forest Service Resour. Bull. RMRS-RB-15. 2012

71

X. References

Amacher, M. C.; Perry, C. H. 2011. Background technical report for Criterion 4. Conservation and maintenance of soil water resources: Indicator 19. Area and percent of forest land with significant soil degradation. National Report on Sustainable Forests - 2010. FS-979. Washington, DC: U.S. Department of Agriculture, Forest Service.

Amman, G. D. 1973. Population changes of the mountain pine beetle in relation to elevation. Environmental Entomology. 2: 541-547.

Arner, S. L.; Woudenberg, S.; Waters, S.; [and others]. 2001. National algorithms for determining stocking class, stand size class, and forest type for Forest Inventory and Analysis plots. Unpublished report on file at: U.S. Department of Agriculture, Forest Service, Rocky Mountain Research Station, Forestry Sciences Lab, Ogden, UT. Available online at http://www.fs.fed.us/fmsc/ftp/fvs/docs/gtr/Arner2001.pdf. Accessed 2/2/2012.

Arno, S. F. 1986. Whitebark pine cone crops: A diminishing source of wildlife food? Western Journal of Applied Forestry. 1(3): 92-94.

Arno, S. F.; Hoff, R. J. 1989. Silvics of whitebark pine (Pinus albicaulis). Gen. Tech. Rep. INT-253. U.S. Department of Agriculture, Forest Service, Intermountain Research Station. 14 p.

Bailey, R. G. 1995. Descriptions of the ecoregions of the United States. (2nd ed. rev. and expanded). Misc. Publ. No. 1391. Washington, DC: U.S. Department of Agriculture, Forest Service.

Bartos, D. L.; Campbell, R. B., Jr. 1998. Decline of quaking aspen in the Interior West— examples from Utah. Rangelands. 20(1): 17-24.

Bechtold, W. A.; Patterson, P. L., eds. 2005. The enhanced Forest Inventory and Analysis program—National sampling design and estimation procedures. Gen. Tech. Rep. SRS-80. Asheville, NC: U.S. Department of Agriculture, Forest Service, Southern Research Station. 85 p.

Beers, T. W.; Miller, C. I. 1964. Point sampling; research results, theory and applications. Res. Bull. 786. Purdue University Agricultural Experiment Station. 55 p.

Brickell, J. E. 1970. Equations and computer subroutines for estimating site quality of eight Rocky Mountain species. Res. Pap. INT-75. Ogden, UT: U.S. Department of Agriculture, Forest Service, Intermountain Research Station.

Carroll, A. L.; Safranyik, L. 2004. The bionomics of the mountain pine beetle in lodgepole pine forests: Establishing a context. In: Shore, T. L.; Brooks, J. E.; Stone, J. E., eds. Mountain pine beetle symposium: Challenges and solutions; Proceedings: Challenges and solutions; October 30-31, 2003; Kelowna, British Columbia, Canada: 19-30.

Chojnacky, D. C. 1984. Volume and biomass for curlleaf cercocarpus in Nevada. Res. Pap. INT-332. Ogden, UT: U.S. Department of Agriculture, Forest Service, Intermountain Forest and Range Experiment Station. 8 p.

Chojnacky, D. C. 1985. Pinyon-juniper volume equations for the central Rocky Mountain States. Res. Note INT-339. Ogden, UT: U.S. Department of Agriculture, Forest Service, Intermountain Forest and Range Experiment Station.

Chojnacky, D. C. 1994. Volume equations for New Mexico pinyon-juniper dryland forests. Res. Note INT-471. Ogden, UT: U.S. Department of Agriculture, Forest Service, Intermountain Research Station.

Chojnacky, D. C.; Moisen, G. G. 1993. Converting wood volume to biomass for pinyon and juniper. Res. Note INT-411. Ogden, UT: U.S. Department of Agriculture, Forest Service, Intermountain Research Station. 5 p.

Cohen, S.; Miller, D. 1978. The big burn: The Northwest's fire of 1910. Missoula, MT: Pictorial Histories Publishing Co. 96 p.

Conner, R. C.; O'Brien, R. A. 1993. Montana's forest resources. Resour. Bull. INT-81. Ogden, UT: U.S. Department of Agriculture, Forest Service, Intermountain Research Station. 96 p.

DeBlander, L. T.; Shaw, J. D.; Witt, C.; [and others]. 2010. Utah's forest resources, 2000–2005. Resour. Bull. RMRS-RB-10. Fort Collins, CO: U.S. Department of Agriculture, Forest Service, Rocky Mountain Research Station. 144 p.

Di Orio, A. P.; Callasa, R.; Schaefer, R. J. 2005. Forty-eight year decline and fragmentation of aspen (*Populus tremuloides*) in the South Warner Mountains of California. Forest Ecology and Management. 206(1-3): 307-313.

Dobkin, D. S.; Rich, A. C.; Pretare, J. A.; Pyle, W. H. 1995. Nest-site relationships among cavity-nesting birds of riparian and snowpocket aspen woodlands in the Northwestern Great Basin. Condor. 97: 694-707.

Edminster, C. B.; Mowrer, H. T.; Sheppard, W. D. 1985. Site index curves for aspen in the central Rocky Mountains. Res. Note RM-453. Ogden, UT: U.S. Department of Agriculture, Forest Service, Intermountain Research Station. 4 p.

Egan, T. 2009. The big burn: Teddy Roosevelt and the fire that saved America. Boston: Houghton Mifflin Harcourt. 324 p.

Eidenshenk, J.; Schwind, B.; Brewer, K.; [and others]. 2007. A project for monitoring trends in burn severity. Fire Ecology Special Issue. 3(1) [online] http://fireecology.net/docs/Journal/pdf/Volume03/Issue01/003.pdf. Accessed 5/2/2012.

Fiedler, C. E.; Friederici, P.; Petruncio, M. 2007. Monitoring old growth in frequent-fire landscapes. Ecology and Society. 12(2): 22. [online] http://www.ecologyandsociety.org/vol12/iss2/art22/ Accessed 7/25/2011.

Flack, J. A. D. 1976. Bird populations of aspen forests in western North America. Ornithological Monographs 19. Washington, DC: American Ornithologist's Union.

Gillespie, A. J. R. 1999. Rationale for a national annual forest inventory program. Journal of Forestry. 97(12): 16-20.

Gingrich, S. F. 1967. Measuring and evaluating stocking and stand density in uplandh forests in the Central States. Forest Science. 13: 38-53.

Green, A. W.; O'Brien, R. A.; Schaefer, J. C. 1985. Montana's forests. Resour. Bull. INT-38. Ogden, UT: U.S. Department of Agriculture, Forest Service, Intermountain Research Station. 70 p.

Green, P.; Joy, J.; Sirucek, D.; [and others]. 1992. Old-growth forest types of the northern region. R-1 SES 4/92. Missoula, MT: U.S. Department of Agriculture, Forest Service, Northern Region,

Hawksworth, F. G. 1977. The 6-class dwarf mistletoe rating system. Gen. Tech. Rep. RM-48. Fort Collins, CO: U.S. Department of Agriculture, Forest Service, Rocky Mountain Forest and Range Experiment Station. 7 p.

Hessl, A. E.; Graumlich, L. J. 2002. Interactive effects of human activities, herbivory and fire on quaking aspen (*Populus tremuloides*) age structures in western Wyoming. Journal of Biogeography. 29: 889–902.

Hutchison, B. S.; Kemp, P. D. 1952. Forest Resources of Montana. Forest Resource Report No. 5. Washington, DC: U.S. Department of Agriculture, Forest Service, Northern Rocky Mountain Forest and Range Experiment Station. 76 p.

Jenny, H. 1994. Factors of soil formation—a system of quantitative pedology. Dover Edition. New York: Dover Publications. 191 p.

Johnson, M. 1994. Changes in Southwestern forests: Stewardship implications. Journal of Forestry. 92: 16-19.

Kaufmann, M. R.; Binkley, D.; Fulé, P. Z.; [and others]. 2007. Defining old growth for fire-adapted forests of the western United States. Ecology and Society. 12(2): 15. [online] http://www.ecologyandsociety.org/vol12/iss2/art15/ Accessed 7/25/2011.

Kay, C. E. 1997. Is aspen doomed? Journal of Forestry. 95(5): 4–11.

Keane, R. E.; Arno, S. F. 1993. Rapid decline of whitebark pine in western Montana: Evidence from 20-year remeasurements. Western Journal of Applied Forestry. 8(2): 44-46.

Kegley, S.; Schwandt, J.; Gibson, K.; Perkins, D. 2011. Health of whitebark pine forests after mountain pine beetle outbreaks. In: Keane, R. E.; Tomback, D. F.; Murray, M. P.; Smith, C. M., eds. The future of high-elevation, five-needle white pines in Western North America: Proceedings of the High Five Symposium; 28-30 June 2010; Missoula, MT. Proceedings RMRS-P-63. Fort Collins: 85-93.

Kemp, P. D., 1956. Region 1 volume tables for ADP cruise computations. Timber Cruising Handbook, R1-2430-31. Missoula, MT: U.S. Department of Agriculture, Forest Service, Northern Region.

Kendall, K. C. 1980. Use of pine nuts by grizzly and black bears in the Yellowstone area. International Conference on Bear Research and Management. 5:166-173.

Kulakowski, D.; Veblen, T. T.; Drinkwater, S. 2004. The persistence of quaking aspen (*Populus tremuloides*) in the Grand Mesa area, Colorado. Ecological Applications. 14 (5): 1603-1614.

Lilieholm, R. J.; Long, J. N.; Patla, S. 1994. Assessing goshawk nest stand habitat using stand density index. Cooper Ornithological Society. Studies in Avian Biology. 16: 18-24.

Long, J. N. 1985. A practical approach to density management. Forest Chronicle. 61: 23-37.

Long, J. N.; Daniel, T. W. 1990. Assessment of growing stock in uneven-aged stands. Western Journal of Applied Forestry. 5: 93-96.

Long, J. N.; Shaw J. D. 2005. A density management diagram for even-aged ponderosa pine stands. Western Journal of Applied Forestry. 20: 205-215.

Lutes, D. C.; Keane, R. E.; Caratti, J. F. 2009. A surface fuel classification for estimating fire effects. International Journal of Wildland Fire. 18: 802-814.

Martin, K.; Aitken, K. E. H.; Weibe, K. L. 2004. Nest sites and nest webs for cavity-nesting communities in interior British Columbia, Canada: Nest characteristics and niche partitioning. Condor. 106 (1): 5-19.

McClelland, R. B.; Frissell, S. S.; Fischer, W. C.; Halvorson, C. H. 1979. Habitat management for hole-nesting birds in forests of western larch and Douglas-fir. Journal of Forestry. 77: 480-483.

McNab, W. H.; Cleland, D. T.; Freeouf, J. A.; [and others], comps. 2007. Description of ecological subregions: Sections of the conterminous United States. Gen. Tech. Report WO-76B. Washington, DC: U.S. Department of Agriculture, Forest Service. 80 p. [CD-ROM].

Moisen, G. G. 1990. Volume equations for timber species in western Montana and northern Idaho. Unpublished report on file at U.S. Department of Agriculture, Forest Service, Rocky Mountain Research Station, Inventory and Monitoring Program, Ogden, UT.

Myers, C. A. 1964. Volume tables and point-sampling factors for ponderosa pine in the Black Hills. Res. Note RM-8. U.S. Department of Agriculture, Forest Service, Rocky Mountain Forest and Range Experiment Station, Fort Collins, CO.

Pollard, J. E.; Westfall, J. A.; Patterson, P. L.; [and others]. 2006. Forest inventory and analysis national data quality assessment report 2000 to 2003. Gen. Tech. Rep. RMRS-GTR-181. Fort Collins, CO: U.S. Department of Agriculture, Forest Service, Rocky Mountain Research Station. 43 p.

Pyne, S. J. 2008. Year of the fires: The story of the great fires of 1910. Revised ed. Missoula, MT: Mountain Press Publishing Company. 320 p.

Reineke, L. H. 1933. Perfecting a stand density index for even-aged forests. Journal of Agricultural Research. 46(7): 627-638.

Rudinsky, J. A. 1962. Ecology of Scolytidae. Annual Review of Entomology. 7: 327-348.

Schmidt, W. C.; McDonald, K. J., comps. 1990. Proceedings—Symposium on white-bark pine ecosystems: Ecology and management of a high-mountain resource. Gen. Tech. Rep. INT-270. Ogden, UT: U.S. Department of Agriculture, Forest Service, Intermountain Research Station. 386 p.

Shaw, J. D. 2000. Application of stand density index to irregularly structured stands, Western Journal of Applied Forestry. 15: 40-42.

Shaw, J. D.; Steed, B. E.; DeBlander, L. T. 2005. Forest Inventory and Analysis (FIA) annual inventory answers the question: What is happening to pinyon-juniper woodlands? Journal of Forestry. 103(6): 280-285.

Shaw, J. D.; Long, J. N. [In preparation]. Consistent definition and use of stand density index.

Smith, F. W.; Long, J. N. 1987. Elk hiding and thermal cover guidelines in the context of lodgepole pine stand density. Western Journal of Applied Forestry. 2: 6-10.

Spoelma, T. P.; Morgan, T. A.; Dillon, T.; [and others]. 2008. Montana's forest products industry and timber harvest, 2004. Resour. Bull. RMRS-RB-8. Fort Collins, CO: U.S. Department of Agriculture, Forest Service, Rocky Mountain Research Station. 36 p.

Stage, A. R. 1966. Simultaneous derivation of site-curve and productivity rating procedures. Society of American Foresters Proceedings. 1966: 134-136. [Original equations were reformulated by J. Shaw; documentation on file at Rocky Mountain Research Station, Ogden, UT.]

Stage, A. R. 1969. Computing procedure for grand fir site evaluation and productivity estimation. Res. Note INT-98. U.S. Department of Agriculture, Forest Service, Intermountain Forest and Range Experiment Station.

Thompson, M. T. 2009. Analysis of conifer mortality in Colorado using Forest Inventory and Analysis's annual forest inventory. Western Journal of Applied Forestry. 24(4): 193-197.

Thompson, M. T.; Duda, J. A.; DeBlander, L. T.; [and others]. 2010. Colorado's forest resources, 2002-2006. Resour. Bull. RMRS-RB-11. Fort Collins, CO: U.S. Department of Agriculture, Forest Service, Rocky Mountain Research Station. 108 p.

USDA Forest Service. 1993. RMSTAND and RMRIS User's guide. Ogden, UT: U.S. Department of Agriculture, Forest Service , Intermountain Region.

USDA Forest Service. 2003-2009a. IWFIA Forest Survey field procedures. Unpublished field guide on file at: U.S. Department of Agriculture, Forest Service, Rocky Mountain Research Station, Forestry Sciences Laboratory, Interior West Forest Inventory and Analysis Program, Ogden, UT. Available online at: http://www.fs.fed.us/rm/ogden/data-collection/field-manuals.shtml. Accessed 5/2/2012.

USDA Forest Service. 2003-2009b. IWFIA Phase 3 field procedures. Unpublished field guide on file at: U.S. Department of Agriculture, Forest Service, Rocky Mountain Research Station, Forestry Sciences Laboratory, Interior West Forest Inventory and Analysis Program, Ogden, UT. Available online at: http://www.fs.fed.us/rm/ogden/data-collection/field-manuals.shtml. Accessed 5/2/2012.

USDA Forest Service. 2006-2009. Forest Survey field procedures. Unpublished field guide on file at: U.S. Department of Agriculture, Forest Service, Rocky Mountain Research Station, Forestry Sciences Laboratory, Interior West Forest Inventory and Analysis Program, Ogden, UT. Available online at: http://fsweb.ogden.rmrs fs.fed.us/manual/manual.html. Accessed 5/2/2012.

USDA Forest Service. 2011. IWFIA Forest Survey field procedures, Ver. 5.0. Unpublished field guide on file at: U.S. Department of Agriculture, Forest Service, Rocky Mountain Research Station, Forestry Sciences Laboratory, Interior West Forest Inventory and Analysis Program, Ogden, UT. Available online at: http://www.fs.fed.us/rm/ogden/data-collection/field-manuals.shtml; last accessed August 2011.

USDA Forest Service Resour. Bull. RMRS-RB-15. 2012

75

Van Hooser, D. D.; Chojnacky, D. C. 1983. Whole tree volume estimates for the Rocky Mountain States. Res. Bull. INT-29. U.S. Department of Agriculture, Forest Service, Intermountain Forest and Range Experiment Station.

Vosick, D.; Ostergren, D. M.; Murfitt, L. 2007. Old-growth policy. Ecology and Society. 12(2): 19. [online] http://www.ecologyandsociety.org/vol12/iss2/art19. Accessed 7/25/2011.

Wilson, M. J.; Deblander, L. T.; Halverson, K. A. 2010. Resource impacts of the 1910 fires: A Forest Inventory and Analysis (FIA) perspective. Powerpoint presentation given at: 1910 Fires: A Century Later. Wallace, Idaho, May 20-22, 2010. On file at: U.S. Department of Agriculture, Forest Service, Rocky Mountain Research Station, Forestry Sciences Laboratory, Interior West Forest Inventory and Analysis Program, Ogden, UT.

Woodall, C. W.; Monleon, V. J. 2008. Sampling protocol, estimation, and analysis procedures for the down woody materials indicator of the FIA program. Gen. Tech. Rep. NRS-22. Newtown Square, PA: U.S. Department of Agriculture, Forest Service, Northern Research Station. 68 p.

Worrall, J. J.; Egeland, L.; Eager, T.; [and others]. 2008. Rapid mortality of *Populus tremuloides* in southwestern Colorado, USA. Forest Ecology and Management. 255(3-4): 686-696.

Woudenberg, S. W.; Conkling, B. L.; O'Connell, B. M.; [and others]. 2010. The Forest Inventory and Analysis Database: Database description and users manual version 4.0 for Phase 2. Gen. Tech. Rep. RMRS-GTR- 245. Fort Collins, CO: U.S. Department of Agriculture, Forest Service, Rocky Mountain Research Station. 339 p.

Appendix A: Inventory History

It is often desirable to compare data from new inventories with data from earlier inventories to determine trends in forest resources. However, for the comparisons to be valid, the procedures used in the two inventories must be compatible. There are several differences between the data used for this report and older data that need to be considered before comparing inventory data or estimates. These can be grouped as issues of sampling frame, the spatial and temporal sequence of sampling, and sampling or data compilation protocols.

In considering these factors, the point needs to be made that the 1989 Montana report (Connor and O'Brien 1993) and the "1989" data available through the FIA database (FIADB) tools and download do not represent the same inventory. The differences between the two are detailed below.

Appendix A figure 1(A and B) compares the sampling frame for the 1989 report and the 1989 inventory in FIADB. The report was based on data from field plots only on non-reserved lands (area estimates for reserved areas were obtained through aerial photo interpretation) and non-National Forest lands. Summarized data for National Forests were taken from the Resource Planning Act (RPA) database. No detailed FIA plot-level data were available for reserved lands or National Forest lands. Most areas were sampled at the standard (1x) grid intensity, and State lands west of the Continental Divide had extra plots installed. Because of the spatial distribution of State lands, a standard double intensity (2x) grid was not effective, and the extra plots equate to a little less than a 2x intensity. The Connor and O'Brien (1993) report details differences in data sources in the introduction, procedure description, and various inventory tables.

Beginning in 1993, the Forest Service Northern Region Inventory Service Center, with cooperation from what was then the FIA unit of the Intermountain Research Station, sampled field plots on all Montana National Forest lands, including wilderness areas. In addition, during the most recent Wyoming periodic inventory (nominally the 2000 inventory), plots in the Montana and Idaho portions of Yellowstone National Park were sampled. These subsequent plots were installed at the standard 1x intensity. All of the plots sampled after the 1989 report were added to the FIADB under the "1989" inventory. These data filled in many of the areas missing from the report; but some heavily forested areas, including Glacier National Park and various tribal timber reserves, do not have data in the FIADB. Some less-forested non-sampled areas include the Bighorn Canyon National Recreation Area, the Upper Missouri Wild and Scenic River, and U.S. Fish and Wildlife Service wilderness areas. In contrast, all areas and ownerships in Montana have been sampled in the 2003-2009 inventory, but because the full cycle is not yet complete, the sampling intensity is currently only 70 percent (0.7x). Differences in sampling intensity will influence the sampling error for inventory estimates, with higher errors for smaller samples. Non-sampled areas introduce bias and imbalance in inventory estimates.

The differences in spatial and temporal sequence of plot sampling between annual and periodic inventories can be important when comparing some data. Appendix A figure 2(A and B) compares plot measurement year for forested plots for the 1989 and 2003-2009 Montana inventories. In Appendix A figure 2A, it is possible to see how field crews moved about the State while completing the inventory. For the report data, crews worked on plots in the east and south in 1988, and moved to the northwest in 1989. Crews completing plots on National Forests began in the

USDA Forest Service Resour. Bull. RMRS-RB-15. 2012

77

northwest in 1993 and worked to the southeast, finishing on the Gallatin National Forest in 1998. Yellowstone National Park plots were done in 1999, and a few plots on the Montana portions of the Idaho Panhandle National Forest were completed with that Forest in 2000 and 2001. As a result, plots from any given measurement year will be spatially biased (see "Damage to Live Trees" in Section VI). In contrast, Appendix A figure 2B shows how, under the annual system, the plots in any given measurement year are spread evenly across the State, so that plots and estimates from different measurement years can be compared without introducing as much spatial bias.

There have been several changes in sampling and compilation protocols from 1988 to 2009 that affect inventory comparisons. Sampling protocols include the plot design or layout, determination of whether a plot is forested, and how to determine which trees get measured. The most relevant compilation protocol is the calculation of forest type.

For most of the 1989 inventory sampling period, two basic plot designs were used: a variable-radius, multi-point plot for timber-type stands (see "Whitebark Pine Status" in Section V) and a single fixed-radius plot for woodland-type stands. It should be noted that both designs employed rules to ensure that the entire plot was in a single condition: variable-radius sampling points were rotated into the central condition if they occurred on contrasting conditions, and fixed-radius plots were shifted so that the entire plot fell within the condition occurring at the center point. Appendix A figure 3(A and B) shows the various plot designs used during the periodic inventory compared to the consistent use of the mapped plot design (described in Section II, "Plot Configuration") during the 2003-2009 annual inventory. In the 1989 inventory, only 15 plots were installed using the fixed-radius woodland design. These were a single plot with a radius of 26.3, 37.2, or 52.7 feet (1/20, 1/10, or 1/5 of an acre, respectively), depending on woodland type or tree density. They had four 6.8-foot radius microplots, at 45, 135, 225, and 315 degrees from the main plot center at 15 or 25 feet, depending on the size of the main plot. The timber-type variable radius plots used a 40 basal area factor (BAF) and 6.8-foot radius microplots, but the number of sampling points in the cluster and microplots changed over time. In 1988 and 1989, a ten-point cluster with three microplots (centered on points 1, 2, and 3) was used. The National Forest inventory began in 1993 with a seven-point cluster, each with a centered microplot. This changed to a five-point cluster with centered microplots on every point, beginning in 1994. The five-point cluster was used exclusively for timber-type plots from 1995 to 1998. In 1999, the mapped plot design was introduced, and used for all plots in Yellowstone National Park and the Idaho Panhandle National Forest. Some of the mapped plots had microplots centered on the subplot, rather than offset 12 feet. Differences in plot design alone do not introduce major difficulties in comparing inventory results and estimates, since tree and area expanders are set appropriately; however, these design changes were also accompanied by changes in sampling and compilation protocols that, when paired with non-sampled areas, present reason for caution.

Over the course of the 1989 and 2003-2009 inventories, the field determination of whether a plot is forested, and therefore whether to measure it, has varied. This is based on crown cover, or evidence of recent crown cover such as stumps or dead trees. For variable-radius timber-type plots measured from 1988 to 1997, the requirement was 5 percent crown cover of timber species. For fixed-radius woodland plots in the same time frame, the requirement was 10 percent crown cover of all trees, but less than 5 percent of timber species. For periodic mapped plots measured from 1998 to 2001, 5 percent cover of all qualifying, or tally, trees was required for forested conditions. In the annual inventory (2003-2009), a minimum crown cover of 10 percent for all tally species is required (see definition of forest land in Section IX). Since IWFIA continues to collect data for conditions with 5 to 9 percent cover (now called "other wooded land," see Section IX "Standard Forest Inventory and Analysis Terminology"; also see DeBlander and others 2010, Appendix A), we know that the area estimate for Montana is only 655 thousand acres in this cover range. The impact on tree-based estimates (number of trees, biomass, volume, growth, and mortality) is minimal, since these acres support few trees.

The amount of crown cover will depend somewhat on what qualifies as a tree in the inventory. This has also varied over the course of the two inventories. All of the major timber-type conifers in Montana have been consistently included in all recent inventories; however, the inclusion and measurement of woodland types and hardwoods have been less consistent. On plots measured from 1988 to 1997, woodland trees were evaluated according to growth form, and trees were excluded that did not meet specified tree-form requirements (the capacity to produce at least one stem 3 inches or larger in diameter at root collar, and 8 feet or more in length to a minimum branch diameter of 1.5 inches). This would have more impact on hardwood woodland types like Rocky Mountain maple and curlleaf mountain-mahogany than it would on junipers. From 1998 and during the 2003-2009 annual inventory, qualifying trees were determined by species, and whether the species was on the inventory list. For many hardwoods, inclusion on the inventory list changed over time. Only paper birch, curlleaf mountain-mahogany, quaking aspen, and cottonwoods (balsam, plains, black, and narrowleaf) have consistently been included in species lists. Species added for periodic mapped plots and/or annual inventories include boxelder, red alder, green ash, American elm, and water birch. Rocky Mountain maple was included from 1988 to 1997, but dropped for mapped plot design. Over the same period, crews were allowed to record a generic code for cottonwoods (*Populus* spp.), but after 1998 they were required to identify cottonwoods to species (or subspecies in the case of black cottonwood). The same would appear to be true for generic maples (*Acer* spp.), but in the 1988-1989 field manual, the code used for Rocky Mountain maple is the same code that was later used for *Acer* spp.

Data compilation changes resulting in different forest types for annual and periodic inventories have also occurred. In the 1989 report, the sample-based data used different forest types than the RPA and photo-interpreted data. Most of these differences are explained in the report (Connor and O'Brien 1993). With annual inventory, several new forest types were introduced. The most significant of these is the subalpine fir forest type, the most abundant type in the fir-spruce-mountain hemlock group, which is Montana's second most common type in the current report. Stands with this species composition are included in the Engelmann spruce-subalpine fir forest type in the periodic data (referred to as "spruce-fir" in the 1989 report). Also new is the Rocky Mountain juniper forest type, which is included in juniper woodland in periodic data. Since several hardwoods have been included in species lists, there are a few hardwood forest types that are new to IWFIA inventories, including sugarberry-hackberry-elm-green ash, elm-ash-black locust, and red alder. Reporting for the nonstocked forest type is also somewhat different in annual inventories. If there are not enough live trees encountered on a condition, the forest type algorithm assigns a type of nonstocked. However, field crews use evidence in the plot vicinity to assign a forest type. In many periodic reports the nonstocked forest type was replaced with the field forest type, and nonstocked was

USDA Forest Service Resour. Bull. RMRS-RB-15. 2012

79

retained only as a stand size class. For RPA data in the 1989 report, nonstocked stands are included in "miscellaneous western softwoods."

Another factor influencing apparent increases in forest land has been the improvement of aerial photography for identifying plot locations that may have small or isolated forest areas in the vicinity. It would appear that many plots in areas like eastern Montana have been missed in past inventories, as pre-field personnel identify plots for field visits. Appendix A figures 2(A and B) and 3(A and B) show that although the overall density of forested plots is lower in the 2003-2009 inventory than in the 1989 inventory, there are more forested plots in the eastern portion of the State. Inclusion of more hardwood species and dropping the growth form criteria from Rocky Mountain juniper may also be contributing to this increase.

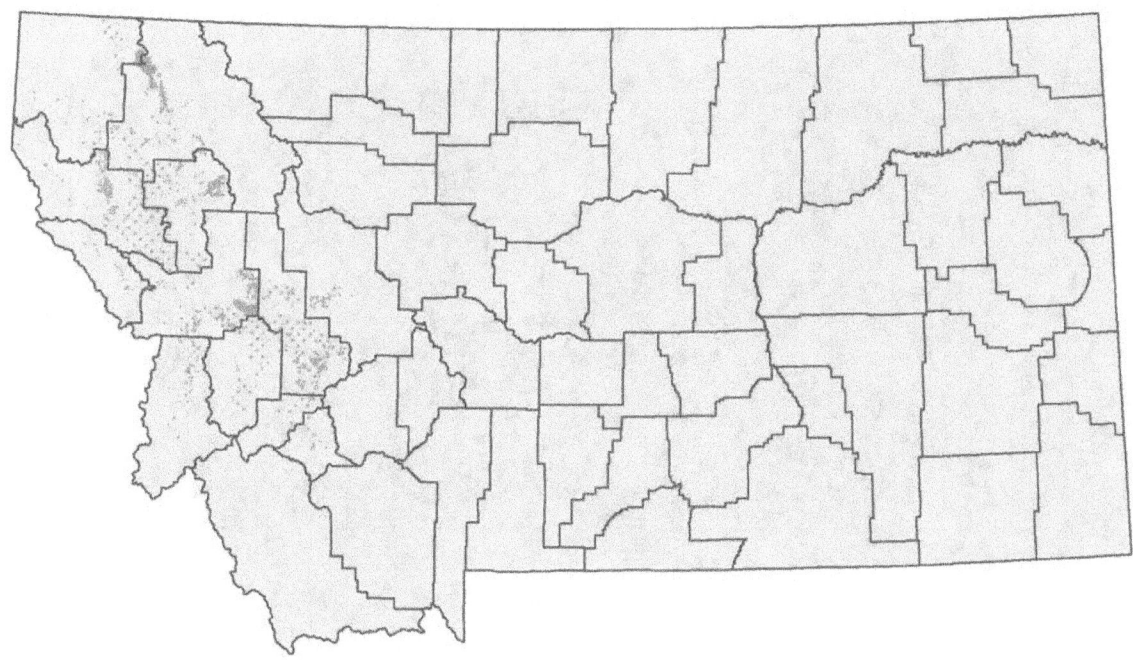

A. 1989 state report

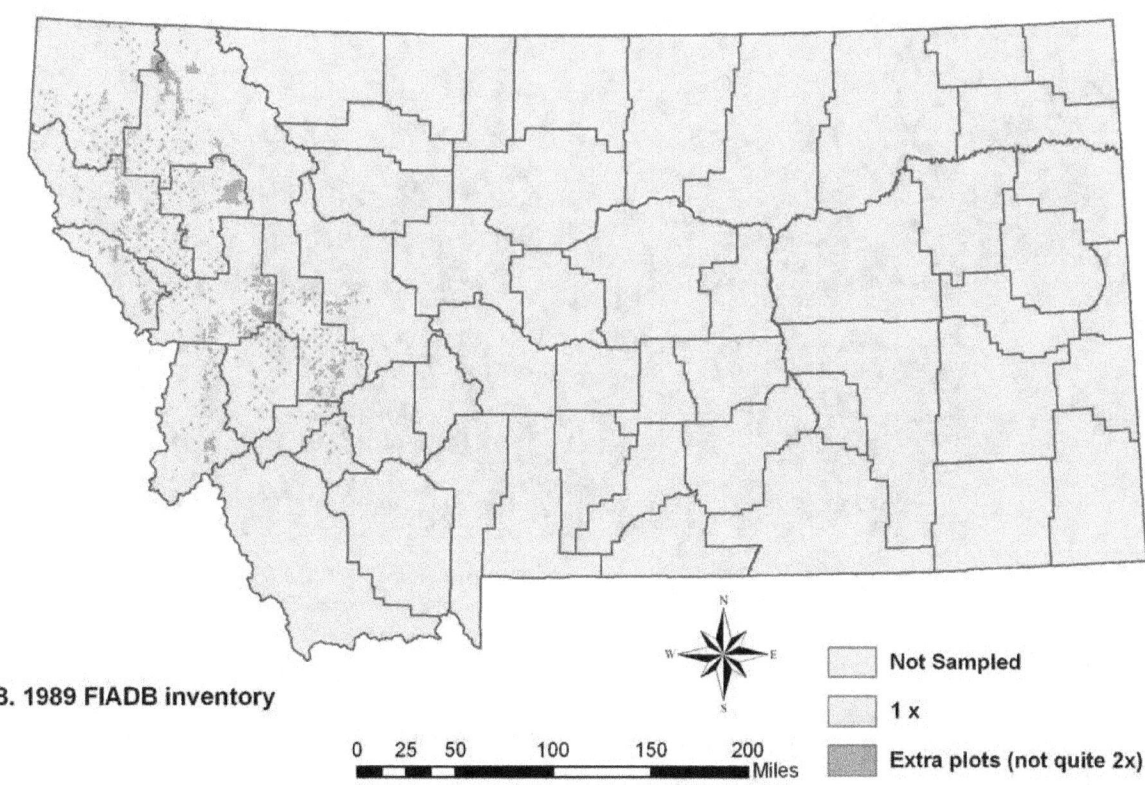

B. 1989 FIADB inventory

| Not Sampled |
| 1 x |
| Extra plots (not quite 2x) |

0 25 50   100   150   200
Miles

Figure A1—Comparison of sampling frames for Montana's 1989 report (A) and 1989 database inventory (B), showing areas sampled, and sampling intensity.

USDA Forest Service Resour. Bull. RMRS-RB-15. 2012

81

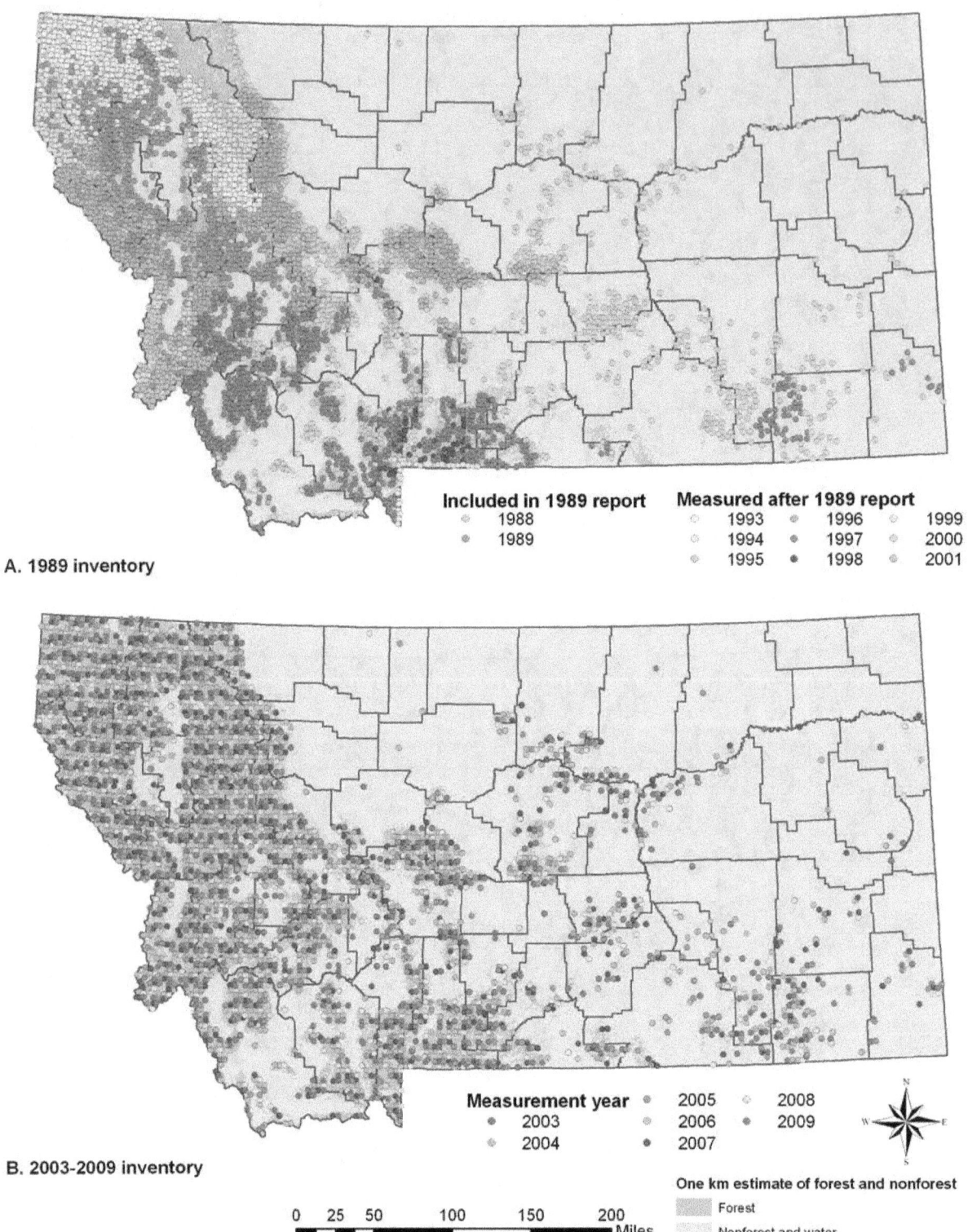

Figure A2—Location of forested plots for Montana's 1989 inventory (A) compared to Montana's 2003-2009 inventory (B) showing year of measurement for each, with generalized model (1 km pixels) of predicted forest and non-forest.

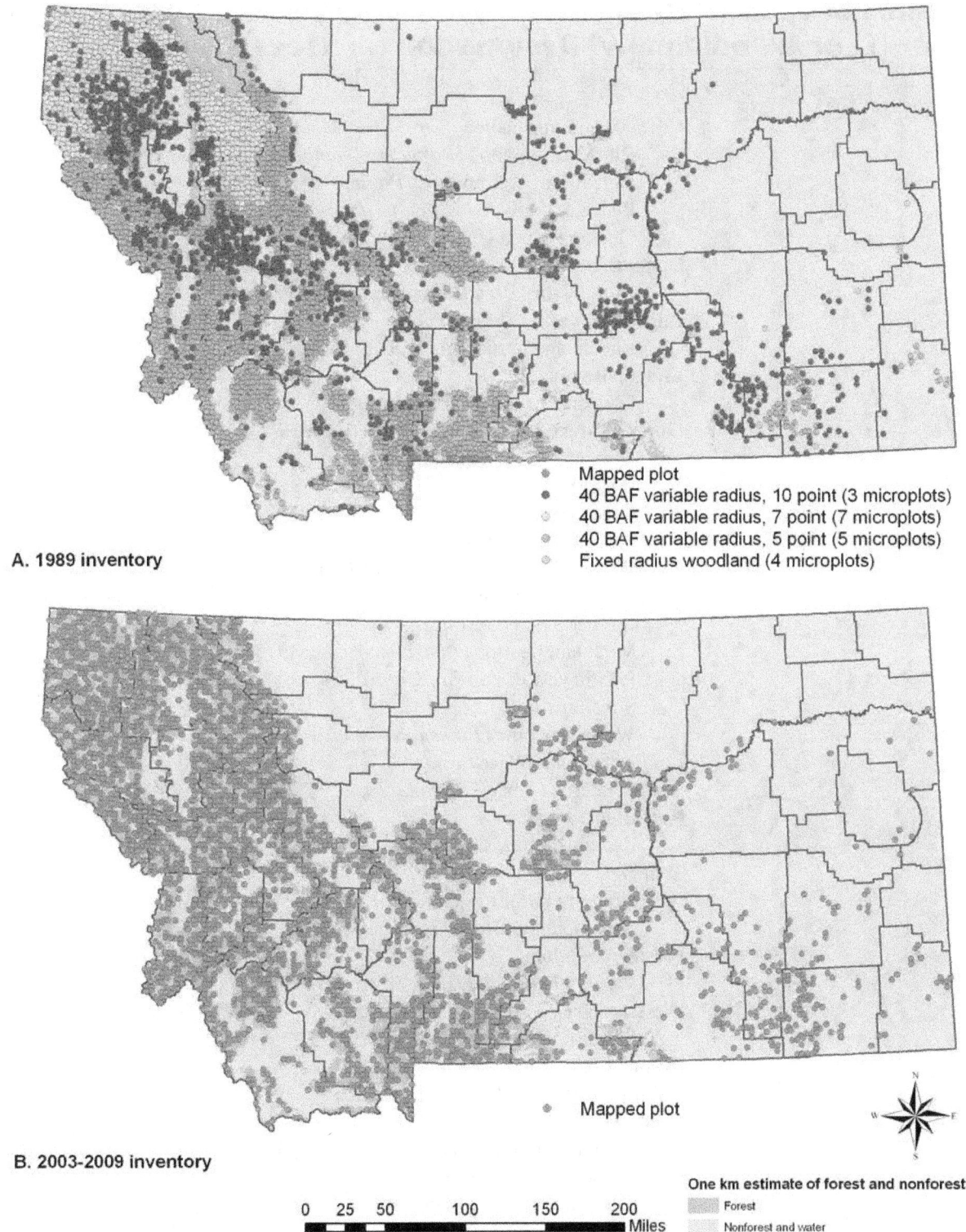

A. 1989 inventory

Legend:
- Mapped plot
- 40 BAF variable radius, 10 point (3 microplots)
- 40 BAF variable radius, 7 point (7 microplots)
- 40 BAF variable radius, 5 point (5 microplots)
- Fixed radius woodland (4 microplots)

B. 2003-2009 inventory

- Mapped plot

One km estimate of forest and nonforest
- Forest
- Nonforest and water

0 25 50 100 150 200 Miles

Figure A3—Location of forested plots for Montana's 1989 inventory (A) compared to Montana's 2003-2009 inventory (B) showing plot designs for each, with generalized model (1 km pixels) of predicted forest and non-forest.

USDA Forest Service Resour. Bull. RMRS-RB-15. 2012

83

Appendix B: Species Groups, Common Names, Scientific Names, and Timber (T) or Woodland (W) Designation for Trees

Cottonwood and aspen
  Black cottonwood (*Populus basamifera* ssp. *trichocarpa*) T
  Narrowleaf cottonwood (*Populus angustifolia*) T
  Plains cottonwood (*Populus deltoides* ssp. *monilifera*) T
  Quaking aspen (*Populus temuloides*) T
Douglas-fir
  Douglas-fir (*Pseudotsuga menziesii*) T
Engelmann and other spruces
  Engelmann spruce (*Picea engelmannii*) T
Lodgepole pine
  Lodgepole pine (*Pinus contorta*) T
Other western hardwoods
  American elm (*Ulmus americana*) T
  Boxelder (*Acer negundo*) T
  Green ash (*Fraxinus pennsylvanica*) T
  Paper birch (*Betula papyrifera*) T
  Water birch (*Betula occidentalis*) T
Other western softwoods
  Limber pine (*Pinus flexilis*) T
  Mountain hemlock (*Tsuga mertensiana*) T
  Pacific yew (*Taxus brevifolia*) T
  Subalpine larch (*Larix lyallii*) T
  Whitebark pine (*Pinus albicaulis*) T
Ponderosa and Jeffrey pines
  Ponderosa pine (*Pinus ponderosa*) T
Red alder
  Red alder (*Alnus rubra*) T
True fir
  Grand fir (*Abies grandis*) T
  Subalpine fir (*Abies lasiocarpa*) T
Western hemlock
  Western hemlock (*Tsuga heterophylla*) T
Western larch
  Western larch (*Larix occidentalis*) T
Western redcedar
  Western redcedar (*Thuja plicata*) T
Western white pine
  Western white pine (*Pinus monticola*) T
Western woodland hardwoods
  Curlleaf mountain-mahogany (*Cercocarpus ledifolius*) W
Western woodland softwoods
  Rocky Mountain juniper (*Juniperus scopulorum*) W
  Utah juniper (*Juniperus osteosperma*) W

Appendix C: Forest Type Groups, Forest Type Names, and Timber (T) or Woodland (W) Designation for Forest Types

Alder-maple group
Red alder T
Aspen-birch group
Aspen T
Paper birch T
Douglas-fir group
Douglas-fir T
Elm-ash-cottonwood group
Cottonwood T
Cottonwood-willow T
Sugarberry-hackberry-elm-green ash T
Fir-spruce-mountain hemlock group
Engelmann spruce T
Engelmann spruce-subalpine fir T
Grand fir T
Mountain hemlock T
Subalpine fir T
Hemlock-Sitka spruce group
Western hemlock T
Western redcedar T
Lodgepole pine group
Lodgepole pine T
Nonstocked
Nonstocked T or W
Oak-hickory group
Elm-ash-black locust T
Other western softwoods group
Limber pine T
Miscellaneous western softwoods T
Whitebark pine T
Pinyon-juniper group
Juniper woodland W
Rocky Mountain juniper W
Ponderosa pine group
Ponderosa pine T
Western larch group
Western larch T
Woodland hardwoods group
Cercocarpus (mountain brush) woodland W

Appendix D: Volume, Biomass, and Site Index Equation Sources

Volume

Chojnacky (1985) was used for curlleaf mountain-mahogany volume estimation.

Chojnacky (1994) was used for Rocky Mountain juniper and Utah juniper volume estimation.

Kemp (1956) was used for black cottonwood, Engelmann spruce, mountain hemlock, narrowleaf cottonwood, paper birch, plains cottonwood, quaking aspen, red alder, subalpine fir, water birch, western hemlock, and western redcedar volume estimation.

Moisen (1990) was used for Douglas-fir, grand fir, limber pine, lodgepole pine, Pacific yew, subalpine larch, western larch, western white pine, and whitebark pine volume estimation; and for ponderosa pine volume estimation in eastern Montana.

Myers (1964) was used for ponderosa pine volume estimation in western Montana.

Volume equations provided by the USDA Forest Service's Northern Research Station were used for American elm, boxelder, and green ash volume estimation. [Documentation on file at U.S. Department of Agriculture, Forest Service, Rocky Mountain Research Station, Ogden, UT.]

Biomass

Chojnacky (1984) was used for curlleaf mountain mahogany biomass estimation.

Chojnacky and Moisen (1993) was used for Rocky Mountain juniper and Utah juniper biomass estimation.

Van Hooser and Chojnacky (1983) was used for all timber (T) species biomass estimation.

Site Index

Brickell (1970) was used for Douglas-fir, Engelmann spruce, limber pine, lodgepole pine, ponderosa pine, subalpine fir, subalpine larch, western larch, western white pine, and whitebark pine site index estimation.

Edminster and others (1985) was used for American elm, black cottonwood, boxelder, green ash, narrowleaf cottonwood, paper birch, plains cottonwood, quaking aspen, and red alder site index estimation.

Stage (1966, 1969) was used for grand fir site index estimation. [Original equations were reformulated by J. Shaw; documentation on file at U.S. Department of Agriculture, Forest Service, Rocky Mountain Research Station, Ogden, UT.]

Equations from RMSTAND (USDA Forest Service 1993) were used for mountain hemlock, western hemlock, and western redcedar site index estimation.

Appendix E: Forest Resource Tables.

Table 1: Percentage of area by land status.

Table 2: Area of accessible forest land by owner class and forest land status.

Table 3: Area of accessible forest land by forest type group and productivity class.

Table 4: Area of accessible forest land by forest type group, ownership group, and land status.

Table 5: Area of accessible forest land by forest type group and stand-size class.

Table 6: Area of accessible forest land by forest type group and stand-age class.

Table 7: Area of accessible forest land by forest type group and stand origin.

Table 8: Area of forest land by forest type group and primary disturbance class.

Table 9: Area of timberland by forest type group and stand-size class.

Table 10: Number of live trees on forest land by species group and diameter class.

Table 11: Number of growing stock trees on timberland by species group and diameter class.

Table 12: Net volume of all live trees by owner class and forest land status.

Table 13: Net volume of all live trees on forest land by forest type group and stand-size class.

Table 14: Net volume of all live trees on forest land by species group and ownership group.

Table 15: Net volume of all live trees on forest land by species group and diameter class.

Table 16: Net volume of all live trees on forest land by forest type group and stand origin.

Table 17: Net volume of growing stock trees on timberland by species group and diameter class.

Table 18: Net volume of growing stock trees on timberland by species group and ownership group.

Table 19: Net volume of sawtimber trees (International 1/4 inch rule) on timberland by species group and diameter class.

Table 20: Net volume of sawtimber trees on timberland by species group and ownership group.

Table 21: Average annual net growth of all live trees by owner class and forest land status.

Table 22: Average annual net growth of all live trees on forest land by forest type group and stand-size class.

Table 23: Average annual net growth of all live trees on forest land by species group and ownership group.

Table 24: Average annual net growth of growing stock trees on timberland by species group and ownership group.

Table 25: Average annual mortality of all live trees by owner class and forest land status.

Table 26: Average annual mortality of all live trees on forest land by forest type group and stand-size class.

Table 27: Average annual mortality of all live trees on forest land by species group and ownership group.

Table 1--Percentage of area by land status, Montana, cycle 2, 2003-2009.

Land status	Percentage of area
Accessible forest land	
Unreserved forest land	
Timberland	20.1
Unproductive	1.6
Total unreserved forest land	21.7
Reserved forest land	
Productive	3.8
Unproductive	0.3
Total reserved forest land	4.1
All accessible forest land	25.8
Nonforest and other land	
Nonforest land	69.8
Water	
Census	0.8
Non-Census	0.1
All nonforest and other land	70.8
Nonsampled land	
Access denied	2.4
Hazardous conditions	0.5
Other	0.5
All land	100.0

Total area (thousands of acres)	94,107

All table cells without observations in the inventory sample are indicated by --. Table value of 0.0 indicates the percentage rounds to less than 0.1 percent. Columns and rows may not add to their totals due to rounding.

USDA Forest Service Resour. Bull. RMRS-RB-15. 2012

89

Table 2--Area of accessible forest land by owner class and forest land status, Montana, cycle 2, 2003-2009.
(In thousand acres)

Owner class	Unreserved forests			Reserved forests			All forest land
	Timberland	Unproductive	Total	Productive	Unproductive	Total	
Forest Service							
National forest	12,239.6	471.4	12,711.1	2,596.1	92.7	2,688.9	15,399.9
Other Federal							
National Park Service	--	--	--	863.5	44.6	908.1	908.1
Bureau of Land Management	851.6	256.1	1,107.7	73.4	50.5	123.9	1,231.6
Fish and Wildlife Service	--	--	--	93.7	93.2	186.9	186.9
Other Federal	--	--	--	8.2	--	8.2	8.2
State and local government							
State	825.5	103.1	928.6	--	--	--	928.6
Local (county, municipal, etc.)	10.2	--	10.2	--	--	--	10.2
Private							
Undifferentiated private	5,947.5	804.0	6,751.5	156.4	9.2	165.7	6,917.2
All owners	19,874.5	1,634.7	21,509.1	3,791.5	290.2	4,081.7	25,590.8

All table cells without observations in the inventory sample are indicated by --. Table value of 0.0 indicates the acres round to less than 0.1 thousand acres. Columns and rows may not add to their totals due to rounding.

Table 3--Area of accessible forest land by forest type group and productivity class, Montana, cycle 2, 2003-2009.
(In thousand acres)

Forest-type group	Site-productivity class (cubic feet/acre/year)							All classes
	0-19	20-49	50-84	85-119	120-164	165-224	225+	
Pinyon / uniper group	805.1	--	--	--	--	--	--	805.1
Douglas-f r group	84.3	4,627.5	2,339.6	421.1	44.5	--	--	7,517.0
Ponderosa pine g oup	153.7	2,245.6	533.6	63.7	22.0	--	--	3,018.6
Fir / spruc / mountain hemlock group	77.4	2,537.4	1,930.4	462.0	23.9	--	--	5,031.2
Lodgepole pine group	109.4	3,330.3	885.5	40.8	--	--	--	4,365.9
Hemlock / Sitka spruce group	--	8.7	109.3	114.4	8.9	--	--	241.4
Western larch group	--	142.0	577.9	163.5	43.6	8.9	--	936.0
Other western ofw ods group	270.0	678.8	--	--	--	--	--	948.8
Oak / hicko y group	15.0	8.6	--	--	--	--	--	23.6
Elm / ash / cottonwood group	51.0	105.9	41.6	40.0	--	--	--	238.5
Aspen / birch group	85.2	331.8	100.1	5.0	--	--	--	522.1
Alder / maple group	--	--	6.7	--	--	--	--	6.7
Woodland hardwoods group	18.0	--	--	--	--	--	--	18.0
Nonstocked	255.8	--	254.6	26.7	--	--	--	1,918.0
All forest-type groups	1,924.8	15,397.5	6,779.3	1,337.3	143.0	8.9	--	25,590.8

All table cells without observations in the inventory sample are indicated by --. Table value of 0.0 indicates the acres round to less than 0.1 thousand acres. Columns and rows may not add to their totals due to rounding.

Table 4—Area of accessible forest land by forest type group, ownership group, and land status, Montana, cycle 2, 2003-2009.

(In thousand acres)

Forest-type group	Forest Service		Other Federal		State and local government		Undifferentiated private		All forest land
	Timber-land	Other forest land	Timber-land	Other forest land	Timber-land	Other forest land	Timber-land	Other forest land	
Pinyon / juniper group	--	62.2	--	294.7	--	45.4	--	402.8	805.1
Douglas-fir group	3,824.3	415.2	379.2	162.1	293.7	--	2,335.6	106.8	7,517.0
Ponderosa pine group	653.5	8.9	217.7	119.0	233.3	24.4	1,659.6	102.3	3,018.6
Fir / spruce / mountain hemlock group	2,879.7	1,266.2	24.6	435.2	67.1	--	351.8	6.5	5,031.2
Lodgepole pine group	2,999.3	662.9	101.4	154.1	56.9	9.4	348.7	33.3	4,365.9
Hemlock / Sitka spruce group	197.8	8.9	--	8.7	--	--	17.8	8.2	241.4
Western larch group	638.9	20.0	6.8	52.3	65.7	--	152.2	--	936.0
Other western softwoods group	416.0	411.0	8.2	36.7	8.7	9.4	9.4	49.4	948.8
Oak / hickory group	--	--	--	--	--	--	8.6	15.0	23.6
Elm / ash / cottonwood group	5.8	10.9	--	--	17.3	2.2	153.5	48.8	238.5
Aspen / birch group	95.6	44.1	2.3	43.1	13.3	--	247.1	76.6	522.1
Alder / maple group	6.7	--	--	--	--	--	--	--	6.7
Woodland hardwoods group	--	--	--	15.9	--	--	--	2.1	18.0
Nonstocked	522.1	250.1	111.3	161.4	79.7	12.3	663.1	118.0	1,918.0
All forest-type groups	**12,239.6**	**3,160.3**	**851.6**	**1,483.2**	**835.7**	**103.1**	**5,947.5**	**969.7**	**25,590.8**

All table cells without observations in the inventory sample are indicated by --. Table value of 0.0 indicates the acres round to less than 0.1 thousand acres. Columns and rows may not add to their totals due to rounding.

Table 5—Area of accessible forest land by forest type group and stand-size class, Montana, cycle 2, 2003-2009.

(In thousand acres)

Forest-type group	Large diameter	Medium diameter	Stand-size class Small diameter	Chaparral	Nonstocked	All size classes
Pinyon / juniper group	558.2	134.7	112.1	--	--	805.1
Douglas-fir group	5,273.5	1,059.1	1,184.4	--	--	7,517.0
Ponderosa pine group	2,062.5	387.0	569.1	--	--	3,018.6
Fir / spruce / mountain hemlock group	3,230.1	701.0	1,100.1	--	--	5,031.2
Lodgepole pine group	1,500.1	1,796.5	1,069.3	--	--	4,365.9
Hemlock / Sitka spruce group	205.7	26.8	8.9	--	--	241.4
Western larch group	588.9	134.1	213.0	--	--	936.0
Other western softwoods group	549.8	214.8	184.1	--	--	948.8
Oak / hickory group	8.6	15.0	--	--	--	23.6
Elm / ash / cottonwood group	183.2	31.0	24.2	--	--	238.5
Aspen / birch group	58.8	154.4	308.9	--	--	522.1
Alder / maple group	--	6.7	--	--	--	6.7
Woodland hardwoods group	--	--	18.0	--	--	18.0
Nonstocked	--	--	--	--	1,918.0	1,918.0
All forest-type groups	14,219.4	4,661.2	4,792.1	--	1,918.0	25,590.8

All table cells without observations in the inventory sample are indicated by --. Table value of 0.0 indicates the acres round to less than 0.1 thousand acres. Columns and rows may not add to their totals due to rounding.

USDA Forest Service Resour. Bull. RMRS-RB-15. 2012

93

Table 6—Area of accessible forest land by forest type group and stand-age class, Montana, cycle 2, 2003-2009.
(In thousand acres)

Forest-type group	Non stocked	Stand-age class (years)											All classes
		1-20	21-40	41-60	61-80	81-100	101-120	121-140	141-160	161-180	181-200	201+	
Pinyon / juniper group	--	64.1	86.2	138.3	160.6	119.8	126.3	46.4	29.3	16.9	17.2	--	805.1
Douglas-fir group	--	951.7	217.7	275.3	839.0	1,693.9	1,371.7	794.3	488.7	515.0	202.6	167.0	7,517.0
Ponderosa pine group	--	526.0	76.9	200.5	456.4	715.2	589.1	186.7	138.9	50.0	49.5	29.4	3,018.6
Fir / spruce / mountain hemlock group	--	731.5	337.8	135.3	249.6	565.0	531.9	775.1	508.2	457.8	348.0	391.0	5,031.2
Lodgepole pine group	--	866.2	96.3	197.8	471.7	951.4	725.9	476.7	303.6	168.4	78.0	29.9	4,365.9
Hemlock / Sitka spruce group	--	8.9	--	8.9	29.0	60.9	73.6	46.6	13.4	--	--	--	241.4
Western larch group	--	195.3	26.5	69.0	132.0	152.9	138.7	63.1	22.1	52.8	36.6	46.8	936.0
Other western softwoods group	--	94.3	80.4	18.2	17.7	88.9	126.4	58.8	113.3	121.3	50.5	179.1	948.8
Oak / hickory group	--	--	--	6.4	8.6	--	8.6	--	--	--	--	--	23.6
Elm / ash / cottonwood group	--	24.2	6.9	32.9	33.1	83.9	42.1	2.2	13.0	--	--	--	238.5
Aspen / birch group	--	256.7	42.4	73.5	64.5	60.0	15.8	9.1	--	--	--	--	522.1
Alder / maple group	--	--	--	--	6.7	--	--	--	--	--	--	--	6.7
Woodland hardwoods group	--	--	11.1	7.0	--	--	--	--	--	--	--	--	18.0
Nonstocked	1,918.0	--	--	--	--	--	--	--	--	--	--	--	1,918.0
All forest-type groups	1,918.0	3,718.9	982.2	1,163.1	2,468.9	4,492.0	3,750.2	2,459.0	1,630.7	1,382.3	782.3	843.1	25,590.8

All table cells without observations in the inventory sample are indicated by --. Table value of 0.0 indicates the acres round to less than 0.1 thousand acres. Columns and rows may not add to their totals due to rounding.

Table 7--Area of accessible forest land by forest type group and stand origin, Montana, cycle 2, 2003-2009.
(In thousand acres)

| | Stand origin | | |
Forest-type group	Natural stands	Artificial regeneration	All forest land
Pinyon / juniper group	805.1	- -	805.1
Douglas-fir group	7,473.6	43 4	7 517.0
Ponderosa pine group	2,982.5	36.1	3 018.6
Fir / spruce / mountain hemlock group	5,013.6	17.6	5,031.2
Lodgepole pine group	4,348.5	17 4	4,365.9
Hemlock / Sitka spruce group	241.4	- -	241.4
Western larch group	924.9	11.1	936.0
Other western softwoods group	948.8	- -	948.8
Oak / hickory group	23.6	- -	23.6
Elm / ash / cottonwood group	238.5	- -	238.5
Aspen / birch group	513.5	8.6	522.1
Alder / maple group	6.7	- -	6.7
Woodland hardwoods group	18.0	- -	18.0
Nonstocked	1,913.6	4.5	1,918.0
All forest-type groups	25,452.1	138.7	25,590.8

All table cells without observations in the inventory sample are indicated by --. Table value of 0.0 indicates the
acres round to less than 0.1 thousand acres. Columns and rows may not add to their totals due to rounding.

Table 8—Area of forest land by forest type group and primary disturbance class, Montana, cycle 2, 2003-2009.
(In thousand acres)

Forest-type group	Disturbance class									All forest land
	None	Insects	Disease	Weather	Fire	Domestic animals	Wild animals	Human	Other	
Pinyon / juniper group	766.4	--	22.2	12.4	4.0	--	--	--	--	805.1
Douglas-fir group	6,274.2	690.0	312.2	8.9	166.8	64.9	--	--	--	7,517.0
Ponderosa pine group	2,640.3	57.0	35.3	41.8	172.2	35.1	36.9	--	--	3,018.6
Fir / spruce / mountain hemlock group	4,127.6	323.5	426.6	12.1	97.2	2.1	--	--	8.7	5,031.2
Lodgepole pine group	3,682.8	291.5	228.9	--	130.1	--	18.1	--	8.9	4,365.9
Hemlock / Sitka spruce group	214.6	--	17.9	--	--	--	--	--	8.9	241.4
Western larch group	745.7	39.7	64.1	8.9	68.6	--	8.9	--	--	936.0
Other western softwoods group	777.2	64.1	81.2	1.3	22.9	--	--	--	--	948.8
Oak / hickory group	17.2	--	6.4	--	--	--	--	--	--	23.6
Elm / ash / cottonwood group	202.7	--	--	17.5	--	11.4	6.8	--	--	238.5
Aspen / birch group	371.1	14.2	32.5	4.9	81.8	17.7	--	--	--	522.1
Alder / maple group	6.7	--	--	--	--	--	--	--	--	6.7
Woodland hardwoods group	18.0	--	--	--	--	--	--	--	--	18.0
Nonstocked	1,293.6	28.6	11.0	--	565.3	7.1	3.5	--	--	1,918.0
All forest-type groups	21,138.0	1,508.6	1,238.3	107.9	1,308.9	138.3	74.2	--	26.6	25,590.8

All table cells without observations in the inventory sample are indicated by --. Table value of 0.0 indicates the acres round to less than 0.1 thousand acres. Columns and rows may not add to their totals due to rounding.

Table 9.--Area of timberland by forest type group and stand-class, Montana, cycle 2, 2003-2009.

(In thousand acres)

Forest-type group	Stand-size class					All size classes
	Large diameter	Medium diameter	Small diameter	Chaparral	Nonstocked	
Douglas-fir group	4,765.0	926.2	1,141.7	--	--	6,832.9
Ponderosa pine group	1,924.4	322.7	517.0	--	--	2,764.0
Fir / spruce / mountai hemlock group	2,159.6	467.9	695.8	--	--	3,323.3
Lodgepole pine group	1,214.3	1,518.8	773.1	--	--	3,506.2
Hemlock / Sitka sp uce group	179.9	26.8	8.9	--	--	215.6
Western la ch g oup	534.0	134.1	195.5	--	--	863.6
Other western softwoods gr up	292.5	88.6	61.3	--	--	442.4
Oak / hickory group	8.6	--	--	--	--	8.6
Elm / ash / cottonwood group	137.1	26.1	13.3	--	--	176.6
Aspen / birch group	50.3	94.1	213.9	--	--	358.4
Alder / maple group	--	6.7	--	--	--	6.7
Nonstocked	--	--	--	--	1,376.3	1,376.3
All forest-type groups	11,265.9	3,611.8	3,620.5	--	1,376.3	19,874.5

All table cells without observations in the inventory sample are indicated by --. Table value of 0.0 indicates the acres round to less than 0.1 thousand acres. Columns and rows may not add to their totals due to rounding.

Table 10--Number of live trees on forest land by species group and diameter class, Montana, cycle 2, 2003-2009.
(In thousand trees)

Species group	Diameter class (inches)															All classes
	1.0-2.9	3.0-4.9	5.0-6.9	7.0-8.9	9.0-10.9	11.0-12.9	13.0-14.9	15.0-16.9	17.0-18.9	19.0-20.9	21.0-24.9	25.0-28.9	29.0-32.9	33.0-36.9	37.0+	
Softwood species groups																
Western softwood species groups																
Douglas-fir	1,093,546	518,680	317,943	233,774	168,089	110,322	73,371	47,159	30,054	16,805	16,887	5,189	2,163	494	496	2,634,970
Ponderosa and Jeffrey pines	347,587	147,847	89,363	65,102	47,559	31,357	23,189	13,464	7,996	4,591	3,941	1,265	654	--	167	784,082
True fir	1,648,139	582,652	265,340	143,833	80,096	42,835	20,529	10,448	5,528	1,990	2,161	486	54	--	57	2,804,146
Western hemlock	35,924	11,986	7,708	4,176	2,516	1,447	1,070	1,232	214	321	54	107	--	54	54	66,863
Western white pine	6,622	3,976	1,391	1,386	801	801	321	215	49	107	52	106	53	--	--	15,882
Engelmann and other spruces	366,709	183,288	99,082	72,862	48,635	35,336	23,935	14,667	10,305	6,980	6,546	3,407	1,233	488	207	873,681
Western larch	119,521	51,399	38,948	32,269	22,863	15,922	10,764	6,372	3,862	2,873	3,393	2,173	956	371	107	311,793
Lodgepole pine	925,829	612,837	524,116	365,375	184,148	79,590	31,082	10,738	3,796	999	549	50	--	--	--	2,739,108
Western redcedar	169,289	44,661	17,820	9,777	5,374	3,133	2,881	1,382	905	589	856	375	--	161	53	257,256
Western woodland softwoods	209,593	107,507	52,607	30,905	18,442	9,903	4,659	3,509	1,015	634	726	257	55	--	--	439,812
Other western softwoods	317,477	153,997	100,330	67,147	43,407	25,095	12,722	5,465	3,548	1,781	1,314	218	164	--	--	732,664
All softwoods	5,240,234	2,418,830	1,514,648	1,026,607	621,930	355,740	204,523	114,651	67,272	37,670	36,479	13,632	5,333	1,567	1,141	11,660,257
Hardwood species groups																
Western hardwood species groups																
Cottonwood and aspen	140,830	49,048	24,262	14,399	7,387	4,678	3,174	1,009	853	950	969	214	105	52	--	247,932
Red alder	--	--	374	53	--	53	--	--	--	--	--	--	--	--	--	481
Other western hardwoods	26,550	9,787	7,174	4,576	1,674	535	477	210	213	108	52	--	--	--	--	51,358
Western woodland hardwoods	6,122	8,165	1,637	424	42	--	--	--	--	--	--	--	--	--	--	16,389
All hardwoods	173,502	67,000	33,448	19,452	9,103	5,267	3,651	1,219	1,066	1,058	1,022	214	105	52	--	316,160
All species groups	5,413,736	2,485,830	1,548,097	1,046,059	631,033	361,007	208,174	115,870	68,339	38,728	37,501	13,846	5,438	1,620	1,141	11,976,417

All table cells without observations in the inventory sample are indicated by --. Table value of 0 indicates the number of trees rounds to less than 1 thousand trees. Columns and rows may not add to their totals due to rounding.

Table 11—Number of growing-stock trees on timberland by species group and diameter class, Montana, cycle 2, 2003-2009.

(In thousand trees)

Species group	Diameter class (inches)													All classes
	5.0-6.9	7.0-8.9	9.0-10.9	11.0-12.9	13.0-14.9	15.0-16.9	17.0-18.9	19.0-20.9	21.0-24.9	25.0-28.9	29.0-32.9	33.0-36.9	37.0+	
Softwood species groups														
Western softwood species groups														
Douglas-fir	273,815	205,428	149,766	98,536	64,419	41,814	25,929	14,936	14,441	4,472	1,722	328	331	895,936
Ponderosa and Jeffrey pines	72,775	55,312	41,926	28,700	21,333	13,022	7,750	4,591	3,835	1,265	654	--	167	251,329
True fir	179,539	99,605	57,373	31,246	15,284	7,884	4,150	1,717	1,538	428	54	--	--	398,820
Western hemlock	7,281	4,069	2,196	1,233	857	964	161	268	54	107	--	54	54	17,297
Western white pine	1,391	1,386	695	696	321	215	49	107	52	106	53	--	--	5,073
Engelmann and other spruces	67,263	51,103	34,767	25,629	17,149	9,654	7,318	4,433	4,648	2,151	857	213	159	225,344
Western larch	37,900	31,018	21,711	14,654	10,026	5,678	3,489	2,820	2,756	1,746	690	371	--	132,861
Lodgepole pine	436,148	305,330	150,080	62,205	22,821	7,547	2,874	836	378	50	--	--	--	988,268
Western redcedar	15,832	8,794	4,597	2,723	2,412	1,179	749	536	695	375	--	161	53	38,107
Other western softwoods	56,757	41,443	27,684	14,800	7,086	3,363	1,809	817	700	107	--	--	--	154,566
All softwoods	1,148,702	803,489	490,797	280,422	161,706	91,321	54,278	31,061	29,096	10,807	4,030	1,127	764	3,107,600
Hardwood species groups														
Western hardwood species groups														
Cottonwood and aspen	14,294	8,785	5,746	3,515	2,266	692	746	795	703	160	--	52	--	37,754
Red alder	374	53	--	53	--	--	--	--	--	--	--	--	--	481
Other western hardwoods	3,135	2,475	843	324	319	103	213	56	--	--	--	--	--	7,468
All hardwoods	17,803	11,314	6,589	3,893	2,585	796	959	850	703	160	--	52	--	45,703
All species groups	1,166,504	814,803	497,386	284,314	164,291	92,116	55,237	31,911	29,800	10,966	4,030	1,180	764	3,153,303

All table cells without observations in the inventory sample are indicated by --. Table value of 0 indicates the number of trees rounds to less than 1 thousand trees. Columns and rows may not add to their totals due to rounding.

Table 12—Net volume of all live trees by owner class and forest land status, Montana, cycle 2, 2003-2009.

(In million cubic feet)

Owner class	Unreserved forests			Reserved forests			All forest land
	Timberland	Unproductive	Total	Productive	Unproductive	Total	
Forest Service							
National forest	27,972.6	406.5	28,379.1	5,202.5	76.9	5,279.4	33,658.5
Other Federal							
National Park Service	--	--	--	1,644.3	6.9	1,651.2	1,651.2
Bureau of Land Management	1,201.8	100.4	1,302.2	36.1	9.8	45.9	1,348.2
Fish and Wildlife Service	--	--	--	42.3	27.4	69.7	69.7
Other Federal	--	--	--	20.1	--	20.1	20.1
State and local government							
State	1,280.4	24.8	1,305.2	--	--	--	1,305.2
Local (county, municipal, etc.)	2.0	--	2.0	--	--	--	2.0
Private							
Undifferentiated private	5,965.4	273.5	6,238.8	287.7	--	287.7	6,526.5
All owners	36,422.2	805.2	37,227.4	7,233.1	121.0	7,354.1	44,581.4

All table cells without observations in the inventory sample are indicated by --. Table value of 0.0 indicates the volume rounds to less than 0.1 million cubic feet. Columns and rows may not add to their totals due to rounding.

Table 13—Net volume of all live trees on forest land by forest type group and stand-size class. Montana, cycle 2, 2003-2009.

(In million cubic feet)

Forest-type group	Stand-size class					All size classes
	Large diameter	Medium diameter	Small diameter	Chaparral	Nonstocked	
Pinyon / juniper group	223.4	36 0	6.9	--	--	266.3
Douglas-fir group	12,010.4	1,420.7	367.2	--	--	13,798.3
Ponderosa pine group	2,620.1	199 2	90.3	--	--	2,909.7
Fir / spruce / mountain hemlock group	10,314.1	1,353 1	374.1	--	--	12,041.2
Lodgepole pine group	5,011.7	4,342 4	298.6	--	--	9,652.8
Hemlock / Sitka spruce group	1,087.4	46 6	6.7	--	--	1,140.7
Western larch group	2,186.3	265.6	96.5	--	--	2,548.3
Other western softwoods group	1,137.2	254.6	33.3	--	--	1,425.0
Oak / hickory group	8.3	5.1	--	--	--	13.3
Elm / ash / cottonwood group	301.6	19.2	0.6	--	--	321.4
Aspen / birch group	139.6	134.5	71.7	--	--	345.8
Alder / maple group	--	3.3	--	--	--	3.3
Woodland hardwoods group	--	--	1.3	--	--	1.3
Nonstocked	--	--	--	--	114.0	114.0
All forest-type groups	35,040.0	8,080.2	1,347.2	--	114.0	44,581.4

All table cells without observations in the inventory sample are indicated by --. Table value of 0.0 indicates the volume rounds to less than 0.1 million cubic feet. Columns and rows may not add to their totals due to rounding.

USDA Forest Service Resour. Bull. RMRS-RB-15. 2012

101

Table 14—Net volume of all live trees on forest land by species group and ownership group, Montana, cycle 2, 2003-2009.
(In million cubic feet)

Species group	Ownership group				All owners
	Forest Service	Other Federal	State and local government	Undifferentiated private	
Softwood species groups					
Western softwood species groups					
Douglas-fir	8,601.8	821.4	476.6	2,644.0	12,543.8
Ponderosa and Jeffrey pines	1,116.5	291.9	218.1	1,625.0	3,251.5
True fir	4,465.3	381.3	132.2	268.3	5,247.1
Western hemlock	278.8	2.0	--	7.9	288.6
Western white pine	96.6	3.2	--	3.4	103.3
Engelmann and other spruces	5,211.7	572.3	49.1	268.4	6,101.4
Western larch	2,194.2	182.4	235.8	287.9	2,900.3
Lodgepole pine	9,154.0	592.0	105.8	763.8	10,615.6
Western redcedar	490.7	35.8	2.2	44.2	572.9
Western woodland softwoods	32.1	96.4	15.3	147.7	291.3
Other western softwoods	1,884.5	72.4	19.3	49.3	2,025.5
All softwoods	33,526.2	3,051.2	1,254.2	6,109.8	43,941.4
Hardwood species groups					
Western hardwood species groups					
Cottonwood and aspen	104.6	25.0	37.3	376.3	543.2
Red alder	2.0	--	--	--	2.0
Other western hardwoods	25.7	12.5	15.4	40.0	93.6
Western woodland hardwoods	--	0.6	0.2	0.4	1.2
All hardwoods	132.3	38.0	53.0	416.7	640.0
All species groups	33,658.5	3,089.2	1,307.2	6,526.5	44,581.4

All table cells without observations in the inventory sample are indicated by --. Table value of 0.0 indicates the volume rounds to less than 0.1 million cubic feet. Columns and rows may not add to their totals due to rounding.

Table 15—Net volume of all live trees on forest land by species group and diameter class, Montana, cycle 2, 2003-2009.

(In million cubic feet)

Species group	Diameter class (inches)													All classes
	5.0-6.9	7.0-8.9	9.0-10.9	11.0-12.9	13.0-14.9	15.0-16.9	17.0-18.9	19.0-20.9	21.0-24.9	25.0-28.9	29.0-32.9	33.0-36.9	37.0+	
Softwood species groups														
Western softwood species groups														
Douglas-fir	715	1,224	1,618	1,697	1,667	1,450	1,218	848	1,146	485	284	81	111	12,544
Ponderosa and Jeffrey pines	118	255	381	415	476	408	334	248	306	142	107	--	61	3,251
True fir	986	979	926	769	544	389	270	122	177	65	5	--	15	5,247
Western hemlock	16	25	34	31	30	57	13	25	6	19	--	15	18	289
Western white pine	4	9	9	16	10	10	3	8	6	17	10	--	--	103
Engelmann and other spruces	321	493	590	692	708	623	581	517	675	470	244	117	70	6,101
Western larch	103	226	303	346	337	275	212	202	326	283	181	87	19	2,900
Lodgepole pine	1,723	2,862	2,563	1,733	962	457	196	70	44	6	--	--	--	10,616
Western redcedar	60	61	58	54	73	48	41	33	62	38	--	33	12	573
Western woodland softwoods	40	49	51	43	33	32	11	9	14	7	1	--	--	291
Other western softwoods	191	323	392	360	261	160	133	80	85	25	14	--	--	2,026
All softwoods	4,277	6,507	6,925	6,156	5,101	3,911	3,012	2,162	2,848	1,557	846	332	307	43,941
Hardwood species groups														
Western hardwood species groups														
Cottonwood and aspen	47	67	71	72	71	29	37	52	57	22	8	11	--	543
Red alder	1	0	--	1	--	--	--	--	--	--	--	--	--	2
Other western hardwoods	16	25	17	10	10	3	7	4	2	--	--	--	--	94
Western woodland hardwoods	1	0	0	--	--	--	--	--	--	--	--	--	--	1
All hardwoods	65	92	87	82	80	32	44	56	59	22	8	11	--	640
All species groups	4,342	6,599	7,013	6,238	5,182	3,943	3,057	2,217	2,907	1,579	854	344	307	44,581

All table cells without observations in the inventory sample are indicated by --. Table value of 0 indicates the volume rounds to less than 1 million cubic feet. Columns and rows may not add to their totals due to rounding.

USDA Forest Service Resour. Bull. RMRS-RB-15. 2012

103

Table 16--Net volume of all live trees on forest land by forest type group and stand origin, Montana, cycle 2, 2003-2009.
(In million cubic feet)

| Forest-type group | Stand origin | | All forest land |
	Natural stands	Artificial regeneration	
Pinyon / juniper group	266.3	- -	266.3
Douglas-fir group	13,786.4	11.9	13 798.3
Ponderosa pine group	2,899.1	10 6	2,909.7
Fir / spruce / mountain hemlock group	12,003.0	38 2	12,041.2
Lodgepole pine group	9,652.2	0.6	9,652.8
Hemlock / Sitka spruce group	1,140.7	- -	1,140.7
Western larch group	2,532.1	16.3	2,548.3
Other western softwoods group	1,425.0	-	1,425.0
Oak / hickory group	13.3	- -	13.3
Elm / ash / cottonwood group	321.4	- -	321.4
Aspen / birch group	345.4	0.4	345.8
Alder / maple group	3.3	- -	3.3
Woodland hardwoods group	1.3	- -	1.3
Nonstocked	110.3	3.7	114.0
All forest-type groups	44,499.9	81.6	44,581.4

All table cells without observations in the inventory sample are indicated by --. Table value of 0.0 indicates the volume rounds to less than 0.1 million cubic feet. Columns and rows may not add to their totals due to rounding.

Table 17--Net volume of growing-stock trees on timberland by species group and diameter class, Montana, cycle 2, 2003-2009.

(In million cubic feet)

Species group	Diameter class (inches)													All classes
	5.0-6.9	7.0-8.9	9.0-10.9	11.0-12.9	13.0-14.9	15.0-16.9	17.0-18.9	19.0-20.9	21.0-24.9	25.0-28.9	29.0-32.9	33.0-36.9	37.0+	
Softwood species groups														
Western softwood species groups														
Douglas-fir	629	1,090	1,446	1,525	1,473	1,301	1,061	754	985	436	226	56	86	11,067
Ponderosa and Jeffrey pines	104	228	346	385	448	397	329	248	299	142	107	--	61	3,093
True fir	673	692	681	585	425	303	214	105	138	58	5	--	--	3,879
Western hemlock	15	24	29	25	24	43	9	20	6	19	--	15	18	247
Western white pine	4	9	9	13	10	10	3	8	6	17	10	--	--	100
Engelmann and other spruces	220	350	424	505	514	416	421	338	486	305	189	46	59	4,274
Western larch	99	218	287	319	316	247	194	198	259	230	133	87	--	2,589
Lodgepole pine	1,463	2,422	2,105	1,363	707	315	145	59	30	6	--	--	--	8,614
Western redcedar	53	55	49	46	61	40	34	29	52	38	--	33	12	503
Other western softwoods	114	209	251	215	141	97	71	38	49	15	--	--	--	1,200
All softwoods	3,375	5,297	5,627	4,982	4,117	3,170	2,480	1,798	2,310	1,266	669	237	236	35,565
Hardwood species groups														
Western hardwood species groups														
Cottonwood and aspen	32	48	59	58	59	22	33	46	46	18	--	11	--	432
Red alder	1	0	--	1	--	--	--	--	--	--	--	--	--	2
Other western hardwoods	9	16	10	6	8	2	7	2	--	--	--	--	--	62
All hardwoods	42	65	69	65	67	24	40	48	46	18	--	11	--	496
All species groups	3,417	5,362	5,696	5,047	4,184	3,194	2,521	1,846	2,357	1,284	669	248	236	36,061

All table cells without observations in the inventory sample are indicated by --. Table value of 0 indicates the volume rounds to less than 1 million cubic feet. Columns and rows may not add to their totals due to rounding.

Table 18--Net volume of growing-stock trees on timberland by species group and ownership group, Montana, cycle 2, 2003-2009.

(In million cubic feet)

Species group	Ownership group				All owners
	Forest Service	Other Federal	State and local government	Undifferentiated private	
Softwood species groups					
Western softwood species groups					
Douglas-fir	7,620.2	515.1	474.7	2,457.0	11,066.9
Ponderosa and Jeffrey pines	1,104.2	225.0	212.0	1,552.3	3,093.4
True fir	3,479.5	43.1	130.6	225.6	3,878.7
Western hemlock	239.0	- -	- -	7.9	246.8
Western white pine	96.5	- -	- -	3.4	99.9
Engelmann and other spruces	3,912.2	58.7	49.1	254.3	4,274.2
Western larch	2,061.8	10.8	234.9	281.3	2,588.9
Lodgepole pine	7,529.5	293.6	100.0	690.9	8,614.0
Western redcedar	473.9	- -	2.2	26.5	502.5
Other western softwoods	1,126.4	20.5	17.9	35.3	1,200.0
All softwoods	27,643.1	1,166.8	1,221.2	5,534.3	35,565.4
Hardwood species groups					
Western hardwood species groups					
Cottonwood and aspen	86.8	6.3	35.7	302.9	431.8
Red alder	2.0	- -	- -	- -	2.0
Other western hardwoods	24.6	- -	11.2	26.2	62.0
All hardwoods	113.4	6.3	46.9	329.1	495.8
All species groups	27,756.5	1,173.1	1,268.1	5,863.5	36,061.2

All table cells without observations in the inventory sample are indicated by --. Table value of 0.0 indicates the volume rounds to less than 0.1 million cubic feet. Columns and rows may not add to their totals due to rounding.

Table 19—Net volume of sawtimber trees (International 1/4-inch rule) on timberland by species group and diameter class, Montana, cycle 2, 2003-2009.

(In million board feet)

Species group	Diameter class (inches)											All classes
	9.0-10.9	11.0-12.9	13.0-14.9	15.0-16.9	17.0-18.9	19.0-20.9	21.0-24.9	25.0-28.9	29.0-32.9	33.0-36.9	37.0+	
Softwood species groups												
Western softwood species groups												
Douglas-fir	5,560	7,023	7,484	7,011	6,022	4,444	5,994	2,722	1,449	382	599	48,690
Ponderosa and Jeffrey pines	764	1,513	2,237	2,263	2,049	1,600	2,050	1,063	858	--	567	14,965
True fir	3,443	3,158	2,389	1,749	1,274	634	875	375	29	--	--	13,926
Western hemlock	132	132	130	254	54	125	38	121	--	94	116	1,195
Western white pine	45	77	60	65	19	53	42	122	74	--	--	556
Engelmann and other spruces	2,336	2,866	2,957	2,412	2,460	1,987	2,928	1,950	1,252	305	400	21,854
Western larch	1,577	1,797	1,810	1,455	1,164	1,202	1,616	1,396	790	519	--	13,326
Lodgepole pine	11,966	7,591	3,929	1,734	797	318	154	32	--	--	--	26,522
Western redcedar	242	243	330	223	191	168	300	217	--	193	74	2,181
Other western softwoods	1,359	1,146	737	506	373	208	243	94	--	--	--	4,665
All softwoods	27,422	25,547	22,063	17,672	14,404	10,738	14,240	8,091	4,452	1,493	1,757	147,880
Hardwood species groups												
Western hardwood species groups												
Cottonwood and aspen	--	291	299	111	174	233	239	103	--	41	--	1,490
Red alder	--	4	--	--	--	--	--	--	--	--	--	4
Other western hardwoods	--	29	40	9	35	9	--	--	--	--	--	121
All hardwoods	--	324	339	119	209	242	239	103	--	41	--	1,616
All species groups	27,422	25,871	22,402	17,791	14,613	10,980	14,479	8,194	4,452	1,534	1,757	149,496

All table cells without observations in he inventory sample are indicated by --. Table value of 0 indicates the volume rounds to less than 1 million board feet. Columns and rows may not add to heir totals due to rounding.

Table 20—Net volume of sawtimber trees on timberland by species group and ownership group, Montana, cycle 2, 2003-2009.

(In million cubic feet)

| Species group | Ownership group | | | | |
	Forest Service	Other Federal	State and local government	Undifferentiated private	All owners
Softwood species groups					
Western softwood species groups					
Douglas-fir	5,872.0	351.4	353.7	1,698.7	8,275.9
Ponderosa and Jeffrey pines	922.1	159.3	174.6	1,168.9	2,424.9
True fir	1,957.7	17.7	81.2	122.3	2,178.8
Western hemlock	171.9	- -	- -	4.0	175.9
Western white pine	80.0	- -	- -	2.0	81.9
Engelmann and other spruces	3,062.0	32.6	32.5	175.3	3,302.4
Western larch	1,644.7	9.0	195.0	191.7	2,040.5
Lodgepole pine	3,702.6	164.5	44.1	382.8	4,294.0
Western redcedar	310.4	- -	1.1	14.8	326.3
Other western softwoods	741.8	13.1	13.0	19.4	787.3
All softwoods	18,465.3	747.6	895.2	3,779.8	23,887.9
Hardwood species groups					
Western hardwood species groups					
Cottonwood and aspen	43.1	1.8	20.2	162.6	227.8
Red alder	0.6	- -	- -	- -	0.6
Other western hardwoods	10.4	- -	- -	10.5	20.8
All hardwoods	54.1	1.8	20.2	173.1	249.3
All species groups	18,519.4	749.5	915.4	3,952.9	24,137.2

All table cells without observations in the inventory sample are indicated by --. Table value of 0.0 indicates the volume rounds to less than 0.1 million cubic feet. Columns and rows may not add to their totals due to rounding.

Table 21--Average annual net growth of all live trees by owner class and forest land status, Montana, cycle 2, 2003-2009.

(In million cubic feet)

Owner class	Unreserved forests			Reserved forests			All forest land
	Timberland	Unproductive	Total	Productive	Unproductive	Total	
Forest Service							
National forest	223.3	-2.1	221.2	-50.0	0.2	-49.8	171.4
Other Federal							
National Park Service	--	--	--	-33.2	0.3	-33.0	-33.0
Bureau of Land Management	10.1	1.3	11.4	0.6	0.1	0.7	12.1
Fish and Wildlife Service	--	--	--	0.2	0.1	0.3	0.3
Other Federal	--	--	--	-0.1	--	-0.1	-0.1
State and local government							
State	11.7	0.4	12.1	--	--	--	12.1
Local (county, municipal, etc.)	0.0	--	0.0	--	--	--	0.0
Private							
Undifferentiated private	124.6	4.4	129.1	-1.8	-0.4	-2.2	126.9
All owners	369.8	4.1	373.9	-84.3	0.3	-84.0	289.8

All table cells without observations in the inventory sample are indicated by --. Table value of 0.0 indicates the volume rounds to less than 0.1 million cubic feet. Columns and rows may not add to their totals due to rounding.

Table 22—Average annual net growth of all live trees on forest land by forest type group and stand-size class, Montana, cycle 2, 2003-2009.

(In million cubic feet)

Forest-type group	Stand-size class					All size classes
	Large diameter	Medium diameter	Small diameter	Chaparral	Non stocked	
Pinyon / juniper group	2.3	0.8	0.2	--	--	3.3
Douglas-fir group	117.1	35.5	12.7	--	--	165.3
Ponderosa pine group	36.3	7.6	2.8	--	--	46.7
Fir / spruce / mountain hemlock group	71.7	31.9	-1.2	--	--	102.4
Lodgepole pine group	58.9	86.7	-19.9	--	--	125.7
Hemlock / Sitka spruce group	22.3	2.4	0.3	--	--	25.0
Western larch group	22.3	12.3	-12.9	--	--	21.7
Other western softwoods group	-5.8	4.6	0.8	--	--	-0.4
Oak / hickory group	0.1	0.2	--	--	--	0.3
Elm / ash / cottonwood group	6.4	0.7	0.0	--	--	7.1
Aspen / birch group	4.0	3.4	-29.2	--	--	-21.9
Alder / maple group	--	0.2	--	--	--	0.2
Woodland hardwoods group	--	--	-0.5	--	--	-0.5
Nonstocked	--	--	--	--	-185.2	-185.2
All forest-type groups	**335.5**	**186.4**	**-46.8**	**--**	**-185.2**	**289.8**

All table cells without observations in the inventory sample are indicated by --. Table value of 0.0 indicates the volume rounds to less than 0.1 million cubic feet. Columns and rows may not add to their totals due to rounding.

Table 23--Average annual net growth of all live trees on forest land by species group and ownership group, Montana, cycle 2, 2003-2009.

(In million cubic feet)

Species group	Ownership group				
	Forest Service	Other Federal	State and local government	Undifferentiated private	All owners
Softwood species groups					
Western softwood species groups					
Douglas-fir	38.5	2.5	3.4	55.2	99.5
Ponderosa and Jeffrey pines	12.2	2.1	0.2	29.1	43.6
True fir	34.8	-9.6	3.1	6.1	34.4
Western hemlock	8.0	0.0	- -	0.4	8.4
Western white pine	1.5	0.1	- -	0.4	2.0
Engelmann and other spruces	42.9	-2.2	1.6	9.2	51.5
Western larch	34.3	-7.7	3.4	6.5	36.6
Lodgepole pine	4.6	-1.5	-0.8	7.7	10.0
Western redcedar	15.7	0.0	0.2	1.3	17.2
Western woodland softwoods	0.0	1.0	0.2	1.7	2.9
Other western softwoods	-25.6	-2.7	-0.5	0.0	-28.8
All softwoods	166.9	-17.9	10.7	117.8	277.5
Hardwood species groups					
Western hardwood species groups					
Cottonwood and aspen	3.5	-2.0	0.7	7.9	10.2
Red alder	0.1	- -	- -	- -	0.1
Other western hardwoods	0.8	-0.7	0.7	1.2	2.0
Western woodland hardwoods	- -	0.0	0.0	0.0	0.0
All hardwoods	4.4	-2.7	1.5	9.1	12.3
All species groups	171.4	-20.6	12.2	126.9	289.8

All table cells without observations in the inventory sample are indicated by --. Table value of 0.0 indicates the volume rounds to less than 0.1 million cubic feet. Columns and rows may not add to their totals due to rounding.

USDA Forest Service Resour. Bull. RMRS-RB-15. 2012

111

Table 24--Average annual net growth of growing-stock trees on timberland by species group and ownership group, Montana, cycle 2, 2003-2009.

(In million cubic feet)

Species group	Ownership group				
	Forest Service	Other Federal	State and local government	Undifferentiated private	All owners
Softwood species groups					
Western softwood species groups					
Douglas-fir	52.3	8.1	3.4	52.2	116.0
Ponderosa and Jeffrey pines	13.4	1.5	0.0	27.3	42.1
True fir	37.3	0.8	3.1	5.9	47.1
Western hemlock	7.0	--	--	0.4	7.4
Western white pine	1.5	--	--	0.4	1.8
Engelmann and other spruces	34.8	1.9	1.6	9.0	47.3
Western larch	34.7	0.4	3.4	6.4	44.9
Lodgepole pine	22.6	-1.3	-0.9	12.8	33.2
Western redcedar	15.5	--	0.2	0.9	16.6
Other western softwoods	-4.6	-1.8	-0.5	-0.3	-7.3
All softwoods	214.4	9.6	10.2	115.0	349.2
Hardwood species groups					
Western hardwood species groups					
Cottonwood and aspen	2.8	0.1	0.7	6.4	10.0
Red alder	0.1	--	--	--	0.1
Other western hardwoods	0.7	--	0.7	0.8	2.2
All hardwoods	3.7	0.1	1.3	7.2	12.3
All species groups	218.1	9.7	11.5	122.2	361.5

All table cells without observations in the inventory sample are indicated by --. Table value of 0.0 indicates the volume rounds to less than 0.1 million cubic feet. Columns and rows may not add to their totals due to rounding.

Table 25—Average annual mortality of all live trees by owner class and forest land status, Montana, cycle 2, 2003-2009.
(In million cubic feet)

Owner class	Unreserved forests			Reserved forests			All forest land
	Timberland	Unproductive	Total	Productive	Unproductive	Total	
Forest Service							
National forest	410.8	11.2	422.1	155.1	0.8	156.0	578.0
Other Federal							
National Park Service	--	--	--	71.4	0.0	71.4	71.4
Bureau of Land Management	17.4	0.7	18.1	0.1	0.0	0.1	18.2
Fish and Wildlife Service	--	--	--	0.7	0.4	1.1	1.1
Other Federal	--	--	--	0.4	--	0.4	0.4
State and local government							
State	18.3	0.1	18.4	--	--	--	18.4
Private							
Undifferentiated private	47.7	1.4	49.2	9.2	0.4	9.7	58.8
All owners	494.3	13.5	507.8	236.9	1.7	238.6	746.3

All table cells without observations in the inventory sample are indicated by --. Table value of 0.0 indicates the volume rounds to less than 0.1 million cubic feet. Columns and rows may not add to their totals due to rounding.

Table 26--Average annual mortality of all live trees on forest land by forest type group and stand-size class, Montana, cycle 2, 2003-2009.

(In million cubic feet)

Forest-type group	Stand-size class					All size classes
	Large diameter	Medium diameter	Small diameter	Chaparral	Non stocked	
Pinyon / juniper group	1.3	0.0	0.1	--	--	1.4
Douglas-fir group	107.2	15.6	5.8	--	--	128.5
Ponderosa pine group	17.9	1.4	1.1	--	--	20.4
Fir / spruce / mountain hemlock group	130.0	17.6	23.1	--	--	170.8
Lodgepole pine group	37.1	52.4	40.0	--	--	129.6
Hemlock / Sitka spruce group	2.4	0.1	--	--	--	2.5
Western larch group	21.8	0.4	19.0	--	--	41.2
Other western softwoods group	23.7	2.8	0.5	--	--	27.0
Elm / ash / cottonwood group	0.4	0.1	--	--	--	0.5
Aspen / birch group	0.1	1.4	32.9	--	--	34.4
Woodland hardwoods group	--	--	0.5	--	--	0.5
Nonstocked	--	--	--	--	189.7	189.7
All forest-type groups	341.8	91.8	123.1	--	189.7	746.3

All table cells without observations in the inventory sample are indicated by --. Table value of 0.0 indicates the volume rounds to less than 0.1 million cubic feet. Columns and rows may not add to their totals due to rounding.

Table 27--Table 26--Average annual mortality of all live trees on forest land by species group and ownership group, Montana, cycle 2, 2003-2009.

(In million cubic feet)

Species group	Ownership group				All owners
	Forest Service	Other Federal	State and local government	Undifferentiated private	
Softwood species groups					
Western softwood species groups					
Douglas-fir	122.3	15.3	6.2	17.3	161.0
Ponderosa and Jeffrey pines	8.1	4.1	4.4	13.1	29.7
True fir	110.3	22.0	1.1	5.1	138.5
Western white pine	1.2	0.0	--	--	1.2
Engelmann and other spruces	55.8	17.1	0.1	0.8	73.8
Western larch	4.8	10.0	0.5	2.6	17.9
Lodgepole pine	217.7	13.8	4.7	16.4	252.6
Western redcedar	0.1	0.8	--	0.1	1.1
Western woodland softwoods	0.7	0.3	0.1	0.8	1.8
Other western softwoods	56.7	3.7	0.9	1.1	62.4
All softwoods	577.6	87.2	17.9	57.3	740.0
Hardwood species groups					
Western hardwood species groups					
Cottonwood and aspen	0.4	2.8	0.5	1.4	5.1
Other western hardwoods	--	1.1	0.0	0.1	1.3
All hardwoods	0.4	3.9	0.5	1.5	6.3
All species groups	578.0	91.1	18.4	58.8	746.3

All table cells without observations in the inventory sample are indicated by --. Table value of 0.0 indicates the volume rounds to less than 0.1 million cubic feet. Columns and rows may not add to their totals due to rounding.

Table 28—Average annual mortality of growing-stock trees on timberland by species group and ownership group, Montana, cycle 2, 2003-2009.
(In million cubic feet)

Species group	Ownership group				All owners
	Forest Service	Other Federal	State and local government	Undifferentiated private	
Softwood species groups					
Western softwood species groups					
Douglas-fir	90.8	2.9	6.1	15.4	115.2
Ponderosa and Jeffrey pines	6.4	3.0	4.4	12.8	26.6
True fir	75.9	1.0	1.0	4.1	82.0
Western white pine	1.2	--	--	--	1.2
Engelmann and other spruces	42.1	0.0	0.1	0.7	42.9
Western larch	3.4	--	0.5	2.6	6.5
Lodgepole pine	164.5	8.0	4.7	9.6	186.8
Western redcedar	0.1	--	--	--	0.1
Other western softwoods	24.7	2.2	0.8	0.9	28.6
All softwoods	409.1	17.2	17.5	46.1	489.9
Hardwood species groups					
Western hardwood species groups					
Cottonwood and aspen	0.4	0.1	0.5	1.2	2.2
Other western hardwoods	--	--	0.0	0.0	0.1
All hardwoods	0.4	0.1	0.5	1.2	2.2
All species groups	409.5	17.3	18.1	47.3	492.1

All table cells without observations in the inventory sample are indicated by --. Table value of 0.0 indicates the volume rounds to less than 0.1 million cubic feet. Columns and rows may not add to their totals due to rounding.

Table 29a—Aboveground dry weight (regional equations method) of all live trees by owner class and forest land status, Montana, cycle 2, 2003-2009.
(In thousand dry tons)

Owner class	Unreserved forests			Reserved forests			All forest land
	Timberland	Unproductive	Total	Productive	Unproductive	Total	
Forest Service							
National Forest	534,178	9,343	543,522	95,971	1,738	97,709	641,231
Other Federal							
National Park Service	--	--	--	30,221	283	30,503	30,503
Bureau of Land Management	25,138	2,336	27,474	1,013	287	1,300	28,773
Fish and Wildlife Service	--	--	--	1,118	776	1,894	1,894
Other Federal	--	--	--	350	--	350	350
State and local government							
State	26,460	561	27,021	--	--	--	27,021
Local (county, municipal, etc.)	50	--	50	--	--	--	50
Private							
Undifferentiated private	128,750	6,072	134,822	5,786	--	5,786	140,608
All owners	714,576	18,312	732,888	134,459	3,084	137,543	870,430

All table cells without observations in the inventory sample are indicated by --. Table value of 0 indicates the aboveground tree biomass rounds to less than 1 thousand dry tons. Columns and rows may not add to their totals due to rounding.

Table 29b—Aboveground dry weight (component ratio method) of all live trees by owner class and forest land status, Montana, cycle 2, 2003-2009.
(In thousand dry tons)

Owner class	Unreserved forests			Reserved forests			All forest land
	Timberland	Unproductive	Total	Productive	Unproductive	Total	
Forest Service							
National forest	512,024	8,177	520,201	91,351	1,477	92,828	613,029
Other Federal							
National Park Service	--	--	--	28,361	189	28,551	28,551
Bureau of Land Management	23,112	1,974	25,086	793	259	1,051	26,138
Fish and Wildlife Service	--	--	--	893	619	1,512	1,512
Other Federal	--	--	--	327	--	327	327
State and local government							
State	25,053	428	25,480	--	--	--	25,480
Local (county, municipal, etc.)	37	--	37	--	--	--	37
Private							
Undifferentiated private	117,865	5,286	123,151	5,432	--	5,432	128,583
All owners	678,090	15,865	693,955	127,157	2,545	129,702	823,657

All table cells without observations in the inventory sample are indicated by --. Table value of 0 indicates the aboveground tree biomass rounds to less than 1 thousand dry tons. Columns and rows may not add to their totals due to rounding.

USDA Forest Service Resour. Bull. RMRS-RB-15. 2012

117

Table 30a—Aboveground dry weight (regional equations method) of all live trees on forest land by species group and diameter class, Montana, cycle 2, 2003-2009.
(In thousand dry tons)

Species group	Diameter class (inches)															All classes
	1.0-2.9	3.0-4.9	5.0-6.9	7.0-8.9	9.0-10.9	11.0-12.9	13.0-14.9	15.0-16.9	17.0-18.9	19.0-20.9	21.0-22.9	23.0-24.9	25.0-26.9	27.0-28.9	29.0+	
Softwood species groups																
Western softwood species groups																
Douglas-fir	6,015	12,708	17,476	26,893	33,690	34,344	33,056	28,512	23,759	16,493	12,643	9,578	6,069	3,408	9,102	273,746
Ponderosa and Jeffrey pine	1,738	2,957	3,813	5,188	7,149	7,815	9,082	7,818	6,506	4,852	3,252	2,824	1,777	1,103	3,317	69,191
True fir	9,011	12,527	16,222	15,656	14,374	11,713	8,269	5,854	4,107	1,879	1,645	1,223	652	276	276	103,685
Western hemlock	180	228	377	496	618	550	565	989	233	428	98	100	--	--	548	5,655
Western white pine	30	83	83	150	152	265	159	167	49	131	--	--	159	138	174	1,839
Engelmann and other spruces	2,200	3,941	5,576	7,957	9,084	10,279	10,263	8,844	8,214	7,207	5,047	4,305	3,929	2,768	5,969	95,584
Western larch	598	1,285	2,415	4,713	6,033	6,697	6,486	5,275	4,107	3,847	3,552	2,639	2,868	2,801	5,828	59,141
Lodgepole pine	4,629	12,257	34,667	45,553	39,686	27,218	15,196	7,041	3,049	1,062	616	76	--	89	--	191,139
Western redcedar	762	849	964	956	857	771	1,023	658	562	455	630	246	442	76	645	9,894
Western woodland softwoods	439	895	886	992	992	818	594	582	204	162	114	123	30	93	23	6,947
Other western softwoods	1,587	3,068	4,839	5,856	6,752	6,324	4,565	2,711	2,248	1,399	933	550	201	231	264	41,529
All softwoods	27,188	50,797	87,318	114,410	119,387	106,794	89,260	68,451	53,036	37,916	28,531	21,664	16,127	11,327	26,147	858,350
Hardwood species groups																
Western hardwood species groups																
Cottonwood and aspen	282	466	800	1,154	1,211	1,267	1,230	486	621	788	648	214	85	293	306	9,851
Red alder	--	--	17	4	--	15	--	--	--	--	--	--	--	--	--	37
Other western hardwoods	53	93	302	467	326	187	215	97	151	94	--	73	--	--	--	2,058
Western woodland hardwoods	10	53	45	23	5	--	--	--	--	--	--	--	--	--	--	135
All hardwoods	344	612	1,164	1,648	1,542	1,470	1,445	583	772	883	648	287	85	293	306	12,081
All species groups	27,532	51,409	88,482	116,058	120,928	108,263	90,705	69,034	53,808	38,798	29,178	21,951	16,212	11,619	26,452	870,430

All table cells without observations in the inventory sample are indicated by --. Table value of 0 indicates the aboveground tree biomass rounds to less than 1 thousand dry tons. Columns and rows may not add to their totals due to rounding.

USDA Forest Service Resour. Bull. RMRS-RB-15. 2012

Table 30b--Aboveground dry weight (component ratio method) of all live trees on forest land by species group and diameter class, Montana, cycle 2, 2003-2009.

(In thousand dry tons)

| Species group | Diameter class (inches) | | | | | | | | | | | | | | All classes |
	1.0-2.9	3.0-4.9	5.0-6.9	7.0-8.9	9.0-10.9	11.0-12.9	13.0-14.9	15.0-16.9	17.0-18.9	19.0-20.9	21.0-22.9	23.0-24.9	25.0-26.9	27.0-28.9	29.0+	
Softwood species groups																
Western softwood species groups																
Douglas-fir	2,900	8,299	15,058	25,216	32,868	34,151	33,332	28,848	24,136	16,747	12,823	9,730	6,071	3,433	9,285	262,896
Ponderosa and Jeffrey pines	577	1,360	2,214	4,695	6,901	7,455	8,494	7,243	5,915	4,372	2,890	2,491	1,489	1,001	2,918	60,015
True fir	3,650	8,056	14,491	14,126	13,219	10,951	7,806	5,538	3,863	1,756	1,456	1,124	671	272	269	87,248
Western hemlock	64	208	316	489	653	595	576	1,082	239	468	112	--	--	349	600	5,750
Western white pine	9	41	65	149	153	257	158	166	48	123	--	96	147	122	160	1,692
Engelmann and other spruces	793	2,191	4,972	7,474	8,816	10,251	10,409	9,118	8,477	7,507	5,309	4,471	4,011	2,774	6,194	92,766
Western larch	352	1,069	2,162	4,648	6,150	6,956	6,749	5,470	4,200	3,990	3,667	2,754	2,752	2,806	5,621	59,346
Lodgepole pine	3,073	12,384	28,518	46,367	40,975	27,436	15,126	7,157	3,052	1,088	611	78	--	89	--	185,955
Western redcedar	496	763	844	839	763	725	967	631	537	432	610	200	416	73	581	8,899
Western woodland softwoods	477	902	581	678	724	617	467	457	171	146	105	113	28	80	17	5,544
Other western softwoods	553	1,682	3,703	6,140	7,365	6,713	4,846	2,976	2,430	1,468	958	588	213	229	271	40,136
All softwoods	12,944	36,955	72,904	110,821	118,608	106,106	88,929	68,686	53,069	38,096	28,541	21,644	15,798	11,230	25,918	810,249
Hardwood species groups																
Western hardwood species groups																
Cottonwood and aspen	508	873	946	1,239	1,245	1,208	1,146	482	578	813	674	227	42	303	284	10,568
Red alder	--	--	21	5	--	14	--	--	--	--	--	--	--	--	--	40
Other western hardwoods	129	223	441	635	399	223	225	78	156	92	--	43	--	--	--	2,643
Western woodland hardwoods	28	109	11	5	3	--	--	--	--	--	--	--	--	--	--	157
All hardwoods	666	1,205	1,419	1,884	1,646	1,445	1,371	560	734	904	674	270	42	303	284	13,408
All species groups	13,610	38,160	74,323	112,705	120,254	107,551	90,300	69,246	53,803	39,000	29,215	21,914	15,839	11,533	26,202	823,657

All table cells without observations in the inventory sample are indicated by --. Table value of 0 indicates the aboveground tree biomass rounds to less than 1 thousand dry tons. Columns and rows may not add to their totals due to rounding.

USDA Forest Service Resour. Bull. RMRS-RB-15. 2012

119

Table 31—Area of accessible forest land by Forest Survey Unit, county and forest land status, Montana, cycle 2, 2003-2009.
(In thousand acres)

Forest Survey Unit and county	Unreserved forests			Reserved forests			All forest land
	Timberland	Unproductive	Total	Productive	Unproductive	Total	
Northwestern							
Flathead	1,694.8	- -	1,694.8	1,066.5	11.4	1,078.0	2,772.8
Lake	463.7	16.7	480.4	71.4	- -	71.4	551.8
Lincoln	2,139.4	- -	2,139.4	20.3	8.9	29.2	2,168.6
Sanders	1,355.4	17.9	1,373.3	44.5	- -	44.5	1,417.8
Total	5,653.3	34.6	5,687.9	1,202.8	20.3	1,223.1	6,911.0
Eastern							
Big Horn	222.6	34.9	257.4	45.4	9.2	54.6	312.0
Blaine	91.8	8.7	100.4	52.2	19.6	71.7	172.2
Carbon	132.1	104.0	236.2	58.0	16.6	74.6	310.7
Carter	120.1	4.9	125.0	- -	- -	- -	125.0
Chouteau	48.8	8.5	57.3	- -	- -	- -	57.3
Custer	123.0	56.4	179.4	- -	- -	- -	179.4
Dawson	- -	22.3	22.3	- -	- -	- -	22.3
Fergus	454.7	42.7	497.3	27.1	36.1	63.1	560.4
Garfield	123.1	16.0	139.1	25.6	17.0	42.6	181.7
Glacier	132.8	59.6	192.4	206.5	19.5	226.0	418.4
Golden Valley	63.5	8.2	71.7	- -	- -	- -	71.7
Hill	26.2	- -	26.2	8.9	- -	8.9	35.0
Liberty	2.2	8.7	10.8	- -	- -	- -	10.8
McCone	2.7	- -	2.7	- -	- -	- -	2.7
Musselshell	227.2	81.1	308.2	- -	- -	- -	308.2
Petroleum	58.7	40.5	99.2	17.9	- -	17.9	117.0
Phillips	58.2	- -	58.2	33.3	53.9	87.2	145.4
Pondera	94.6	- -	94.6	6.5	- -	6.5	101.1
Powder River	439.2	66.1	505.3	- -	- -	- -	505.3
Prairie	- -	14.5	14.5	- -	- -	- -	14.5
Richland	17.1	8.6	25.7	- -	- -	- -	25.7
Roosevelt	6.7	2.2	8.9	- -	- -	- -	8.9
Rosebud	272.7	103.3	375.9	- -	- -	- -	375.9
Stillwater	137.0	32.6	169.6	63.0	- -	63.0	232.5
Sweet Grass	265.5	88.6	354.0	38.9	13.2	52.2	406.2
Teton	119.5	20.1	139.6	112.3	- -	112.3	251.9
Toole	8.7	- -	8.7	- -	- -	- -	8.7
Treasure	71.5	5.1	76.6	- -	- -	- -	76.6
Valley	13.8	8.5	22.4	- -	17.1	17.1	39.5
Yellowstone	143.2	45.6	188.8	- -	- -	- -	188.8
Total	3,477.1	891.5	4,368.6	695.3	202.2	897.5	5,266.0

(Table 31 continued on next page)

USDA Forest Service Resour. Bull. RMRS-RB-15. 2012

(Table 31 continued)

Forest Survey Unit and county	Unreserved forests			Reserved forests			All forest land
	Timberland	Unproductive	Total	Productive	Unproductive	Total	
Western							
Granite	778.9	31.2	810.0	35.6	--	35.6	845.6
Mineral	735.6	--	735.6	--	--	--	735.6
Missoula	1,264.3	2.3	1,266.6	121.1	8.8	130.0	1,396.6
Ravalli	991.1	26.5	1,017.7	208.3	--	208.3	1,225.9
Total	3,769.9	60.1	3,829.9	365.0	8.8	373.8	4,203.7
West Central							
Broadwater	224.9	52.4	277.3	--	--	--	277.3
Cascade	313.8	14.5	328.3	--	--	--	328.3
Jefferson	581.5	44.4	625.9	--	--	--	625.9
Judith Basin	252.4	48.4	300.8	--	--	--	300.8
Lewis and Clark	870.5	70.4	940.9	444.5	17.9	462.4	1,403.3
Meagher	640.4	44.2	684.6	--	--	--	684.6
Powell	689.5	18.2	707.7	254.7	6.8	261.5	969.2
Wheatland	51.5	24.6	76.2	--	--	--	76.2
Total	3,624.6	317.2	3,941.8	699.2	24.7	723.9	4,665.7
Southwestern							
Beaverhead	1,165.2	80.2	1,245.4	16.5	--	16.5	1,261.9
Deer Lodge	220.3	32.6	252.9	34.7	8.7	43.4	296.3
Gallatin	684.6	52.0	736.6	131.7	--	131.7	868.4
Madison	639.1	84.2	723.3	120.5	--	120.5	843.8
Park	391.4	75.3	466.7	525.7	25.5	551.1	1,017.8
Silver Bow	249.1	7.0	256.0	--	--	--	256.0
Total	3,349.7	331.3	3,681.0	829.1	34.1	863.3	4,544.3
All counties	19,874.5	1,634.7	21,509.1	3,791.5	290.2	4,081.7	25,590.8

All table cells without observations in the inventory sample are indicated by --. Table value of 0.0 indicates the acres round to less than 0.1 thousand acres. Columns and rows may not add to their totals due to rounding.

Table 32--Area of accessible forest land by Forest Survey Unit, county, ownership group and forest land status, Montana, cycle 2, 2003-2009.

(In thousand acres)

Forest Survey Unit and county	Forest Service		Other Federal		State and local government		Undifferentiated private		All forest land
	Timber-land	Other forest land	Timber-land	Other forest land	Timber-land	Other forest land	Timber-land	Other forest land	
Northwestern									
Flathead	1,121.9	558.2	- -	519.7	154.8	- -	418.1	- -	2,772.8
Lake	157.4	16.7	- -	- -	41.2	- -	265.1	71.4	551.8
Lincoln	1,720.5	29.2	- -	- -	42.3	- -	376.6	- -	2,168.6
Sanders	854.9	44.4	- -	9.0	62.2	- -	438.3	9.0	1,417.8
Total	3,854.7	648.6	- -	528.7	300.5	- -	1,498.1	80.4	6,911.0

(Table 32 continued on next page)

(Table 32 continued)

Forest Survey Unit and county	Forest Service		Other Federal		State and local government		Undifferentiated private		All forest land
	Timber-land	Other forest land	Timber-land	Other forest land	Timber-land	Other forest land	Timber-land	Other forest land	
Eastern									
Big Horn	--	--	--	--	33.2	2.3	189.4	87.2	312.0
Blaine	--	--	8.7	71.7	--	--	83.1	8.7	172.2
Carbon	78.0	66.3	26.8	78.7	8.9	--	18.5	33.6	310.7
Carter	74.0	--	--	--	--	--	46.1	4.9	125.0
Chouteau	19.3	--	--	--	1.9	--	27.6	8.5	57.3
Custer	--	--	18.0	9.0	11.3	--	93.7	47.4	179.4
Dawson	--	--	--	7.2	--	4.3	--	10.8	22.3
Fergus	74.2	9.0	106.2	72.1	16.8	--	257.4	24.7	560.4
Garfield	--	--	71.2	49.0	8.5	1.1	43.3	8.5	181.7
Glacier	33.9	--	--	226.0	--	--	98.8	59.6	418.4
Golden Valley	8.2	--	--	--	--	--	55.3	8.2	71.7
Hill	--	--	--	--	--	--	26.2	8.9	35.0
Liberty	--	--	--	8.7	--	--	2.2	--	10.8
McCone	--	--	--	--	--	--	2.7	--	2.7
Musselshell	--	--	21.6	44.5	--	14.0	205.5	67.1	308.2
Petroleum	--	--	34.2	87.2	6.7	4.9	17.9	8.9	117.0
Phillips	--	--	8.6	--	--	--	49.6	--	145.4
Pondera	86.0	6.5	--	--	--	--	8.6	--	101.1
Powder River	241.9	10.7	26.7	44.2	15.1	--	155.4	11.2	505.3
Prairie	--	--	--	14.5	--	--	--	--	14.5
Richland	--	--	--	--	8.6	2.1	8.6	6.4	25.7
Roosevelt	--	--	--	--	--	--	6.7	2.2	8.9
Rosebud	61.5	23.3	28.0	10.5	15.5	23.3	167.7	46.2	375.9
Stillwater	47.1	68.9	--	--	7.9	--	82.0	26.7	232.5
Sweet Grass	167.9	78.6	13.2	--	--	--	84.3	62.1	406.2
Teton	93.9	121.7	9.4	--	--	9.4	16.2	1.3	251.9
Toole	--	--	8.7	--	--	--	--	--	8.7
Treasure	--	--	--	--	2.5	--	69.0	5.1	76.6
Valley	--	--	--	25.6	--	--	13.8	--	39.5
Yellowstone	--	--	15.6	9.1	--	--	127.6	36.5	188.8
Total	985.9	384.9	397.1	758.0	137.0	61.5	1,957.0	584.6	5,266.0

(Table 32 continued on next page)

(Table 32 continued)

Forest Survey Unit and county	Forest Service		Other Federal		State and local government		Undifferentiated private		All forest land
	Timber-land	Other forest land	Timber-land	Other forest land	Timber-land	Other forest land	Timber-land	Other forest land	
Western									
Granite	519.0	66.8	26.8	--	42.3	--	190.7	--	845.6
Mineral	637.0	--	--	--	17.9	--	80.6	--	735.6
Missoula	574.6	99.1	17.6	--	133.4	--	538.6	33.2	1,396.6
Ravalli	837.8	225.4	--	--	25.8	--	127.5	9.4	1,225.9
Total	2,568.4	391.3	44.4	--	219.5	--	937.5	42.6	4,203.7
West Central									
Broadwater	149.8	--	18.1	8.4	--	--	57.0	44.0	277.3
Cascade	199.1	12.3	8.7	--	10.1	--	95.9	2.2	328.3
Jefferson	412.1	18.7	60.0	--	7.0	9.4	102.3	16.4	625.9
Judith Basin	232.0	40.1	--	--	--	8.4	20.4	--	300.8
Lewis and Clark	475.4	516.0	35.3	--	37.5	--	322.3	16.8	1,403.3
Meagher	435.2	19.2	--	--	17.5	--	187.7	25.0	684.6
Powell	337.5	279.8	70.7	--	29.7	--	251.6	--	969.2
Wheatland	35.8	17.9	--	--	--	--	15.7	6.7	76.2
Total	2,276.9	904.0	192.8	8.4	101.9	17.8	1,053.0	111.0	4,665.7
Southwestern									
Beaverhead	1,003.9	68.9	107.4	23.9	12.7	3.9	41.1	--	1,261.9
Deer Lodge	141.7	69.4	8.7	--	32.3	--	37.7	6.5	296.3
Gallatin	528.3	56.8	--	77.5	--	6.3	156.3	43.3	868.4
Madison	461.4	136.8	80.4	16.2	9.3	--	87.9	51.8	843.8
Park	236.8	499.6	--	70.5	19.0	13.8	135.6	42.5	1,017.8
Silver Bow	181.5	--	20.9	--	3.5	--	43.2	7.0	256.0
Total	2,553.7	831.4	217.4	188.1	76.7	23.9	501.9	151.1	4,544.3
All counties	12,239.6	3,160.3	851.6	1,483.2	835.7	103.1	5,947.5	969.7	25,590.8

All table cells without observations in the inventory sample are indicated by --. Table value of 0.0 indicates the acres round to less than 0.1 thousand acres. Columns and rows may not add to their totals due to rounding.

Table 33–Area of timberland by Forest Survey Unit, county, and stand-class, Montana, cycle 2, 2003-2009.

(In thousand acres)

Forest Survey Unit and county	Large diameter	Medium diameter	Stand-size class Small diameter	Chaparral	Nonstocked	All size classes
Northwestern						
Flathead	917.8	257.8	426.0	--	93.3	1,694.8
Lake	257.7	86.6	107.0	--	12.3	463.7
Lincoln	1,233.8	375.8	483.0	--	46.8	2,139.4
Sanders	858.2	169.9	276.0	--	51.3	1,355.4
Total	3,267.5	890.1	1,292.0	--	203.6	5,653.3
Eastern						
Big Horn	114.1	26.9	33.9	--	47.6	222.6
Blaine	21.7	34.8	8.7	--	26.5	91.8
Carbon	84.2	15.6	32.3	--	--	132.1
Carter	81.8	4.3	10.6	--	23.4	120.1
Chouteau	25.3	15.0	--	--	8.5	48.8
Custer	55.4	--	29.3	--	38.4	123.0
Fergus	279.9	94.9	51.1	--	28.8	454.7
Garfield	42.6	21.2	10.6	--	48.6	123.1
Glacier	30.7	26.0	67.6	--	8.5	132.8
Golden Valley	36.4	8.2	19.0	--	--	63.5
Hill	17.4	8.7	--	--	--	26.2
Liberty	--	--	2.2	--	--	2.2
McCone	--	--	--	--	2.7	2.7
Musselshell	95.4	26.5	48.1	--	57.1	227.2
Petroleum	25.2	11.2	8.9	--	13.4	58.7
Phillips	22.3	8.6	6.5	--	20.8	58.2
Pondera	51.6	17.2	25.8	--	--	94.6
Powder River	256.6	43.8	68.3	--	70.5	439.2
Richland	8.6	8.6	--	--	--	17.1
Roosevelt	6.7	--	--	--	--	6.7
Rosebud	112.8	2.5	45.8	--	111.6	272.7
Stillwater	94.4	15.9	19.6	--	7.0	137.0
Sweet Grass	176.1	41.7	15.8	--	31.8	265.5
Teton	25.9	40.6	43.6	--	9.4	119.5
Toole	8.7	--	--	--	--	8.7
Treasure	53.1	--	4.8	--	13.6	71.5
Valley	13.8	--	--	--	--	13.8
Yellowstone	65.8	25.1	16.0	--	36.5	143.2
Total	1,806.7	496.9	568.5	--	605.0	3,477.1

(Table 33 continued on next page)

(Table 33 continued)

Forest Survey Unit and county	Stand-size class					All size classes
	Large diameter	Medium diameter	Small diameter	Chaparral	Nonstocked	
Western						
Granite	414.5	185.1	135.5	--	43.7	778.9
Mineral	503.8	60.6	126.3	--	44.9	735.6
Missoula	644.6	160.8	358.9	--	100.0	1,264.3
Ravalli	643.1	150.3	156.6	--	41.2	991.1
Total	2,206.0	556.8	777.3	--	229.8	3,769.9
West Central						
Broadwater	133.1	47.1	15.7	--	29.1	224.9
Cascade	179.9	63.3	65.9	--	4.7	313.8
Jefferson	361.4	154.7	56.0	--	9.3	581.5
Judith Basin	92.8	92.1	59.0	--	8.4	252.4
Lewis and Clark	493.1	167.5	138.8	--	71.0	870.5
Meagher	419.4	150.4	66.2	--	4.3	640.4
Powell	324.2	203.2	125.4	--	36.7	689.5
Wheatland	42.6	--	9.0	--	--	51.5
Total	2,046.4	878.5	536.1	--	163.6	3,624.6
Southwestern						
Beaverhead	573.5	441.6	99.9	--	50.2	1,165.2
Deer Lodge	82.1	41.3	96.9	--	--	220.3
Gallatin	430.2	92.1	96.2	--	66.1	684.6
Madison	433.5	126.8	61.0	--	17.7	639.1
Park	261.6	34.8	63.1	--	32.0	391.4
Silver Bow	158.2	53.0	29.4	--	8.4	249.1
Total	1,939.2	789.6	446.6	--	174.3	3,349.7
All counties	11,265.9	3,611.8	3,620.5	--	1,376.3	19,874.5

All table cells without observations in the inventory sample are indicated by --. Table value of 0.0 indicates the acres round to less than 0.1 thousand acres. Columns and rows may not add to their totals due to rounding.

Table 34--Area of timberland by Forest Survey Unit, county, and stocking class, Montana, cycle 2, 2003-2009.

(In thousand acres)

| Forest Survey Unit and county | | Stocking class of growing-stock trees | | | | |
	Nonstocked	Poorly stocked	Moderately stocked	Fully stocked	Over-stocked	All classes
Northwestern						
Flathead	98.8	357.2	750.9	421.7	66.2	1,694.8
Lake	12.3	134.0	213.6	95.6	8.2	463.7
Lincoln	47.8	537.3	778.3	710.9	65.0	2,139.4
Sanders	60.1	409.8	608.8	257.8	18.8	1,355.4
Total	219.1	1,438.3	2,351.7	1,486.0	158.2	5,653.3
Eastern						
Big Horn	54.6	92.4	53.2	22.4	--	222.6
Blaine	26.5	47.8	17.4	--	--	91.8
Carbon	6.2	32.6	47.6	45.7	--	132.1
Carter	27.6	58.8	25.1	8.5	--	120.1
Chouteau	8.5	12.8	27.6	--	--	48.8
Custer	51.9	27.1	44.1	--	--	123.0
Fergus	28.8	120.6	114.9	187.2	3.2	454.7
Garfield	59.0	47.0	10.6	6.4	--	123.1
Glacier	10.6	30.0	47.3	27.6	17.3	132.8
Golden Valley	--	30.7	24.6	8.2	--	63.5
Hill	--	8.7	--	17.4	--	26.2
Liberty	--	--	--	--	2.2	2.2
McCone	2.7	--	--	--	--	2.7
Musselshell	74.8	103.5	39.3	8.8	0.7	227.2
Petroleum	13.4	26.8	17.9	0.7	--	58.7
Phillips	20.8	32.3	--	5.0	--	58.2
Pondera	--	--	43.0	34.4	17.2	94.6
Powder River	110.4	202.2	86.6	40.0	--	439.2
Richland	--	--	8.6	8.6	--	17.1
Roosevelt	--	--	6.7	--	--	6.7
Rosebud	114.1	88.3	37.7	32.6	--	272.7
Stillwater	7.0	53.9	49.4	26.7	--	137.0
Sweet Grass	41.0	43.0	81.9	81.0	18.6	265.5
Teton	9.4	23.2	18.0	68.9	--	119.5
Toole	--	8.7	--	--	--	8.7
Treasure	13.6	42.2	15.6	--	--	71.5
Valley	--	--	13.8	--	--	13.8
Yellowstone	45.6	56.6	20.5	18.2	2.3	143.2
Total	726.7	1,189.3	851.4	648.2	61.4	3,477.1

(Table 34 continued on next page)

USDA Forest Service Resour. Bull. RMRS-RB-15. 2012

127

(Table 34 continued)

Forest Survey Unit and county	Stocking class of growing-stock trees					All classes
	Nonstocked	Poorly stocked	Moderately stocked	Fully stocked	Over-stocked	
Western						
Granite	43.7	175.9	278.0	260.4	20.9	778.9
Mineral	44.9	132.4	336.3	208.6	13.5	735.6
Missoula	100.0	436.3	488.4	215.7	23.8	1,264.3
Ravalli	43.5	288.7	425.9	214.9	18.1	991.1
Total	232.1	1,033.2	1,528.6	899.7	76.2	3,769.9
West Central						
Broadwater	29.1	34.9	46.0	104.4	10.6	224.9
Cascade	4.7	35.5	143.3	120.1	10.1	313.8
Jefferson	10.1	142.6	229.8	198.9	--	581.5
Judith Basin	8.4	20.4	82.2	124.4	16.9	252.4
Lewis and Clark	71.0	221.7	357.7	184.9	35.2	870.5
Meagher	4.3	177.1	240.6	196.7	21.6	640.4
Powell	36.7	224.8	196.1	204.5	27.4	689.5
Wheatland	--	--	33.6	9.0	9.0	51.5
Total	164.4	857.0	1,329.5	1,142.9	130.7	3,624.6
Southwestern						
Beaverhead	50.2	184.1	500.8	373.5	56.6	1,165.2
Deer Lodge	--	41.2	87.8	82.6	8.7	220.3
Gallatin	68.8	128.6	347.3	132.5	7.4	684.6
Madison	29.2	159.3	195.1	223.1	32.5	639.1
Park	33.0	116.0	139.0	97.2	6.3	391.4
Silver Bow	8.4	95.3	82.8	62.6	--	249.1
Total	189.6	724.4	1,352.8	971.5	111.4	3,349.7
All counties	1,531.8	5,242.4	7,414.0	5,148.3	538.0	19,874.5

All table cells without observations in the inventory sample are indicated by --. Table value of 0.0 indicates the acres round to less than 0.1 thousand acres. Columns and rows may not add to their totals due to rounding.

USDA Forest Service Resour. Bull. RMRS-RB-15. 2012

Table 35—Net volume of growning-stock and sawtimber (International 1/4 inch rule) on timberland by Forest Survey Unit, county, and major species group, Montana, cycle 2, 2003-2009.

| Forest Survey Unit and county | Growing stock (In million cubic feet) | | | | | Sawtimber (In million board feet) | | | | |
| | Major species group | | | | | Major species group | | | | |
	Pine	Other softwoods	Soft hardwoods	Hard hardwoods	All species	Pine	Other softwoods	Soft hardwoods	Hard hardwoods	All species
Northwestern										
Flathead	433.0	2,893.4	22.1	52.6	3,401.1	1,329.9	13,435.7	9.7	187.6	14,962.9
Lake	160.1	693.9	1.7	1.1	856.9	715.5	3,034.8	--	--	3,750.4
Lincoln	916.1	4,353.3	55.1	20.3	5,344.8	3,306.6	20,582.2	237.7	93.5	24,220.0
Sanders	664.8	2,101.1	7.8	1.4	2,775.1	3,057.6	9,706.5	28.7	7.7	12,800.5
Total	2,174.0	10,041.8	86.6	75.4	12,377.9	8,409.7	46,759.2	276.1	288.9	55,733.8
Eastern										
Big Horn	122.2	12.6	5.4	7.0	147.1	457.3	51.6	20.9	20.5	550.2
Blaine	32.3	7.9	5.7	--	46.0	65.5	37.5	--	--	103.0
Carbon	120.4	118.8	1.4	--	240.5	442.0	535.2	1.7	--	978.9
Carter	87.9	--	--	1.2	89.2	370.4	--	--	--	370.4
Chouteau	52.0	23.9	2.8	--	78.7	245.7	111.8	3.8	--	361.3
Custer	49.0	--	--	--	49.0	171.3	--	--	--	171.3
Fergus	349.4	264.2	41.6	--	655.2	1,316.5	935.4	80.8	--	2,332.7
Garfield	28.8	3.2	10.7	--	42.7	77.4	10.6	47.1	--	135.0
Glacier	68.7	71.4	8.3	--	148.4	309.4	298.0	3.6	--	611.0
Golden Valley	22.8	13.7	--	--	36.5	36.2	59.3	--	--	95.5
Hill	49.3	33.2	0.4	--	82.9	132.5	139.6	--	--	272.1
Musselshell	96.1	--	--	--	96.1	262.4	--	--	--	262.4
Petroleum	32.8	--	--	--	32.8	92.2	--	--	--	92.2
Phillips	37.7	--	--	--	37.7	158.5	--	--	--	158.5
Pondera	48.0	120.0	1.4	--	169.4	193.7	436.6	--	--	630.3
Powder River	259.8	--	4.4	--	264.3	1,042.3	--	10.9	--	1,053.2
Richland	--	--	11.0	7.7	18.8	--	--	20.8	20.1	40.9
Roosevelt	--	--	5.4	--	5.4	--	--	17.8	--	17.8
Rosebud	165.4	--	--	0.4	165.8	741.6	--	--	--	741.6
Stillwater	93.6	37.1	1.9	--	132.7	307.9	144.1	1.4	--	453.4
Sweet Grass	142.0	314.3	6.7	11.7	474.8	520.8	1,395.4	20.7	51.3	1,988.2
Teton	43.5	152.1	0.1	0.2	195.8	137.2	620.4	--	--	757.5
Toole	1.5	6.4	0.1	--	8.1	--	24.2	--	--	24.2
Treasure	43.6	--	--	--	43.6	186.2	--	--	--	186.2
Valley	--	--	19.3	0.6	19.8	--	--	101.0	--	101.0
Yellowstone	47.4	--	33.2	--	80.6	150.3	--	171.9	--	322.2
Total	1,994.3	1,178.8	160.0	28.8	3,362.0	7,417.2	4,799.8	502.3	91.8	12,811.1

(Table 35 continued on next page)

(Table 35 continued)

Forest Survey Unit and county	Growing stock					Sawtimber				
	Major species group (In million cubic feet)					Major species group (In million board feet)				
	Pine	Other softwoods	Soft hardwoods	Hard hardwoods	All species	Pine	Other softwoods	Soft hardwoods	Hard hardwoods	All species
Western										
Granite	786.5	726.3	1.1	--	1,513.9	2,442.3	2,970.4	5.9	--	5,418.7
Mineral	324.0	1,459.8	--	6.2	1,789.9	1,504.2	6,866.4	--	34.7	8,405.3
Missoula	512.1	1,508.9	19.8	2.6	2,043.4	2,288.0	6,905.4	67.8	10.9	9,272.1
Ravalli	927.2	1,057.1	0.4	13.8	1,998.6	3,944.9	4,901.7	--	57.9	8,904.5
Total	2,549.8	4,752.2	21.2	22.6	7,345.8	10,179.5	21,643.9	73.7	103.5	32,000.7
West Central										
Broadwater	129.0	351.3	--	--	480.3	359.4	1,537.3	--	--	1,896.7
Cascade	235.2	225.5	4.8	--	465.6	757.4	921.1	19.4	--	1,697.8
Jefferson	599.3	521.6	2.6	--	1,123.5	1,651.9	2,204.8	3.5	--	3,860.3
Judith Basin	157.5	281.0	--	--	438.6	423.6	990.8	--	--	1,414.4
Lewis and Clark	514.9	594.9	16.7	14.8	1,141.2	1,911.8	2,339.2	6.8	77.2	4,334.9
Meagher	668.0	579.6	4.6	--	1,252.2	2,361.8	2,505.1	--	--	4,866.9
Powell	461.7	667.7	13.1	15.5	1,158.1	1,663.2	2,612.3	21.3	81.0	4,377.8
Wheatland	29.0	73.2	--	--	102.1	115.9	327.1	--	--	443.0
Total	2,794.7	3,294.8	41.9	30.3	6,161.7	9,245.1	13,437.7	50.9	158.2	22,891.8
Southwestern										
Beaverhead	1,616.3	1,009.7	1.0	--	2,627.0	4,909.4	4,212.2	--	--	9,121.6
Deer Lodge	235.0	75.0	1.5	--	311.5	636.5	286.7	--	--	923.3
Gallatin	469.8	957.7	--	--	1,427.5	1,572.7	4,623.3	--	--	6,196.0
Madison	539.7	805.4	4.5	--	1,349.6	1,980.8	3,449.8	2.9	--	5,433.4
Park	178.9	462.8	13.8	--	655.5	598.8	2,088.0	59.1	--	2,746.0
Silver Bow	241.9	192.9	8.0	--	442.8	792.6	836.8	8.4	--	1,637.8
Total	3,281.6	3,503.4	28.8	--	6,813.9	10,490.9	15,496.9	70.4	--	26,058.1
All counties	12,794.4	22,771.0	338.6	157.2	36,061.2	45,742.4	102,137.4	973.3	642.5	149,495.6

All table cells without observations in the inventory sample are indicated by --. Table value of 0.0 indicates the volume rounds to less than 0.1 million cubic or board feet. Columns and rows may not add to their totals due to rounding.

Table 36--Average annual net growth of growning-stock and sawtimber (International 1/4 inch rule) on timberland by Forest Survey Unit, county, and major species group, Montana, cycle 2, 2003-2009.

Forest Survey Unit and county	Growing stock Major species group (In million cubic feet)					Sawtimber Major species group (In million board feet)				
	Pine	Other softwoods	Soft hardwoods	Hard hardwoods	All species	Pine	Other softwoods	Soft hardwoods	Hard hardwoods	All species
Northwestern										
Flathead	9.7	23.0	1.4	1.9	36.0	21.0	142.5	0.2	9.6	173.4
Lake	2.8	15.4	0.2	0.2	18.6	19.3	90.2	--	--	109.5
Lincoln	25.5	96.6	1.2	0.7	124.0	134.1	486.6	8.9	2.4	632.0
Sanders	1.0	43.3	0.2	0.0	44.5	29.2	250.9	0.8	0.0	280.8
Total	39.0	178.3	3.1	2.7	223.1	203.6	970.2	9.9	12.1	1,195.7
Eastern										
Big Horn	1.8	0.3	0.1	0.1	2.3	9.3	1.4	0.2	0.4	11.3
Blaine	1.1	0.2	0.3	--	1.6	4.4	1.2	--	--	5.5
Carbon	-1.0	1.1	0.0	--	0.1	11.9	6.6	0.0	--	18.5
Carter	1.7	--	--	0.1	1.7	11.2	--	--	--	11.2
Chouteau	0.5	0.6	0.0	--	1.1	5.3	2.5	0.1	--	7.9
Custer	1.2	--	--	--	1.2	5.6	--	--	--	5.6
Fergus	2.8	7.0	0.6	--	10.4	24.2	33.5	-0.8	--	56.9
Garfield	-2.6	0.2	0.2	--	-2.2	-4.2	1.0	0.8	--	-2.4
Glacier	-0.2	0.5	0.4	--	0.7	5.5	0.3	0.0	--	5.9
Golden Valley	0.5	0.3	--	--	0.8	4.3	1.4	--	--	5.8
Hill	1.1	0.6	0.0	--	1.7	3.4	6.0	--	--	9.3
Musselshell	2.2	--	--	--	2.2	7.9	--	--	--	7.9
Petroleum	0.6	--	--	--	0.6	2.7	--	--	--	2.7
Phillips	1.0	--	--	--	1.0	3.8	--	--	--	3.8
Pondera	0.6	2.1	0.2	--	2.9	3.0	11.8	--	--	14.8
Powder River	5.7	--	0.2	--	5.9	35.1	--	0.3	--	35.4
Richland	--	--	0.4	0.1	0.5	--	--	8.3	0.2	8.5
Roosevelt	--	--	0.1	--	0.1	--	--	0.2	--	0.2
Rosebud	2.4	--	--	0.0	2.4	16.9	--	--	--	16.9
Stillwater	1.5	0.9	0.0	--	2.4	12.7	5.0	0.0	--	17.7
Sweet Grass	0.9	3.6	0.4	0.4	5.3	7.9	40.8	0.6	1.8	51.0
Teton	0.9	3.2	0.0	0.0	4.1	19.0	11.6	--	--	30.6
Tode	0.0	0.1	0.0	--	0.2	--	0.4	--	--	0.4
Treasure	0.6	--	--	--	0.6	4.3	--	--	--	4.3
Valley	--	--	0.3	0.0	0.3	--	--	1.5	--	1.5
Yellowstone	0.1	--	0.2	--	0.3	3.1	--	1.1	--	4.2
Total	23.5	20.6	3.2	0.7	48.1	197.3	123.4	12.4	2.3	335.3

(Table 36 continued on next page)

USDA Forest Service Resour. Bull. RMRS-RB-15. 2012

131

(Table 36 con inued)

Forest Survey Unit and county	Growing stock					Sawtimber				
	Major species group					Major species group				
	(In million cubic feet)					(In million board feet)				
	Pine	Other softwoods	Soft hardwoods	Hard hardwoods	All species	Pine	Other softwoods	Soft hardwoods	Hard hardwoods	All species
Western										
Granite	8.2	-5.5	0.0	--	2.7	73.3	-15.2	0.1	--	58.2
Mineral	-12.8	20.7	--	0.2	8.1	-20.6	143.4	--	1.3	124.1
Missoula	-3.6	26.7	0.2	0.1	23.4	6.4	156.6	0.9	0.2	164.1
Ravalli	8.2	-18.1	0.0	0.2	-9.7	121.6	-56.5	--	4.3	69.4
Total	0.0	23.8	0.3	0.5	24.5	180.8	228.3	1.0	5.8	415.9
West Central										
Broadwater	2.5	1.2	--	--	3.7	12.0	18.4	--	--	30.4
Cascade	5.3	3.1	0.1	--	8.6	28.2	16.1	0.1	--	44.4
Jefferson	-12.3	8.4	0.1	--	-3.8	-23.7	49.6	0.1	--	26.0
Judith Basin	3.2	1.8	--	--	5.0	15.3	5.0	--	--	20.3
Lewis and Clark	-9.7	2.7	0.1	0.3	-6.7	7.2	22.0	-1.3	1.2	29.1
Meagher	7.4	8.9	0.2	--	16.5	65.2	53.9	--	--	119.1
Powell	0.4	9.8	0.0	0.3	10.5	13.8	45.6	-0.6	1.4	60.2
Wheatland	0.1	1.3	--	--	1.4	0.8	5.7	--	--	6.5
Total	-3.1	37.2	0.5	0.5	35.1	118.8	216.2	-1.7	2.6	336.0
Southwestern										
Beaverhead	8.8	-1.0	-0.2	--	7.6	60.5	22.9	-0.8	--	82.6
Deer Lodge	-0.8	1.9	0.2	--	1.3	8.1	9.7	--	--	17.8
Gallatin	6.8	16.6	--	--	23.4	27.9	109.4	--	--	137.2
Madison	-2.8	2.3	0.2	--	-0.4	-0.3	23.6	0.1	--	23.4
Park	2.1	0.6	0.4	--	3.1	18.0	10.6	1.3	--	29.9
Silver Bow	-7.7	3.2	0.2	--	-4.3	-20.0	14.7	5.1	--	-0.2
Total	6.3	23.5	0.9	--	30.7	94.2	190.9	5.7	--	290.7
All counties	65.7	283.5	7.9	4.4	361.5	794.6	1,729.0	27.2	22.7	2,573.5

All table cells without observations in the inventory sample are indicated by --. Table value of 0.0 indicates the volume rounds to less than 0.1 million cubic or board feet. Columns and rows may not add to their totals due to rounding.

132

USDA Forest Service Resour. Bull. RMRS-RB-15. 2012

Table 37—Sampling errors by Forest Survey Unit and county for area of timberland, volume, average annual net growth, average annual removals, and average annual mortality on timberland, Montana, cycle 2, 2003-2009.

(Sampling error in percent)

Forest Survey Unit and county	Forest area	Timberland area	Growing stock				Sawtimber			
			Volume	Average annual net growth	Average annual removals	Average annual mortality	Volume	Average annual net growth	Average annual removals	Average annual mortality
Northwestern										
Flathead	1.56	4.66	7.83	43.56	--	23.21	9.09	44.39	--	27.02
Lake	3.45	6.12	12.40	15.10	--	25.21	14.18	17.01	--	34.04
Lincoln	1.49	1.69	5.90	6.52	--	20.37	7.21	7.78	--	28.10
Sanders	2.23	2.54	7.49	17.95	--	24.72	8.54	13.39	--	26.64
Total	0.95	1.73	3.83	8.77	--	14.31	4.53	8.41	--	17.53
Eastern										
Big Horn	13.80	17.44	26.81	43.58	--	62.78	30.75	32.05	--	61.67
Blaine	20.83	29.14	42.30	41.37	--	100.00	45.98	37.17	--	--
Carbon	10.92	18.42	27.64	100.00	--	49.28	32.82	87.42	--	64.14
Carter	24.08	24.30	38.23	32.99	--	53.24	40.76	33.11	--	100.00
Chouteau	35.73	38.32	54.22	41.76	--	59.83	60.08	64.90	--	--
Custer	20.81	25.48	40.72	39.11	--	100.00	45.05	38.89	--	--
Dawson	54.48	--	--	--	--	--	--	--	--	--
Fergus	8.00	8.66	11.27	18.01	--	35.23	14.34	17.53	--	41.99
Garfield	19.53	23.77	37.57	91.45	--	59.79	44.95	100.00	--	73.17
Glacier	8.40	22.38	37.00	100.00	--	55.29	42.56	100.00	--	72.12
Golden Valley	30.69	32.59	49.32	54.68	--	63.97	65.98	49.03	--	--
Hill	49.46	57.46	62.05	72.27	--	74.16	62.61	65.04	--	--
Liberty	82.28	100.00	--	--	--	--	--	--	--	--
McCone	100.00	100.00	--	--	--	--	--	--	--	--
Musselshell	12.24	16.05	21.73	38.23	--	52.16	23.61	42.77	--	54.98
Petroleum	24.47	35.88	39.89	50.26	--	60.98	46.12	51.21	--	91.05
Phillips	22.23	36.55	51.24	54.11	--	77.15	57.79	51.13	--	--
Pondera	27.60	28.88	38.21	35.70	--	52.20	42.64	58.29	--	--
Powder River	8.13	9.04	16.09	16.09	--	68.45	19.78	17.42	--	--
Prairie	71.17	--	--	--	--	--	--	--	--	--
Richland	53.58	70.48	71.27	88.82	--	100.00	70.49	97.98	--	--
Roosevelt	78.92	100.00	100.00	100.00	--	--	100.00	100.00	--	--
Rosebud	10.63	13.98	27.13	55.13	--	79.21	28.37	35.01	--	101.42
Stillwater	12.69	21.75	27.37	30.39	--	58.54	30.72	31.45	--	110.89
Sweet Grass	7.87	12.57	17.13	45.67	--	32.68	18.46	35.65	--	50.94
Teton	7.13	21.98	39.77	50.37	--	77.16	52.62	50.15	--	71.85
Toole	100.00	100.00	100.00	100.00	--	--	100.00	100.00	--	--
Treasure	30.08	31.79	44.16	61.02	--	96.97	46.07	71.48	--	100.00
Valley	45.09	72.55	71.61	75.81	--	--	71.73	77.53	--	--
Yellowstone	19.26	22.84	39.27	100.00	--	79.04	46.47	99.49	--	74.56
Total	2.98	4.03	6.40	12.87	--	15.28	7.61	11.35	--	20.62

(Table 37 continued on next page)

USDA Forest Service Resour. Bull. RMRS-RB-15. 2012

133

(Table 37 continued)

Forest Survey Unit and county	Forest area	Timberland area	Growing stock				Sawtimber			
			Volume	Average annual net growth	Average annual removals	Average annual mortality	Volume	Average annual net growth	Average annual removals	Average annual mortality
Western										
Granite	2.75	4.18	8.75	100.00	--	37.58	10.11	97.83	--	40.94
Mineral	2.47	2.47	8.84	100.00	--	25.74	10.47	38.43	--	32.76
Missoula	2.06	3.32	8.84	31.83	--	26.77	10.15	21.05	--	29.56
Ravalli	2.36	4.58	8.82	100.00	--	23.99	10.85	92.23	--	27.48
Total	1.20	1.91	4.44	86.45	--	14.23	5.32	24.99	--	17.16
West Central										
Broadwater	9.91	9.04	18.02	100.00	--	48.58	20.60	56.96	--	58.44
Cascade	9.11	9.77	17.05	21.63	--	57.04	23.00	28.49	--	72.23
Jefferson	4.75	5.46	10.18	100.00	--	27.56	13.25	100.00	--	35.17
Judith Basin	4.98	8.16	16.93	54.07	--	67.24	23.41	73.14	--	73.56
Lewis and Clark	2.53	6.98	11.30	100.00	--	38.75	12.63	100.00	--	43.53
Meagher	4.98	5.57	9.32	18.38	--	24.96	10.89	18.49	--	32.35
Powell	2.81	6.73	12.14	58.25	--	26.26	14.11	47.28	--	31.98
Wheatland	31.65	40.00	52.67	67.66	--	61.86	54.32	58.41	--	70.48
Total	1.73	2.80	4.74	48.46	--	15.90	5.69	20.64	--	16.89
Southwestern										
Beaverhead	3.44	3.97	6.87	100.00	--	29.65	8.23	83.98	--	35.78
Deer Lodge	6.12	11.97	21.14	100.00	--	67.88	22.26	100.00	--	79.25
Gallatin	4.37	6.23	10.24	14.94	--	28.23	11.73	18.51	--	38.75
Madison	4.55	7.09	11.27	100.00	--	29.09	13.40	100.00	--	38.24
Park	3.65	12.25	16.82	100.00	--	51.20	17.71	100.00	--	55.71
Silver Bow	7.35	7.01	14.84	100.00	--	42.58	16.79	100.00	--	53.16
Total	1.82	2.88	4.59	65.27	--	16.50	5.39	33.51	--	20.01
All counties	0.83	1.17	2.08	10.93	--	7.20	2.49	7.47	--	8.76

Sampling errors thas exceed 100% are reported as 100%.

134

USDA Forest Service Resour. Bull. RMRS-RB-15. 2012

Appendix F: Tables of Mean Soil Properties.

Appendix F Table 1a: Mean water, carbon, and nitrogen contents of forest floor and soil cores by forest type, Montana, soil visit 1, 2003-2007.

Appendix F Table 1b: Mean water, carbon, and nitrogen contents of forest floor and soil cores by forest type, Montana, soil visit 2, 2008-2009.

Appendix F Table 2a: Mean physical and chemical properties of soil cores by forest type, Montana, soil visit 1, 2003-2007.

Appendix F Table 2b: Mean physical and chemical properties of soil cores by forest type, Montana, soil visit 2, 2008-2009.

Appendix F Table 3a: Mean exchangeable cation concentrations in soil cores by forest type, Montana, soil visit 1, 2003-2007.

Appendix F Table 3b: Mean exchangeable cation concentrations in soil cores by forest type, Montana, soil visit 2, 2008-2009.

Appendix F Table 3b: Mean exchangeable cation concentrations in soil cores by forest type, Montana, soil visit 2, 2008-2009.

Appendix F Table 4b: Mean extractable trace element concentrations in soil cores by forest type, Montana, soil visit 2, 2008-2009.

USDA Forest Service Resour. Bull. RMRS-RB-15. 2012

135

Appendix F Table 1a—Mean water, carbon, and nitrogen contents of forest floor and soil cores by forest type, Montana, soil visit 1, 2003-2007.

Forest type	Soil layer	Number of plots	Water content[a]	Organic carbon	Inorganic carbon	Total nitrogen	C/N ratio	Forest floor mass[a]	Organic carbon	Total nitrogen
	cm				Percent				Mg/ha	
Rocky Mountain juniper	Forest floor	7	14.37	27.85		0.899	33.1	3.90	1.13	0.038
	0–10	7	12.18	1.55	0.49	0.152	10.2		13.32	1.311
	10–20	7	13.49	1.07	0.42	0.108	9.9		9.97	1.005
Ponderosa pine	Forest floor	34	13.92	29.68		0.860	34.3	13.68	3.93	0.119
	0–10	34	10.72	1.92	0.44	0.151	12.7		15.18	1.191
	10–20	34	10.04	1.20	0.54	0.098	12.3		9.70	0.791
Lodgepole pine	Forest floor	35	36.45	35.41		0.980	37.3	21.45	7.16	0.195
	0–10	35	14.39	3.98	0.21	0.148	26.8		21.20	0.791
	10–20	35	11.48	1.79	0.18	0.077	23.3		10.91	0.469
Douglas fir	Forest floor	66	27.18	33.14		0.996	34.5	27.67	9.11	0.268
	0–10	66	9.94	3.57	0.28	0.175	20.4		18.29	0.896
	10–20	66	8.59	1.93	0.25	0.104	18.5		11.49	0.621
Cottonwood/aspen/birch	Forest floor	7	31.09	29.21		0.971	30.3	8.16	2.28	0.075
	0–10	7	14.78	3.32	0.32	0.221	15.0		14.42	0.962
	10–20	7	9.36	1.38	0.27	0.089	15.5		7.04	0.454
Spruce/fir group[b]	Forest floor	36	55.30	35.58		1.130	32.7	33.02	11.61	0.353
	0–10	36	21.12	4.69	0.26	0.223	21.0		24.38	1.159
	10–20	36	16.85	2.98	0.25	0.158	18.9		18.04	0.956
Western redcedar/larch	Forest floor	6	58.10	30.46		0.736	42.0	52.86	15.81	0.378
	0–10	6	17.74	2.66	0.24	0.106	25.2		18.29	0.727
	10–20	6	18.89	1.70	0.28	0.095	18.0		13.77	0.766
Limber/whitebark pines	Forest floor	13	28.06	35.93		1.069	36.0	17.19	6.32	0.172
	0–10	13	9.40	2.80	0.35	0.149	18.8		16.05	0.853
	10–20	13	8.74	1.99	0.30	0.112	17.7		11.58	0.653

[a]Water content and forest floor mass are reported on an oven-dry weight basis (105 °C).
[b]Spruce/fir group includes Engelmann spruce, subalpine fir, mixed Engelmann spruce/subalpine fir, and grand fir.

Appendix F Table 1b—Mean water, carbon, and nitrogen contents of forest floor and soil cores by forest type, Montana, soil visit 2, 2008-2009.

Forest type	Soil layer	Number of plots	Water content[a]	Organic carbon	Inorganic carbon	Total nitrogen	C/N ratio	Forest floor mass[a]	Organic carbon	Total nitrogen
	cm		. . . . Percent					. . . . Mg/ha		
Rocky Mountain juniper	Forest floor	0								
	0–10	0								
	10–20	0								
Ponderosa pine	Forest floor	4	10.25	23.14		0.806	30.0	7.36	1.51	0.058
	0–10	4	6.11	1.91	0.46	0.160	11.9		15.48	1.298
	10–20	4	9.05	1.13	0.42	0.100	11.2		6.93	0.617
Lodgepole pine	Forest floor	7	33.56	30.46		0.751	41.2	41.83	11.98	0.285
	0–10	7	12.18	2.33	0.07	0.089	26.2		13.81	0.527
	10–20	7	10.88	1.31	0.09	0.066	19.7		8.39	0.425
Douglas fir	Forest floor	12	32.52	32.03		0.966	34.0	45.13	13.53	0.409
	0–10	12	12.83	2.99	0.09	0.146	20.6		12.95	0.630
	10–20	12	9.99	1.93	0.09	0.090	21.6		10.27	0.476
Cottonwood/aspen/birch	Forest floor	1	12.19	21.35		0.597	34.4	9.67	2.35	0.062
	0–10	1	15.96	1.58	0.72	0.105	15.1		16.53	1.095
	10–20	1	12.09	1.52	0.64	0.142	10.7		17.68	1.647
Spruce/fir group[b]	Forest floor	8	42.79	40.32		1.197	34.6	17.61	6.93	0.195
	0–10	8	25.44	9.42	0.29	0.417	22.6		52.82	2.336
	10–20	8	17.56	4.24	0.10	0.204	20.8		29.16	1.403
Western redcedar/larch	Forest floor	1	133.22	45.16		1.125	42.9	70.73	33.68	0.741
	0–10	1	51.76	10.70	0.13	0.356	30.1		35.35	1.175
	10–20	1	18.68	0.74	0.02	0.043	17.4		8.16	0.470
Limber/whitebark pines	Forest floor	4	38.67	34.45		1.026	34.1	25.23	10.34	0.269
	0–10	4	15.54	5.74	0.15	0.260	22.1		38.29	1.736
	10–20	4	15.38	3.97	0.68	0.271	14.6		24.69	1.686

[a]Water content and forest floor mass are reported on an oven-dry weight basis (105 °C).
[b]Spruce/fir group includes Engelmann spruce, subalpine fir, mixed Engelmann spruce/subalpine fir, and grand fir.

Appendix F Table 2a—Mean physical and chemical properties of soil cores by forest type, Montana, soil visit 1, 2003-2007.

Forest type	Soil layer	Number of plots	SQI[a]	Bulk density	Coarse fragments	pH		Bray 1 extractable phosphorus	Olsen extractable phosphorus
	cm		%	g/cm^3	%	H_2O	$CaCl_2$	. . . . . . .mg/kg.	
Rocky Mountain juniper	0–10	7	69	1.06	16.31	7.02	6.50	12.8	7.8
	10–20	7	60	1.45	31.39	7.12	6.63	8.2	2.9
Ponderosa pine	0–10	34	65	1.10	23.52	7.20	6.71	9.8	6.4
	10–20	34	58	1.30	32.44	7.40	6.81	2.5	3.1
Lodgepole pine	0–10	35	62	0.91	36.38	5.17	4.56	47.4	22.0
	10–20	35	56	1.21	43.65	5.37	4.69	29.1	14.8
Douglas fir	0–10	66	71	1.04	42.41	6.15	5.60	40.0	26.0
	10–20	66	64	1.30	47.94	6.27	5.67	31.3	16.1
Cottonwood/aspen/birch	0–10	7	71	0.89	43.16	6.48	5.99	21.2	9.8
	10–20	7	61	1.33	47.09	6.54	5.85	11.2	4.5
Spruce/fir group	0–10	36	64	0.85	34.26	5.37	4.82	18.7	13.1
	10–20	36	61	1.14	41.88	5.57	4.96	13.9	8.1
Western redcedar/larch	0–10	6	61	1.12	32.25	6.04	5.37	19.1	18.2
	10–20	6	59	1.31	32.42	6.14	5.53	11.3	17.0
Limber/whitebark pines	0–10	13	64	1.01	40.58	5.94	5.38	12.0	12.0
	10–20	13	56	1.16	45.12	5.87	5.23	15.3	9.5

[a]SQI = Soil Quality Index.

Appendix F Table 2b—Mean physical and chemical properties of soil cores by forest type, Montana, soil visit 2, 2008-2009.

Forest type	Soil layer	Number of plots	SQI[a]	Bulk density	Coarse fragments	pH		Bray 1 extractable phosphorus	Olsen extractable phosphorus
	cm		%	g/cm^3	%	H_2O	$CaCl_2$	. . . . . . .mg/kg.	
Rocky Mountain juniper	0–10	0							
	10–20	0							
Ponderosa pine	0–10	4	60	1.19	25.52	7.34	6.78	3.5	4.7
	10–20	4	55	1.41	43.41	7.40	6.78	1.2	2.1
Lodgepole pine	0–10	7	56	0.96	34.65	5.49	4.93	15.1	13.0
	10–20	7	53	1.32	49.50	5.82	5.22	15.1	9.4
Douglas fir	0–10	12	69	0.96	47.90	6.12	5.61	27.9	34.1
	10–20	12	64	1.38	53.04	6.08	5.49	27.6	26.6
Cottonwood/aspen/birch	0–10	1	63	1.05	0.27	7.78	7.35	11.3	7.7
	10–20	1	63	1.17	0.27	8.04	7.59	7.3	4.1
Spruce/fir group	0–10	8	69	0.92	26.40	5.24	4.73	24.9	17.2
	10–20	8	61	1.27	37.69	5.23	4.63	20.2	12.1
Western redcedar/larch	0–10	1	85	0.49	32.05	5.58	5.23	39.5	24.4
	10–20	1	44	1.79	38.30	5.81	5.15	16.1	6.6
Limber/whitebark pines	0–10	4	61	0.93	23.55	5.26	4.73	25.7	17.8
	10–20	4	69	1.32	40.21	6.52	6.07	9.4	10.5

[a]SQI = Soil Quality Index.

Appendix F Table 3a—Mean exchangeable cation concentrations in soil cores by forest type, Montana, soil visit 1, 2003-2007.

Forest type	Soil layer	Number of plots	1 M NH₄Cl Exchangeable cations					ECEC
			Na	K	Mg	Ca	Al	
	cm		................mg/kg................					cmolc/kg
Rocky Mountain juniper	0–10	7	73	322	426	2722	2	18.52
	10–20	7	141	291	611	3076	1	21.79
Ponderosa pine	0–10	34	19	222	347	2786	3	18.08
	10–20	34	20	148	308	2802	1	17.78
Lodgepole pine	0–10	35	9	164	88	779	97	6.94
	10–20	35	7	102	72	600	65	5.19
Douglas fir	0–10	66	10	255	187	2226	17	14.11
	10–20	66	5	186	154	1724	21	11.13
Cottonwood/aspen/birch	0–10	7	9	345	337	2597	10	17.32
	10–20	7	3	164	187	1999	7	12.55
Spruce/fir group	0–10	36	6	132	114	1112	111	9.44
	10–20	36	9	130	107	815	87	7.74
Western redcedar/larch	0–10	6	6	94	94	1082	38	7.37
	10–20	6	10	97	63	778	36	5.48
Limber/whitebark pines	0–10	13	9	164	146	1594	95	14.03
	10–20	13	8	124	112	997	125	11.08

Appendix F Table 3b—Mean exchangeable cation concentrations in soil cores by forest type, Montana, soil visit 2, 2008-2009.

Forest type	Soil layer	Number of plots	1 M NH₄Cl Exchangeable cations					ECEC
			Na	K	Mg	Ca	Al	
	cm		................mg/kg................					cmolc/kg
Rocky Mountain juniper	0–10	0						
	10–20	0						
Ponderosa pine	0–10	4	73	274	211	3473	0	21.12
	10–20	4	74	175	252	3027	1	19.43
Lodgepole pine	0–10	7	49	81	46	315	41	3.31
	10–20	7	46	120	55	331	24	4.00
Douglas fir	0–10	12	106	323	176	1774	30	12.62
	10–20	12	108	247	174	1565	54	11.21
Cottonwood/aspen/birch	0–10	1	27	239	276	2779	0	16.86
	10–20	1	34	211	296	2729	0	16.74
Spruce/fir group	0–10	8	68	192	141	2031	118	14.50
	10–20	8	76	69	95	993	78	7.76
Western redcedar/larch	0–10	1	9	254	590	2487	2	17.97
	10–20	1	21	39	123	459	11	3.62
Limber/whitebark pines	0–10	4	87	244	96	1075	103	9.81
	10–20	4	109	155	105	2828	2	16.94

USDA Forest Service Resour. Bull. RMRS-RB-15. 2012

139

Appendix F Table 4a—Mean extractable trace element concentrations in soil cores by forest type, Montana, soil visit 1, 2003-2007.

Forest type	Soil layer	Number of plots	1 M NH₄Cl Extractable							
			Mn	Fe	Ni	Cu	Zn	Cd	Pb	S
	cm		. . . . mg/kg							
Rocky Mountain juniper	0–10	7	2.51	0.22	0.13	0.00	0.24	0.02	0.28	6.5
	10–20	7	1.96	0.12	0.13	0.01	0.00	0.03	0.08	6.6
Ponderosa pine	0–10	34	3.08	0.34	0.02	0.00	0.32	0.04	0.19	4.2
	10–20	34	2.09	0.07	0.01	0.00	0.00	0.03	0.10	6.8
Lodgepole pine	0–10	35	40.40	8.75	0.04	0.14	2.88	0.17	1.38	7.5
	10–20	35	14.05	2.74	0.02	0.01	0.37	0.03	0.26	4.7
Douglas fir	0–10	66	16.94	2.28	0.04	0.00	0.66	0.12	0.32	5.1
	10–20	66	8.71	0.58	0.02	0.01	0.28	0.03	0.20	5.7
Cottonwood/aspen/birch	0–10	7	9.14	0.23	0.00	0.00	0.01	0.08	0.04	10.1
	10–20	7	8.60	0.00	0.00	0.00	0.00	0.02	0.17	5.9
Spruce/fir group	0–10	36	21.98	7.47	0.08	0.01	1.06	0.13	0.60	16.6
	10–20	36	10.29	5.63	0.04	0.00	0.36	0.05	0.23	5.0
Western redcedar/larch	0–10	6	11.92	1.57	0.00	0.00	0.22	0.05	0.30	4.6
	10–20	6	4.57	1.86	0.02	0.00	0.25	0.01	0.34	5.5
Limber/whitebark pines	0–10	13	3.59	6.19	0.01	0.01	1.02	0.10	0.43	5.5
	10–20	13	3.90	8.03	0.00	0.00	0.45	0.04	0.69	5.2

Appendix F Table 4b—Mean extractable trace element concentrations in soil cores by forest type, Montana, soil visit 2, 2008-2009.

Forest type	Soil layer	Number of plots	1 M NH₄Cl Extractable							
			Mn	Fe	Ni	Cu	Zn	Cd	Pb	S
	cm		. . . . mg/kg							
Rocky Mountain juniper	0–10	0								
	10–20	0								
Ponderosa pine	0–10	4	1.69	0.05	0.00	0.00	0.00	0.01	0.06	1.0
	10–20	4	1.47	0.93	0.00	0.00	0.00	0.00	0.32	0.2
Lodgepole pine	0–10	7	21.27	2.39	0.11	0.00	1.67	0.08	0.98	3.9
	10–20	7	9.70	1.49	0.10	0.00	0.75	0.03	0.69	3.7
Douglas fir	0–10	12	21.33	1.01	0.22	0.00	0.59	0.08	0.31	8.1
	10–20	12	9.79	0.53	0.23	0.00	0.67	0.04	0.05	7.2
Cottonwood/aspen/birch	0–10	1	2.29	0.00	0.00	0.00	0.00	0.05	0.03	7.6
	10–20	1	1.52	0.00	0.00	0.00	0.00	0.02	0.26	8.3
Spruce/fir group	0–10	8	24.66	23.45	0.13	1.01	6.33	0.37	3.86	9.2
	10–20	8	10.07	8.53	0.04	0.38	1.89	0.14	0.61	2.4
Western redcedar/larch	0–10	1	76.94	1.33	0.03	0.00	0.91	0.13	0.00	12.9
	10–20	1	26.01	0.00	0.00	0.00	0.00	0.00	0.38	0.0
Limber/whitebark pines	0–10	4	22.71	23.97	0.09	0.00	3.60	0.17	5.95	10.7
	10–20	4	3.65	0.48	0.00	0.00	0.00	0.03	0.29	3.9